T0360557

EMPLOYMENT RELATIONS AND HRM IN SOUTH KOREA

Employment Relations and HRM in South Korea

DONG-ONE KIM and JOHNGSEOK BAE
College of Business Administration
Korea University

Routledge
Taylor & Francis Group

LONDON AND NEW YORK

First Published 2004 by Ashgate Publishing

Published 2017 by Routledge
2 Park Square, Milton Park, Abingdon, Oxon OX14 4RN
52 Vanderbilt Avenue, New York, NY 10017

Routledge is an imprint of the Taylor & Francis Group, an informa business

British Library Cataloguing in Publication Data
Kim, Dong-One
    Employment relations and HRM in South Korea
    1.Industrial relations - Korea (South) 2.Industrial
    relations - Korea (South) - History 3.Personnel management
    - Korea (South)
    I.Title II.Bae, Johngseok
    331'.095195

Library of Congress Cataloging-in-Publication Data
Employment relations and HRM in South Korea / Dong-One Kim,
    Johngseok Bae.
        p. cm.
    Includes bibliographical references and index.
    ISBN 0-7546-1356-9
    1. Industrial relations--Korea (South) 2. Industrial relations--Korea (South)--History. 3.
Personnel management--Korea (South) 4. Personnel management--Korea (South)--History.
I. Kim, Dong-One. II. Bae, Johngseok, 1963-.

HD8730.5.E47 2003
331'.095195--dc21

                                                                    2003052340

ISBN 13: 978-0-7546-1356-5 (hbk)

Contents

List of Figures

List of Tables

About the Authors

DONG-ONE KIM is an associate professor of employment relations at Korea University, Seoul, Korea. He holds M.S. and Ph.D. degrees in industrial relations from the University of Wisconsin-Madison. Prior to joining the faculty of Korea University in 1997, he was on the faculty of the School of Business at the State University of New York at Oswego. His primary research interests are high performance work organizations and workplace innovations such as skill-based pay, gainsharing, employee involvement, and mutual-gains bargaining. He is also interested in analyzing issues in Asian labour relations from a comparative perspective. He is co-author of *Gainsharing and Goalsharing: Aligning Pay and Strategic Goals* (with Ken Mericle). His research articles have been published in *Industrial and Labor Relations Review, Industrial Relations, Industrial Relations/Relations Industrielles, Advances in Industrial and Labor Relations, Human Resource Management Handbook, Labor Studies Journal, Journal of Applied Behavioral Sciences, European Sociological Review, Asia Pacific Business Review*, and *International Journal of Employment Studies*. He has consulted widely on employment relations and human resource management issues with business, government, and labour organizations, and served as an editorial board member and a reviewer for a few academic journals.

JOHNGSEOK BAE is an associate professor of human resource management (HRM) at the College of Business Administration, Korea University, Seoul. He received a BBA and an MS in Business from Korea University, and an AM and a Ph.D. (1997) in labour and industrial relations from the University of Illinois at Urbana-Champaign. Prior to joining Korea University, he had taught at Hanyang University (Seoul) for 5 years. He teaches on HRM and organizational development. His recent research is focused on strategic management of human resources, global HRM, and corporate venturing. He is co-editor of *Korean Businesses: Internal and External Industrialization* (with Chris Rowley, 1998, Cass) and *Managing Korean Business: Organization, Culture, Human Resources and Change* (with Chris Rowley and Tae Won Sohn, 2002, Cass). His work has been published in many scholarly outlets including *the Academy of Management Journal, Industrial Relations, Journal of World Business, International Journal of Human Resource Management, Human Resource Development Quarterly, and Asia Pacific Business Review*. He is also on the editorial boards of *Asia Pacific*

Business Review and *Korean Personnel Administration Journal* and reviews for many other academic journals.

Preface and Acknowledgements

South Korea (Korea, hereafter) is one of the rare countries that have experienced political democratization, economic development, and industrial democratization simultaneously in a relatively short period. Since the 1960s Korea has documented very rapid economic developments by any international standards. Behind the rapid economic growth, however, the country has been criticized for suppressing harshly the labour movement for the interest of economic development. As pressures for greater democracy and political freedoms get intensified, especially after the 1980s, so do calls for employee voices in workplace governance and liberalization of the trade union movement. The movement toward greater industrial democracy was culminated by the Great Labour Struggle in 1987. After this turning point, human resource management (HRM) also experienced paradigm shifting from paternalistic, seniority-based, and longterm-oriented approaches toward a more performance-based, equity-oriented system.

The 1997-1998 financial crisis served as another turning point in Korean employment relations and HRM. On the one hand, the crisis brought waves of employment restructuring and managerial efforts toward further labour market flexibility, which greatly intensified open conflicts between labour and the state. On the other hand, the financial crisis resulted in crisis consciousness among the three actors, and led them to form the Tripartite Commission. The creation of the Tripartite Commission implied that the Korean government regarded labour at least as a counterpart for negotiations and compromise, which could be considered as a step toward greater industrial democracy. In the case of HRM, the seniority-based system has been further eroded and flexibility-based HRM was pursued after the crisis. As whole industries undergo restructuring, psychological contracts have been also changed.

As implied in these turbulent developments in the last four decades, employment relations in Korea have been displaying two dissimilar faces. One face, bright aspects of Korean employment relations, shows continuing real wage growth based upon a rapid economic growth and heavy investments in human resources in the last four decades. The other face, dark aspects of Korean employment relations, reveals the authoritarian and suppressive labour policy, exploitative working conditions for many workers, and extremely aggressive and violent labour disputes. The HRM side similarly displayed two faces. On the one hand, organizations have emphasized the critical roles of human assets in gaining and sustaining competitive advantage. Hence firms adopted 'people first' or 'respect for people' philosophy and heavily invested in human assets. However, people were not sufficiently empowered and 'brains' and 'hands' were clearly separated. Under the name of 'employability' rather than 'job security', firms more freely laid off employees, and people began to search for jobs. As a necessary consequence, the level of trust between employees and employers has drastically dropped, and firm-specific distinctive strategic competencies may drain away. Ironically, the importance of people (especially top talents) is increasing in this era of knowledge-based economy.

One purpose of this book is to explain these seemingly contradictory outcomes of Korean employment relations and HRM based upon a theoretical framework that incorporates logics of environmental constraints and strategies of actors. Since the 1997-1998 currency crisis, a central task confronting policy-makers in Korea seems to develop models of employment relations and human resource strategies that can best accommodate the demands for both greater industrial democracy and adjustment to a higher value-added economy. Indeed, the Korean policy-makers currently have to create a solution that can enhance both economic competitiveness and industrial democracy simultaneously. Thus, the second purpose of the present book is to provide policy implications that can stimulate constructive debates regarding these 'mutual-gains' strategies.

Work on this book really began in the late 1980s when both of us were studying employment relations at graduate schools, being keenly aware of the pressing issues and acute problems of Korean employment relations and HRM, especially after the 1987 Great Labour Struggle. We clearly recognize that this book is by no means the end of our intellectual journey, but the beginning of our efforts to better understand employment relations and HRM in this unusually dynamic country.

Dong-One Kim thanks Paula Voos, Ken Mericle, and George Strauss for their stimulation during his intellectual journey in the area of employment relations, acknowledges the diligent research assistance of Yoon Ho Kim, Hyun Sik Yun, Sook Kyung Jin, and other research assistants at Korea University. His wife, Kwi-Ok, his daughter, Ji-Eun, and his son, Paul, have been invaluable for their enduring and warmhearted support. Finally, Kim would like to dedicate this book in memory of his parents.

Johngseok Bae gives thanks to John Lawler for his continuous academic stimulation and guidance, and to Chris Rowley for his invaluable insights and initiatives through academic collaboration. He is also grateful to Professor Soo-Shik Shin and the late Professor Linsu Kim for their support and inspiration since he was a graduate student. He also thanks Kyungjae Ryu,

Wook Ko, Won-Jong Choi, Arrie Sohn and Ow-Won Park for their able research assistance. Bae expresses his love and appreciation to his wife, Eundeok, his daughter, Grace (Saeun), and his son, Oswald (Tamin) for their endless prayers and support. Finally, he wishes to express his deepest gratitude to the Almighty who has paved his academic career path and provided wisdom and strength to walk along the path.

List of Abbreviations

3D	Dangerous, Dirty, Difficult
AMG	American Military Government
BT	Biotechnology
CDT	Color Display Tubes
CKTU	Confederation of Korean Trade Unions
CPT	Color Picture Tubes
CRT	Cathode Ray Tube
e-HRM	Electronic Human Resource Management
ELSA	Employment, Labour and Social Affairs
ER	Employment Relations
ERP	Enterprise Resource Planning
ESOP	Employee Stock Ownership Programs
EVA	Economic Value-Added
FDI	Foreign Direct Investment
FKTU	Federation of Korean Trade Unions
GDP	Gross Domestic Product
GNP	Gross National Product
HPWO	High Performance Work Organization
HPWS	High Performance Work System
HRD	Human Resource Development
HRM	Human Resource Management
ICFTU	International Confederation of Free Trade Unions
ILO	International Labour Organization
IMD	International Institute for Management Development
IMF	International Monetary Fund
IRS	Industrial Relations Systems
IT	Information Technology
KAL	Korean Air Lines
KCIA	Korean Central Intelligence Agency
KCTU	Korean Confederation of Trade Unions
KEDI	Korean Educational Development Institute
KEF	Korea Employers Federation
KEPCO	Korea Electric Power Corporation
KLI	Korea Labour Institute
LCD	Liquid Crystal Displays
LFPR	Labour Force Participation Rates

LMC	Labour-Management Committee
MBO	Management by Objectives
MNEs	Multi-national Enterprises
NATU	National Alliance of Trade Unions
NCKTU	National Council of Korean Trade Unions
NCTU	National Conference of Trade Unions
NHRS	New Human Resource System
NICs	Newly Industrialized Countries
NT	Nanotechnology
OECD	Organization for Economic Cooperation and Development
OEM	Original Equipment Manufacturer
OPIC	Overseas Private Investment Corporation
PDP	Plasma Display Panel
PDSS	Personal Decision Support System
PHR	Professional in Human Resources
PI	Process Innovations
PM	Personnel Management
POSCO	Pohang Iron and Steel Co.
R&D	Research and Development
SCM	Supply Chain Management
SEC	Samsung Electronic Company
SHRM	Strategic Human Resource Management
SPHR	Senior Professional in Human Resources
TPC	Total Productivity Control
TPI	Total Productivity Innovations
TPM	Total Production Maintenance
ULPs	Unfair Labour Practices
VFD	Vacuum Fluorescent Displays
WTO	World Trade Organization

PART I
INTRODUCTION AND
CONTEXTS OF EMPLOYMENT
RELATIONS AND HRM

1 Introduction

The term *insamansa* ('personnel matters are everything') has been widely used by people for generations in South Korea (hereafter Korea as shorthand). It means that personnel or human resources are considered the single most critical factor ensuring organizational success. Many Koreans ascribe the nation's successful economic development from the early 1960s to the 1980s to the efficient mobilization of human resources. However, the full story of economic development reveals both positive and negative aspects to the deployment of labour and human resources. This introductory chapter establishes the conceptual frameworks that will be used in this book. Employment relations/human resource management (ER/HRM) systems are so complex that they defy a simple analysis. In an attempt to provide an overview of such systems, we will first explain the roles of labour and human resources during the period of economic growth, before introducing a general model of ER/HRM systems. This will consist of outlining their general and organizational environments, organizational architecture, the nature of ER/HRM systems and the outcomes (ER, HRM, organizational, financial and national), during three key periods of the previous century (i.e., pre-1987, 1987-1997 and post-1997). Finally, some crucial elements of both ER and HRM systems will be explained.

The Korean Economy and the Roles of Labour and Human Resources[1]

During the 20th century, the Korean economy and society experienced its rise and fall. At each stage of the historical cycle, the nation encountered critical issues needing resolution, and responded with the use of dominant ideologies for each (see Table 1.1). During the colonial period, it was necessary for national independence to be the main issue and nationalism dominated society. The Korean War generated a mood of anti-communism and this ideology prevailed throughout during the subsequent Cold War period. Leaving behind these difficulties, the single most urgent issue was to overcome poverty. This led to a strong impetus towards industrialization. Given the fragile infrastructure and immature markets, the government needed to take the initiative. The dominant ideology was neo-mercantilism. 'The Hermit Kingdom' achieved the economic miracle on the Han River for about three decades. During the process of industrialization, and the rapid growth which resulted, other critical issues included political and industrial democracy, since this growth was being realized at the expense of civil and labour rights. From 1987 onwards, these rights were slowly granted to citizens and workers. It seemed that the sun would never set on Korea's economic prosperity, until the Asian Crisis hit Korea in 1997. For many Koreans, the IMF bailout program was a national humiliation and loss of face. During this period, globalization and neo-liberalism prevailed.

Table 1.1   Main issues, dominant ideologies and roles of institutions

Period	Main Issues	Dominant Ideology	Roles of Institutions
Pre-1962	• Independence • Reconstruction	• Nationalism • Anti-communism	• All institutions (government, market and firm) less developed • Flimsy infrastructures
1962-1987	• Overcoming poverty	• Industrialization • Neo-mercantilism	• Governments: authoritarian • Markets: immature • Firms: *chaebol* formation and growth
1987-1997	• Re-configuration	• Democracy • Pluralism	• Government failure • Inefficient labour/financial/product markets • Organizations: lax management
Post-1997	• Overcoming the Asian crisis • Restructuring	• Neo-liberalism • Globalization	• All institutions' efforts directed towards repositioning

In each period, institutions took a different role. Before 1962, none of the main institutions (i.e., government, market and firm) were ready for industrialization. From 1962 onwards, given the immature labour, product and financial markets and firms, the government took the initiative to ensure economic development. In the 1980s, firms, vis-à-vis governments, gradually took more active roles in economic activities. When the Asian Crisis hit Korea in 1997, it was argued that all institutions displayed some sort of problem, such as strong government intervention and regulation, rigid and inefficient markets and lax management.

Scholars and commentators have expressed quite diverse views on the principal engine of industrialization in Korea. Korea's economic success has been attributed to external forces (Castley, 1998), the government (Amsden, 1989), the management and private sectors (Kim, 1997; Westphal, 1982), or well-educated people (see Moore and Jennings, 1995). However, taking a position does not seem to be a matter of choice, but rather of emphasis. In addition, the views of the dominant engine have changed over time. A number of arguments have been advanced in relation to this issue.

Firstly, we have the question of 'internal versus external' factors. While many scholars and commentators have emphasized the conditions within Korea driving industrialization and economic growth, Castley (1998) credits external sources, especially Japanese firms. He argues that the growth of the Korean electronics industry was a regional phenomenon rather than a national one, and that it arose as a result of foreign interests (especially the restructuring of the Japanese electronics industry). Japan's motives for direct investment obviously involved a degree of self-interest in terms of factors such as low wages, upgrading their production facilities, geographical proximity, achieving a triangular trade pattern[2] and so forth. In addition, Cathie (1998) regards the infusion of US economic aid as a critical element of Korean industrialization, at least in its early stages. While these factors played a partial role in the process, their ultimate effectiveness hinged on their wise mobilization by internal Korean factors. Whatever the 'donor' countries' motives, host countries have always taken advantage of such industrial situations by building their own capacities (Rowley and Bae, 1998). Hence, we now turn to the internal factors.

The second argument about the main engine of industrialization is the 'state versus free market' view, which has been an ongoing macro-level debate since the late 1980s (Amsden, 1989; World Bank, 1993). The former position attributes economic growth and success to the critical role of the state, while the latter ascribes it to the influence of the free market (see Cathie, 1998). Many economists have ascribed the economic success of East Asian countries to liberalization, or the freeing of markets from government control (see Amsden, 1989). With some explanations, Amsden (1989: 78) concludes the following:

> In all, liberalization amounted to nothing more than a footnote to the basic text of Korean expansion. To attribute the role of equilibrator in such expansion to the market mechanism rather than to the government's dual policy of discipline and support is to misrepresent a fundamental property of the most successful cases of late industrialization.

The World Bank (1993) also presents similar arguments. According to their report, proponents of the neoclassical view have argued that the successful Asian economies had been more effective in providing a stable macroeconomic environment and a reliable legal framework, both of which promoted both domestic and international competition. In addition, it was possible for these countries to maintain relatively low price distortions due to the absence of price controls and other distortional policies. Adherents of the revisionist view, however, have refuted the neoclassical model by showing that industrial policy and interventions in markets were not fully compatible with it; rather, some policies were more relevant to a state-led development paradigm. The World Bank report also explains that while the neoclassical view rarely recognised cases of market failure, revisionists have contended that markets failed to provide useful guidance for investment by industry and that governments deliberately and strongly intervened to remedy this problem (Amsden, 1989).

The role of the government in the economic development process of East Asian newly industrializing countries (NICs) has been well characterized (Amsden, 1989; Hsiao, 1988; Wilkinson, 1994). The state in late industrializing countries 'can stimulate or stagnate the economy; it is a necessary, if not a sufficient, cause for development' (Lie, 1991, p.502). The economic success of East Asian countries has come under governments that are not democratic but rather authoritarian (Bae, 1997). In addition, this success has been realized by the 'visible hand' of a strong, authoritarian government and system, rather than by the 'invisible hand' of the free market. Given the underdeveloped nature of economic institutions (i.e., labour, product and financial markets) and the weakness of business enterprises, authoritarianism has often been successful in driving economic development and growth (Khanna and Palepu, 1997; Sharma, 1985).

So far we have discussed two sets of arguments (the external vs. internal and market vs. state views) around the main engine of industrialization and economic development in Korea. However, these two arguments are primarily macro-oriented. According to Porter (1990), national competitiveness largely stems from core industries' capacity to innovate and upgrade, which in turn ultimately comes from each individual firm's core competencies. Kim (1997) also suggests that, for firms in latecomer nations, three sources of technical learning are the international community, the domestic community and in-house efforts at firm level. Therefore, finely-tuned, firm level analysis is required in order to capture the whole picture of Korea's economic success (Kim, 1997).

By demonstrating the ways in which Korean firms have built up their capabilities, the nation's overall industrialization and economic growth can be explained. What were the strategies deployed by Korean firms in shifting from imitator to innovator and from OEM (original equipment manufacturer) producer to global player? One explanation focuses on the learning process. A critical process for dynamic learning at firm level is 'absorptive capacity', which requires two critical elements (i.e., an existing knowledge base and intense effort) (Cohen and Levinthal, 1990; Kim, 1997). To expedite learning, visionary entrepreneurs have used crisis construction as a strategic tool in such industries as automobile and semiconductor manufacture (Kim, 1997). Beyond the strategic roles of entrepreneurs, however, expeditious learning is possible only when well-educated human resources continually show commitment and conscious efforts to develop.

In summary, so far we have discussed the main engine of industrialization and economic development in the light of three competing paradigms: external versus internal, state versus markets and macro versus micro perspectives. Firstly, we explained that external forces (e.g., the infusion of US economic aid, the roles of foreign firms such as Japanese electronics manufacturers and benevolent foreign markets) were important to the early period of industrialization. Then the Korean government took the initiative and brought about the story of 'government success'. Lastly, at the micro level, management took up similar roles. Although all these arguments provide some critical illustrative factors, on their own they are not enough to explaining the whole story of industrialization and economic development. Proponents of micro (i.e., firm level) analyses emphasize the critical role of entrepreneurs, but this still leaves one further critical factor – human resources and the labour force. Human resources have showed discretionary efforts towards expeditious learning and the upgrade of technological capabilities. Whilst a great many issues and ideologies have come and gone, human resources have continually developed as a result of a social culture in which education is regarded as important, parents make efforts for and take an interest in their children's education and governments and corporations invest in human capital. This book is about this aspect of the human resources and labour force in Korea.

General Model of ER/HRM Systems

In his pioneering book *Industrial Relations Systems*, Dunlop (1958) presents a model to frame a general theory of industrial relations systems (IRS). In this model, he proposes three groups of actors: managers and their representatives, workers and their organizations and government agencies concerned with industrial relations. He also identifies three critical contextual factors affecting the interactions of such actors, namely technology, the market or budgetary constraints and the power relations operating in society as a whole. An ideology (i.e., set of shared ideas and beliefs) is another critical component that helps integrate the system according to Dunlop's model, as does the web of rules that governs the behaviour and interactions of the actors.

Based on this model as subsequently modified by Adams (1997), Craig (1975), Kochan, Katz and McKersie (1986) and Meltz (1993), we propose here a simple systems model to illustrate Korean ER/HRM systems (see Figure 1.1). The components of the model include the general environments, the alignments of ER/HRM systems with the organizational architecture, outcomes and the feedback loop. The general environments and organizational architecture will be explained in Chapters 2 and 3, ER systems in Chapters 4 through 6, followed by HRM systems in Chapters 7 and 8.

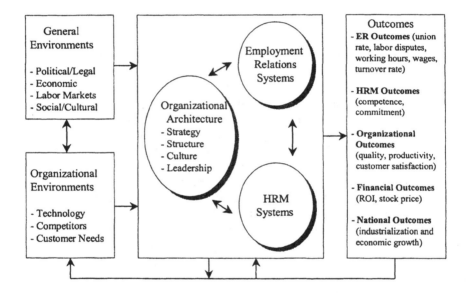

Figure 1.1   A general model of ER/HRM systems

Environments of ER/HRM Systems

Among the three groups of actors involved in ER/HRM systems, the dominant role in framing the basic features of the systems in most developing countries is usually played by the government. Korea is no exception. In this section, we will focus on the political economy as a background to Korean ER/HRM systems. Other important environmental factors will be discussed at length in subsequent chapters.

The role of the state in ER/HRM varies from country to country. A continuum can be envisaged which ranges from a *laissez-faire* approach at one end to complete intervention at the other. Some governments may simply legislate the procedural 'rules of the game' for employers and unions (e.g., the U.S.), some may set protective regulations and/or social welfare benefits for all employees through legislation (e.g., Germany) and others may intervene directly in collective bargaining in order to bring about the desired outcomes (e.g., France).

Governments in the emerging industrial relations system play several roles such as employer, regulator and policymaker both for the system and for the mutual interrelations between itself, the workers and management (Dunlop, 1958). The state actually plays a dominant role in contemporary industrial relations in developing countries (Kassalow, 1978) even though collective agreements are in place (Sturmthal, 1972). The government, as 'the prime agent of industrialization' and 'industrializing elites', is bound to have a profound impact on the evolution of labour movements and patterns of industrial relations in NICs (Kerr et al., 1960; Sharma, 1985).

Korea's labour history is closely related to a change of government, or more precisely, of President. After World War II, the U.S. Military Government ruled over South Korea for three years. Then, Rhee Syngman (1948-1960), Park Chung Hee (1961-1979), Chun Doo Whan (1981-1987), Rho Tae-Woo (1988-1992) and Kim Young Sam (1993-1997), successively, became President of Korea. Actual economic growth has usually been accounted for from the period since the introduction of the first five-year economic development plan by the Korean government in the early 1960s. Rapid economic growth was set as a primary national goal and in order to achieve this, the government intervened in almost every sphere.

The Korean government has adopted mercantilism as a dominant state ideology (Sylvan, 1981). Kihl (1987) also asserts that the economic development of East Asian NICs has been based more on 'neo-mercantilism' (i.e., state-led economic development), rather than either the orthodoxy of the classic economic theory of the market or the neo-Marxian interpretation of dependency. The government has supported the economy by developing the necessary infrastructure, stimulating the private sector, setting up capital-intensive and risky government-owned enterprises, protecting the economy from foreign capital in its early 'import substitution' industrialization, mobilizing foreign capital in its export-oriented industrialization period in the 1970s and controlling labour and small businesses (Kihl, 1987; Kim, 1989). In short, the government has encouraged things that could facilitate the process of economic development and discouraged things that might impede it (Bae, 1997).

Alignments of ER and HRM Systems with Organizational Architecture

Rowley, Bae and Sohn (2001: 4) list the following characteristics of organizational factors in the Korean management model that have contributed to economic growth:

- entrepreneurship/governance: founder-ownership, authoritarian and paternalistic leadership, clan management and competitive goal setting;
- people/HRM: staff who are obedient, industrious and disciplined, well trained or educated, who make efforts towards self-development and enjoy long-term employment;
- structure/system: hierarchical, related and unrelated diversification;
- culture/process: bounded collectivism, *inhwa* (harmony) and solidity, loyalty and seniority-based approach.

In a larger industrial society, an ER system is an analytical subsystem (Dunlop, 1958). In a broad sense, ER/HRM systems are interrelated with other structures such as the economic and legal systems, which we included in the list of general environments in Figure 1.1. However, within a firm, the ER system is also interrelated with the HRM system and the organizational architecture (i.e., strategy, structure, culture, leadership and so on). Recent studies on strategic HRM emphasize both horizontal congruence among the various HRM practices and vertical congruence, which refers to their linkage with strategic management processes (Wright and McMahan, 1992). The ER/HRM outcomes and organizational outcomes can be increased when all these factors are correctly and strongly aligned (MacDuffie, 1995; Tushman and O'Reilly, 1997).

ER systems comprise union organizing, collective bargaining, impasses and their resolution, union-management cooperation, and so forth. HRM systems include such practices as recruitment, training and development, performance evaluation and compensation and employee involvement. Some practices (e.g., wages and benefits, employee participation, etc.) are related to both systems, which themselves are also related to organizational architecture.

Several fundamental values, which have dominated Korean society for several decades, have served as 'linking pins' connecting ER and HRM systems and the organizational architecture. One such example is seniority orientation, which has become a dominant logic in such systems. According to this value, elders should serve as organizational or team leaders regardless of their levels of competence. Seniority is also a basis for pay systems and union operation. Another example is collectivism. In a similar way, this principle has affected various organizational factors such as job assignments, evaluation and pay systems and labour disputes. Authoritarianism, characterized by unquestioning obedience to authority rather than individual freedom of judgment and action, is a third example. This value has formed the underlying basis of leadership style, hierarchical structure, the top-down process, employer-employee relations and negotiation style.

The Korean model of economic development and industrialization had good system alignments at both national and firm levels (Bae, Rowley and Sohn, 2001). Although a good alignment is necessary for success, over time it becomes a trap or restriction which impedes future achievement (Tushman and O'Reilly, 1997; Rowley, Bae and Sohn, 2001). In such a situation, the lack of fit between components of the model becomes a liability, necessitating some new approaches in order to bring about its transformation. This issue is fully explained in Chapter 3.

Outcomes of ER/HRM Systems

The outcomes of the interaction between ER/HRM systems and other aspects of the organizational architecture can be classified into various categories: ER, HRM, organizational, financial and national. Empirical studies usually fix some part of the whole picture as the dependent variable. However, these outcomes are not actually discrete but interrelated. As Kaplan and Norton (1992) note, various performance measures need to be pursued in balance and some causal relationships retained. Relative importance of different outcomes and causal relationships are critical issues in analysing ER/HRM outcomes.

During the period of industrialization and economic development, 'economic growth and well-being' was the most important national goal. This goal has now been achieved successfully. Its single-minded, unquestioning pursuit forced industrial actors to sacrifice other important outcomes, such as quality of life at work, in favour of growth. This unbalanced strategic choice later resulted in some negative impacts for ER/HRM systems. Accordingly, conflicting interests and issues of distributive injustice have become the Achilles' heel of Korean ER/HRM systems.

The Evolution of and Main Issues for, ER/HRM Systems

Transformation of ER/HRM Systems and the Division into Periods

Korean ER/HRM systems have developed and changed since the launch of the first five-year economic development plan (1962-66). The criteria for, and characteristics of, such transformation (Gersick, 1991; Erickson and Kuruvilla, 1998) can be taken as:

- reconsideration and change of the 'deep structure' of the system (i.e., network of fundamental assumptions and principles underlying the basic configuration);

- rapid change in structure and practice relative to the past;
- widespread experimentation and increase in diversity.

While there were many small changes, based on the above criteria we would suggest that there have been two major changes (or transformations) to Korean ER/HRM systems, in 1987 and in 1997. This suggests the existence of three separate periods of history within which ER/HRM systems had unique features: the pre-1987 period, 1987 through 1997 and post-1997. During the pre-1987 period, Korean ER systems were characterized by state corporatism and the HRM systems dominated by the seniority-based approach. What, then, made these periods distinctive? The first transformation occurred in 1987. On June 29 Rho Tae-Woo, the presidential candidate from the then ruling party, announced the Declaration of Democracy which introduced the move towards pluralism and had an impact on many aspects of Korean society. Therefore, during the period 1987-1997, the Korean ER system was characterized by exploratory pluralism, after which time wages dramatically increased and firms made efforts to enhance rationality and efficiency accordingly. The HRM system henceforward can be characterized by an exploratory performance-based approach.

The second discontinuous change occurred in 1997, when the Asian financial crisis hit Korea and heralded another dramatic upheaval for its society. Hence, these two epoch-making events brought about dramatic changes in Korean ER/HRM systems. During the post-1997 period, the Korean ER system shows experiments with social corporatism and the HRM system features a flexibility-based approach. Table 1.2 delineates some characteristics for each period including environmental features, HRM systems, ER systems, organizational issues and ER/HRM issues. The major contents of, and issues for, the ER and HRM systems of each period are discussed in the section which follows.

Pre-1987: State Corporatism and Seniority-based HRM

State corporatism in ER systems   During the first stage of the development of Korean ER systems, the government played a critical role, exercising considerable power. As described in Table 1.2, authoritarian governments took stringent measures to enact their policies for economic development and growth. Employers and employees were relatively weak. The characteristics of macro environments of this stage included authoritarian governments, strategic economic policies, neo-Confucianism, neo-mercantilism, an abundant and cheap but relatively skilled workforce. Organizational factors with an impact on the formation and maintenance of ER/HRM systems were substantial management power, close connection between business and government, a top-down decision-making process, paternalistic leadership and a highly bureaucratic system.

Table 1.2 Historical trajectory of ER/HRM systems in Korea

Period	Pre-1987	1987-1997	Post-1997
Environmental Features	• Authoritarian governments • Industrial-ization	• Deregulation • Competitive pressure	• Financial crisis • Globalization
HRM System	• Seniority-based HRM	• Exploratory performance-based HRM	• Flexibility-based HRM
ER System	• State corporatism	• Exploratory pluralism	• Experiment with social corporatism
Organizational Issues	• *Chaebol* formation and diversification • Catch-up strategy	• Technological/ organizational capability upgrade	• Restructuring • Transparency
HRM/ER Issues	• Labour suppression • Formation of independent HR unit	• Rationalization • New HRM trends • The 1987 Great Labour Struggle	• Professional-ism in HRM • Downsizing • War for talents • The Tripartite Commission

In terms of ER, this initial period of development began back in 1890 and included diverse governments such as the Japanese and American military governments, and subsequent authoritarian Korean governments. The most conspicuous feature of the time was perhaps the suppression of an autonomous labour movement. After the economic development plan had been launched in 1962, a state-led export-oriented strategy led to a labour market characterized by low wages, a disciplined labour force and a subordinated labour movement. In addition, the state controlled the official labour leaders by intervening in union elections. The overall unionization ratio during this period was relatively low. Formal labour organizations were not autonomous or strong since they were often tamed by governments. During this period, labour-management relations were confrontational.

Seniority-based HRM systems   During this stage, firms usually employed an imitating, borrowing, or learning strategy in order to catch up with advanced technology and organizational capabilities in economically advanced countries. Korean *chaebols* began to be formed during this period. Key features of the systems included a seniority-based approach, rank-based job grade system, lifetime employment, recruitment of new graduates, generalist orientation, emphasis on socialization and indoctrination, monthly salary, complex pay structure, traditional boss-subordinate form of appraisal, department- or section-based work organization and broadly-defined jobs.

During this period the HRM system was, to borrow Rousseau's (1995) terminology, much like a relational system. Rousseau (1995) identifies two different contracts: transactional and relational. Both categories are ideal prototypes; so many variants of each may exist. Some of the typical features of relational terms are the following (p.92):

- emotional involvement as well as economic exchange (e.g., personal support, concern for family well-being);
- whole person relations (e.g., growth, development);
- open-ended time frames (i.e., indefinitely);
- both written and unwritten terms (e.g., some terms emerge over time);
- dynamic and subject to change during the life of the contract;
- pervasive conditions (e.g., affects personal and family life);
- ambiguous terms understood subjectively and implicitly by outsiders.

Two key aspects of traditional HRM approaches are the long-term attachment and the seniority-based system. Large Korean companies usually recruited a cohort of new graduates rather than experienced staff, and preferred generalists to specialists. Once hired, employees developed their careers within a firm in the context of its internal labour market. Firms ensured employees' job security and took care of family members. In return, they required the employees to show loyalty and obedience. This meant that the adjustment of employment levels was relatively difficult. In addition, the seniority-based approach, deeply rooted in Korean culture, was a foundation stone of Korean HRM systems pre-1987. It was applied to other HRM functions such as evaluation, promotion and remuneration.

1987-1997: Exploratory Pluralism and Performance-based HRM

Exploratory pluralism in ER systems   After the 1987 Rho's Democracy Declaration, the government suddenly stepped back from ER systems. This sudden withdrawal, together with the immature institutional frameworks, brought about large labour disruptions. Bognanno (1988, p.4) argues that

1987 was a turning point in Korean industrial relations, and explains the situation as follows:

> For decades the ideal of autonomous and democratic unions, free collective bargaining and the right to strike existed only on paper. The institution of collective bargaining in Korea had never before been a viable mechanism open to workers to affect Korea's distribution of income, address issues of industrial justice and/or redress oppressive working conditions. But with the promise of democracy these historically illusive worker rights suddenly became real.

After the mid-1980s, the old industrial order was continually questioned by people as new arrangements were sought out. Growing demands by Korean people for political and industrial democracy through the 1980s culminated in the Great Labour Struggle of 1987, the introduction of autonomous unionism and collective bargaining and experiments with pluralism. During this period, labour disputes became exceptionally severe and explosive. The government also questioned the effectiveness of the traditional oppressive labour policies and authoritarian corporatism. More importantly, during the post-1987 period, collective bargaining became virtually institutionalized and was established as the most important wage-setting mechanism. In addition, there were various attempts to create a second national union federation as an alternative to the conservative Federation of Korean Trade Unions (FKTU). Since the Kim Young Sam administration of the early 1990s, *segyewha*, the Korean term for globalization, has been increasingly used. Given this policy move towards globalization and the sudden increase in labour disputes together with wage rises, many firms have started to establish their operations in other countries, especially in China, other Southeast Asian nations and Eastern Europe (see Bae, Rowley, Kim and Lawler, 1997).

Exploratory performance-based HRM systems Environmental changes pushed Korean companies to transform their HRM systems. During this period, firms adopted *sininsa* (new HRM) systems. The general features of the new paradigms were a move from seniority-based to ability/performance criteria and from lifetime to more flexible employment. Their guiding principles were ability and performance orientation, rationalization and fairness enhancement (Bae, 1997). Specific new HRM practices included in:

*   human resource flow: use of the blind interview, recruiting specialists rather than generalists, promotion by selection, equal promotion opportunities for women, and an honorary retirement system;
*   work systems: use of skill grade systems, separation of post and job grade and single job grade system for both white- and blue-collar workers;

- reward systems: introduction of skill-grade pay, single rate basic pay, individual or group performance bonus, annual salary and monthly salary for production employees;
- performance management: use of multiple-rater performance evaluations, management by objectives, absolute (vis-à-vis relative) appraisal system, appraisal feedback and behaviourally anchored ratings.

These new HRM practices, previously unfamiliar to most Korean firms, have been simultaneously adopted by many companies, or are prepared by firms to adopt in the near future, for the first time in the history of Korean HRM (Bae, 1997). Among these changes, the most critical was the shift in evaluation and pay systems. Because of the changes, the seniority-based tradition was eroded during the 1990s. Bae (1997) suggests four scenarios with regard to this issue: the traditional seniority-based system, the seniority-based system with some performance factors, the performance-based system with some seniority factors and the completely ability/performance-based model. Until the 1980s, the first approach (i.e., the traditional seniority-based system) remained the dominant configuration. However, the dominant model has moved towards the other options with some element of performance coming into rewards – in other words, the second through fourth options have become more widespread in recent years.

Post-1997: Experiment with Social Corporatism and Flexibility-based HRM

Experiment with social corporatism in ER systems   The Asian financial crisis and IMF bailout in 1997 signalled another upheaval for Korean society. Since the economy had experienced both government failure (i.e., too much intervention and regulations) and organizational failure (i.e., lack of adaptability and transparency), the change here was towards a market principle based system. Neo-liberalism and globalization gave some impetus to this transformation. Most companies undertook restructuring and downsizing programs, and pursued labour market flexibility. Most management lost their sense of direction, but retained a change-is-good mentality. Many Korean people suddenly lost their jobs and some of the more competent employees began to move to other companies.

Because of these activities, the unemployment rate soared to 8.6 per cent in February 1999. Wage levels also fell and the growth rate of real wages was -9.3 per cent the same year. Unions' bargaining power was weakened and the main agenda of collective bargaining changed from wage increase to employment security. The number of contingent workers increased. One particularly noticeable result of the financial crisis was the formation of the Tripartite Commission. Given the hostile relationships among ER actors, the creation of this consensual institution seemed bizarre. It also meant that labour had become at least a legitimate actor and furthermore even a partner in ER with government and management. Since the launch of the First Tripartite Commission in January 1998, five different commissions have been subsequently initiated, the current (Fifth) Tripartite Commission beginning in August 2002. The evaluation of the Commission is not an easy task but it seems that it functioned quite effectively early on. However, it malfunctioned in subsequent years. More in-depth analysis is required in terms of the theoretical models previously set out for the explanation of corporatism, which can be found in Chapter 6.

Flexibility-based HRM systems   During the post-1997 period, companies adopted various practices to enhance labour market flexibility: (1) for internal numerical flexibility (changes to working hours without layoffs): reduction in working hours, restriction of overtime and (paid or unpaid) temporary leave of absence; (2) for external numerical flexibility: postponement or reduction of recruitment, dismissal, voluntary (or honorary) retirement and outsourcing; (3) for financial flexibility: base pay reduction, wage freezing, bonus reduction and fringe benefits reduction; and (4) for functional flexibility: dispatch to affiliated company and redeployment to other departments after training (e.g., as salesperson). All these new practices encouraged the existing HRM systems to have more flexibility, in various senses. They also weakened the existing systems.

During this period, firms started to adopt the transactional model of employment systems. Typical features of transactional contract terms include the following (Rousseau, 1995, p.91):

- specific economic conditions (e.g., wage rate) as primary incentive
- limited personal involvement in the job (e.g., working relatively few hours, low emotional investment)
- closed-ended time frame (e.g., seasonal employment, 2 to 3 years on the job at most)
- commitments limited to well-specified conditions (e.g., union contract)
- little flexibility (change requires renegotiation of contract)
- use of existing skills (no development)
- unambiguous terms readily understood by outsiders.

The nature of the contract in Korean ER systems was changing from relational towards transactional terms. The old idea of lifetime employment with a single employer changed to that of a lifetime career working for several firms. This trend was initiated by the government by changes to the labour law, which allowed limited freedom for dismissals. Employers then, after the IMF bailout program in 1997, accelerated early retirement programs and downsizing during periods of corporate restructuring. The outflow of human resources to venture firms accelerated the speed of change. Although the Korean HRM model has not changed completely to the ideal type of transactional contract, the changes have had an impact on many critical facets of the original systems. Firms have tried to keep their core people, and HRM managers, for the first time in Korean labour history, have realized that retention is important.

During this period, the performance-based system was further enhanced. A survey (Park and Ahn, 1999), covering both manufacturing firms (210) and non-manufacturing firms (68) of various sizes, showed that 42.4 per cent had employed the first approach, 24.5 per cent the second (seniority-based model with some performance factors), 29.1 per cent the third (performance-based plus some seniority factor) and about 4 per cent the fourth (pure ability/performance-based) configuration (Bae and Rowley, 2001). This trend was expected to continue through the near future.

Organization of the Book

This book consists of 5 parts and 10 chapters. Part I starts with this introductory chapter containing the analytical frameworks followed by two subsequent chapters on the context of Korean ER and HRM systems. Chapter 2 outlines the basis of Korean economic development, characteristics of labour markets and some features of the three main actors in ER. The chapter also examines basic ER related statistics such as labour force participation rates, unemployment rates and wages and working condition indicators. Chapter 3 discusses both national and organizational culture and organizational strategy. It covers the traditional features of culture and strategy as well as the main aspects of more recent changes.

Part II analyses the historical trajectory of Korean ER/HRM systems, divided into three distinct periods: pre-1987, 1987-1997 and post-1997. Chapter 4 deals with ER systems pre-1987. It covers labour issues, ranging from as far back as the 1890s through the Japanese colonial period, the American military government and the subsequent independent Korean governments. As the title of the chapter suggests, the ER systems of the period were characterized by the suppression of the labour movement. Chapter 5 analyses Korean ER systems during the period 1987-1997. It starts by describing the 1987 Great Labour Struggle and its consequences, focusing primarily on the fundamental transformation of Korean ER from the traditional system towards a new experiment with pluralism. In addition, Chapter 5 also discusses ER systems during the early 1990s, which was characterized by rising labour costs and the decline of the labour movement. It also points out that, as global competition increased, the state took a retrospective strategy by emphasizing earlier measures such as wage controls and union suppression. Finally, Chapter 6 addresses current issues in Korean ER systems. It first explains the 1997-1998 financial crisis and its impacts on labour markets, employment practices and trade unionism and collective bargaining, and then discusses the Tripartite Commission and its effectiveness in Korean contexts.

Part III gives a historical overview of Korean HRM systems. Chapter 7 focuses on a historical sketch of Korean HRM from the Japanese colonial period to 1987. For the purposes of this analysis, the period is divided into three segments: the Japanese colonial period (1910-1945), the transitional and rebuilding period after national independence (1945-1961) and the period of industrialization (1962-1987). To explain the features of HRM for the two earlier periods, we use major firms of the time such as Kyungbang, YuHan and Hwasin as examples. The formation of the HRM unit and establishment of the traditional Korean HRM systems are summarized. Chapter 8 analyses the transformation of Korean HRM systems toward a new paradigm. We argue that the first major change occurred in 1987. Prior to this period HRM was characterized by features such as long-term attachment, the seniority-based approach and an internal labour market. HRM systems after 1987 were mainly performance-based systems with more emphasis on rationality, fairness and competence. After the 1997 financial crisis, Korean HRM moved further towards flexibility-based systems, and the shift to a performance-based approach accelerated. Finally, the chapter explores the new roles of HRM professionals and the roles of HRM units.

Part IV illustrates two cases of Korean firms in the electronic industry (LG Electronics and SDI) to provide more specific and empirical information on Korean ER/HRM systems. One firm is unionized and the other is not, but both are highly innovative, model companies in terms of their sophisticated HRM approaches and cooperative ER. For both firms, organizational and ER/HRM characteristics will be compared and contrasted. Finally, in Part V, Chapter 10, the contents of the book are summarized and conclusions on Korean ER/HRM systems drawn before the implications for the government, firms and unions are discussed. Future scenarios for ER and HRM systems are also proposed.

Chapter Summary

In this chapter, we first introduced the roles of human resources and labour during industrialization and economic development in Korea, before providing a general model for Korean ER/HRM systems. Within this framework, we explained the environments of Korean ER systems, the alignment of ER and HRM systems with organizational architecture and the outcomes of ER/HRM systems. Among the three ER actors, we saw that the government played the most significant role during the industrialization process. Korean *chaebols* then took over these the positions, and now knowledge workers are becoming the critical players in the digital economy. In the next section, we discussed the rationale for setting out three distinctive periods in the evolution of ER/HRM systems and their key features during each. Finally, we outlined the organization of this book.

Notes

1   This part is largely based on one of the authors' other works (Rowley and Bae, 1998).
2   The triangular trade pattern means a process by which Korea imports from Japan then exports to the USA. The Japanese initially preferred this pattern (Castley. 1998).

References

Adams, R.J. (1997), 'Integrating Disparate Strands: An Elaborated Version of Systems Theory as a Framework for Organizing the Field of Industrial Relations', in J. Barbash and N.M. Meltz (eds), Theorizing in Industrial Relations: Approaches and Applications, Centre for Industrial Relations Research and Teaching of the University of Sydney, Sydney, Australia, pp.29-56.
Amsden, A.H. (1989), *Asia's next giant: South Korea and late industrialization*, Oxford University Press, New York.
Bae, J. (1997), 'Beyond seniority-based systems: A paradigm shift in Korean HRM?', *Asia Pacific Business Review*, vol.3, no.4, pp.82-110.
Bae, J. and Rowley, C. (2001), 'The impact of globalization on HRM: The case of Korea', *Journal of World Business*, vol.36, no.4, pp.402-428.
Bae, J., Rowley, C. and Sohn, T. (2001), 'Conclusion – Knowledge, Learning, and Change in Korean Management', *Asia Pacific Business Review*, vol.7, no.4, pp.182-200.
Bae, J., Rowley, C., Kim, D.-H. and Lawler, J. (1997), 'Korean industrial relations at the crossroads: The recent labour troubles', *Asia Pacific Business Review*, vol.3, no.3, pp.148-160.
Bognanno, M.F. (1988), 'Korea's industrial relations at the turning point', *Working Paper No.8816*, Korea Development Institute, Seoul.
Cathie, J. (1998), 'Financial Contagion in East Asia and the Origins of the Economic and Financial Crisis in Korea', *Asia Pacific Business Review*, vol.4, no.2/3, pp.18-28.
Cohen, W.M. and Levinthal, D.A. (1990), 'Absorptive Capacity: A New Perspective on Learning and Innovation', *Administrative Science Quarterly*, vol.35, no.1, pp.128-152.

Craig, A.W. (1975), 'A Framework for the Analysis of Industrial Relations Systems', in B. Barrett, E. Rhodes and J. Beishon (eds), *Industrial Relations and the Wider Society*, Collier Macmillan, London, pp.8-20.

Dunlop, J. (1958), *Industrial Relations Systems*, Henry Holt, New York.

Erickson, C.L. and Kuruvilla, S. (1998), 'Industrial relations system transformation', *Industrial and Labor Relations Review*, vol.52, no.1, pp.3-21.

Gersick, C.J.G. (1991), 'Revolutionary change theories: A multilevel exploration of the punctuated equilibrium paradigm', *Academy of Management Review*, vol.16, no.1, pp.10-36.

Hsiao, H.M. (1988), 'An East Asian development model: Empirical explorations', in P. L. Berger and H. M. Hsiao (eds), *In search of an East Asian development model*, Transaction Books, New Brunswick, NJ, pp.12-23.

Kaplan, R.S. and Norton, D.P. (1992), 'The balanced scorecard: Measures that drive performance', *Harvard Business Review*, vol.70, no.1, pp.71-79.

Kassalow, E.M. (1978), 'Introduction', in E.M. Kassalow and U. Damachi (eds), *The role of trade unions in developing societies*, International Institute for Labour Studies, Geneva.

Kerr, C., Dunlop, J.T., Harbison, F.H. and Myers, C.A. (1960), *Industrialism and industrial man: The problems of labor and management in economic growth*, Harvard University Press, Cambridge, MA.

Khanna, T. and Palepu, K. (1997), 'Why Focused Strategies May Be Wrong for Emerging Markets', *Harvard Business Review*, vol.75, no.4, pp.41-51.

Kihl, Y.W. (1987), 'East Asia's rise to economic prominence: Aspects of the political economy of developments', *Asian Perspective*, vol.11, no.2, pp.248-263.

Kim, L. (1997), *Imitation to Innovation: The Dynamics of Korea's Technological Learning*, Harvard Business School Press, Boston, MA.

Kim, S.J. (1989), 'The political economy of export-led industrialization in Korea', *Asian Perspective*, vol.13, no.2, pp.69-88.

Kochan, T., Katz, H. and McKersie, R. (1986), *The Transformation of American Industrial Relations*, Basic Books, New York.

Lie, J. (1991), 'The prospect for economic democracy in South Korea', *Economic and Industrial Democracy*, vol.12, pp.501-513.

MacDuffie, J.P. (1995), 'Human resource bundles and manufacturing performance: Organizational logic and flexible production systems in the world auto industry', *Industrial and Labor Relations Review*, vol.48, pp.197-221.

Meltz, N.M. (1993), 'Industrial Relations Systems as a Framework for Organizing Contributions to Industrial Relations Theory', in R.J. Adams and N.M. Meltz (eds), *Industrial Relations Theory: Its Nature, Scope, and Pedagogy*, IMLR Press/Rutgers University and The Scarecrow Press, Lanham, MD and London, pp.161-182.

Moore, L.F. and Jennings, P.D. (1995), *Human Resource Management on the Pacific Rim: Institutions, Practices and Attitudes*, Walter de Gruyter, Berlin and New York.

Park, J. and Ahn, H. (1999), *The Changes and Future Direction of Korean Employment Practices*, The Korea Employers' Federation, Seoul. (In Korean.)

Porter, M.E. (1990), *The Competitive Advantage of Nations*, The Free Press, New York.

Rousseau, D.M. (1995), *Psychological contracts in organizations: Understanding written and unwritten agreements*, Sage, London.

Rowley, C., Bae, J. and Sohn, T. (2001), 'Introduction – Capabilities to Liabilities in Korean Management', *Asia Pacific Business Review*, vol.7, no.4, pp.1-21.

Sharma, B. (1985), *Aspects of industrial relations in ASEAN*, Institute of Southeast Asian Studies, Singapore.

Sturmthal, A. (1972), *Comparative labor movements: Ideological roots and industrial development*, Wadsworth, Belmont, CA.

Sylvan, D.J. (1981), 'The newest mercantilism', *International Organization*, vol.35, no.2,

pp.275-393.
Tushman, M.L. and O'Reilly, C.A., III (1997), *Winning through innovation: A practical guide to leading organizational change and renewal,* Harvard Business School Press, Boston, MA.
Westphal, L.E. (1982), 'The Private Sector as 'Principal Engine' of Development: Korea', *Finance and Development,* vol.19, pp.34-38.
Wilkinson, B. (1994), *Labour And Industry In The Asia-Pacific: Lessons From The Newly-Industrialized Countries,* Walter de Gruyter, Berlin and New York.
World Bank (1993), *The East Asian Miracle: Economic Growth and Public Policy,* Oxford, University Press Oxford.
Wright, P.M. and McMahan, G.C. (1992), 'Theoretical perspectives for strategic human resource management', *Journal of Management,* vol.18, pp.295-320.

2 Economic Development, the Labour Market and Actors in Employment Relations

Introduction

This chapter discusses the development of the Korean economy, the characteristics of the Korean labour market and the basic features of the three main actors in employment relations (ER). After three decades of unprecedented economic growth, the Korean economy encountered a serious currency crisis in 1997. This crisis provided an opportunity for policymakers to rethink the Korean development model and to shift the focus from traditional manufacturing to highly value-added information technology and biotechnology industries. More importantly, the economic crisis not only altered employment practices, but also transformed the patterns of interactions among ER actors. In this sense, the 1997-1998 financial crisis was a turning point for the Korean economy and ER.

Economic Performance and the Labour Market

Korea, whose population numbers approximately 47 million, has shown the most remarkable rate of economic growth of the newly industrialized countries. Its growth rates, in terms of real GDP, have averaged almost 10 per cent per year in the 1970s and 1980s and over 7 per cent during 1990-1996. The growth national income per capita also rose from only US$249 in 1970 to US$11,380 in 1996, an almost 50-fold increase in 30 years (see Table 2.1). Although the 1997-1998 financial crisis slowed things down, the economy quickly recovered from the shock to continue growing in 1999 and 2000.

Korea was a typical Asian agricultural country until the 1960s, but three decades later, it has become the 13th biggest international trader in the world (Seoul Economic Daily, 2001). Such economic success might be attributed to export-oriented development based upon price competitiveness in the manufacturing sector. The export-oriented strategy, combined with the gradual process of import liberalization, has been accompanied by a steady increase in trade flows. Import liberalization was heavily influenced by the gradual decline of the import tariff rate from almost 40 per cent in 1970 to less than 10 per cent in the 1990s. Both import and export increased to over US$150 billion in 2000 from around US$ 1 billion in 1970, an approximately 100-fold increase. The ratio of trade to gross domestic product (GDP) increased from about 35 per cent in 1970 to over 50 per cent in the mid-1970s, and rose to over 70 per cent after the 1997-1998 financial crisis (see Table 2.2). As a result, Korea's share of exports in world trade soared from approximately 0.3 per cent in 1970 to around 2.5 per cent in the 1990s (ILO, 1999).

Table 2.1   Economic indicators in Korea

Year	Growth rates of GDP (%)[a]	National income per capita[b]	Year	Growth rates of GDP (%)[a]	National income per capita[b]
1970	-	249	1986	11.0	2,550
1971	8.6	286	1987	11.0	3,201
1972	4.9	316	1988	10.5	4,268
1973	12.3	394	1989	6.1	5,185
1974	7.4	540	1990	9.0	5,886
1975	6.5	592	1991	9.2	6,810
1976	11.2	799	1992	5.4	7,183
1977	10.0	1,009	1993	5.5	7,811
1978	9.0	1,399	1994	8.3	8,998
1979	7.1	1,636	1995	8.9	10,823
1980	-2.1	1,598	1996	6.8	11,380
1981	6.5	1,749	1997	5.0	10,307
1982	7.2	1,847	1998	-6.7	6,723
1983	10.7	2,020	1999	10.9	8,551
1984	8.2	2,190	2000	8.8	9,628
1985	6.5	2,229			

Sources:
[a] Bank of Korea (2002), *http://dbsrv.bok.or.kr/20020320175625.xls*
[b] Korea National Statistical Office (2002), *http://kosis.nso.go.kr/cgi-bin/html-out.cgi*

Foreign direct investment (FDI) flows had been small (approximately US$ 0.5 billion in both inflow and outflow) until the mid-1980s. As a result of a more liberal attitude towards foreign investment, both inflows and outflows showed a more than ten-fold increase: inward investment rose to US$ 7 billion and outward to US$ 5.8 in 1997 (Korea Labour Institute, 2000; ILO, 1999). Thus, in the last decade, Korea's presence in world markets and the economy's reliance on trade and foreign investment have both risen substantially.

Table 2.2   Trade indicators in Korea (in billion US$, %)

Year	Exports[a]	Imports[b]	TDR[c]	Year	Exports[a]	Imports[b]	TDR[c]
1970	0.84	1.98	34.8	1986	34.12	29.83	62.9
1971	1.07	2.39	36.4	1987	46.56	39.03	66.1
1972	1.62	2.52	38.8	1988	59.97	48.69	62.6
1973	3.23	4.24	55.3	1989	61.83	57.47	56.2
1974	4.46	6.85	60.1	1990	63.66	66.11	53.5
1975	5.08	7.27	59.1	1991	70.54	77.34	52.0
1976	7.72	8.77	57.5	1992	76.20	77.95	50.4
1977	10.05	10.81	56.7	1993	82.09	79.77	48.1
1978	12.71	14.97	53.6	1994	94.96	97.82	49.4
1979	15.06	20.34	57.4	1995	124.63	129.08	53.3
1980	17.25	21.86	65.7	1996	129.97	144.93	54.0
1981	20.75	24.60	70.6	1997	138.62	141.80	59.2
1982	20.93	23.76	64.3	1998	132.12	90.49	72.3
1983	23.27	25.12	63.3	1999	145.16	116.79	65.8
1984	26.49	27.58	68.0	2000	175.95	159.08	73.1
1985	26.63	26.65	67.4				

Sources:
[a] Ministry of Industry and Resources (2002), *http:// 152.99.129.80/ 20007-2.htm* (the 1970-1973 period); Korea National Statistical Office (2001), *Major Statistics of Korean Economy* (the 1974-1979 period); Bank of Korea (2002), *http://dbsrv.bok.or.kr/ 20020320175758.xls* (the 1980-2000 period).
[b] Ministry of Industry and Resources (2002), *http:// 152.99.129.80/ 20007-2.htm* (the 1970-1973 period); Korea National Statistical Office (2001), *Major Statistics of Korean Economy* (the 1974-1979 period); Bank of Korea (2002), *http://dbsrv.bok.or.kr/ 20020320175849.xls* (the 1980-2000 period).
[c] Trade dependency ratio. Ministry of Industry and Resources (2002), *http:// 152.99.129.80/ 20007-2.htm* (the 1970-1989 period); Korea National Statistical Office (2002), *http://www.nso.go.kr/ cgi-bin/ html_out.cgi?F=Xa096_r10072.html* (the 1990-2000 period).

In the early stages of industrialization, the Korean economy faced the challenge of creating enough jobs to reduce a relatively high unemployment rate (approximately 8 per cent in the early 1960s) and, more importantly, to absorb large cohorts of new labour market entrants from the rural sector. Since then, the high growth process has translated into the creation of over 10 million jobs. Although men's rate of labour force participation has been more than 70 per cent since the 1960s, the involvement of women has increased significantly over this period, climbing by 10 percentage points to reach 48.8

per cent in 2001 (see Table 2.3). Although at around 50 per cent this rate is similar to that of Japan, it is much smaller than that of the U.S. and EU countries. This suggests that there remains scope to utilize women's human capital in Korea.

Table 2.3   Labour force participation rates (LFPR) in Korea

Year	LFPR (%)	LFPR for male (%)	LFPR for female (%)	Year	LFPR (%)	LFPR for male (%)	LFPR for female (%)
1963	56.6	78.4	37.0	1983	57.7	73.7	42.8
1964	55.7	77.6	36.0	1984	55.8	72.1	40.7
1965	57.0	78.9	37.2	1985	56.6	72.3	41.9
1966	56.9	78.9	37.0	1986	57.1	72.1	43.1
1967	56.9	78.5	37.5	1987	58.3	72.5	45.0
1968	58.0	79.0	39.1	1988	58.5	72.9	45.0
1969	57.8	79.6	38.3	1989	59.6	73.4	46.6
1970	57.6	77.9	39.3	1990	60.0	74.0	47.0
1971	57.4	77.2	39.5	1991	60.6	74.9	47.3
1972	57.7	77.5	39.6	1992	60.9	75.5	47.3
1973	58.4	76.8	41.5	1993	61.1	76.0	47.2
1974	58.9	77.7	41.5	1994	61.7	76.4	47.9
1975	58.3	77.4	40.4	1995	61.9	76.5	48.3
1976	59.7	77.4	43.2	1996	62.0	76.1	48.7
1977	59.4	78.7	41.7	1997	62.2	75.6	49.5
1978	59.9	77.9	43.3	1998	60.7	75.2	47.0
1979	59.5	76.9	43.3	1999	60.5	74.4	47.4
1980	59.0	76.4	42.8	2000	60.7	74.0	48.3
1981	58.5	75.8	42.3	2001	60.8	73.6	48.8
1982	58.6	75.0	43.4				

Source: Korea National Statistical Office (2002), *http://kosis.nso.go.kr/cgi-bin/*

Along with the rapid rate of economic growth, the unemployment rate dropped from 8.1 per cent in 1963 to 4.4 per cent in 1970, remaining below 3 per cent from 1988 until the 1997-1998 financial crisis. From the early 1990s onwards, the labour market has been responding to rising labour costs and economic slowdown. Mid-career employees, even in large corporations, have been forced to accept 'honorary' early retirement and both private firms and public employers have substantially reduced the number of job openings for new college graduates (Park and Lee, 1995). Korean firms have also relocated their production facilities to China and Southeast Asia to benefit from cheap labour, and have imported foreign workers to do low-wage jobs. The Ministry of Labour estimates that the number of foreign workers in Korea reached approximately 300,000 in 2002. After the financial crisis, in 1998 and 1999, the rate of unemployment exceeded 6 per cent. As the economy recovered from the financial crisis, this dropped to around 4 per cent in 2001 and 2002 (see Table 2.4).

One feature captured in the growth process of the Korean economy is the remarkable growth in real wage. Real wages, defined as nominal wages deflated by the consumer price index, grew at an annual rate of 7.8 per cent during the period 1986-1996, higher than any international standard. Although the financial crisis resulted in a 9.3 per cent decrease in real wage in 1998, it rose again by 11.1 per cent in 1999. Such an improvement in real wage is often ascribed to the accumulation of human capital, among other factors.

Table 2.4   Unemployment (UE) rate in Korea

Year	UE rate	Year	UE rate	Year	UE rate
1963	8.1	1976	3.9	1989	2.6
1964	7.7	1977	3.8	1990	2.4
1965	7.3	1978	3.2	1991	2.3
1966	7.1	1979	3.8	1992	2.4
1967	6.1	1980	5.2	1993	2.8
1968	5.0	1981	4.5	1994	2.4
1969	4.7	1982	4.4	1995	2.0
1970	4.4	1983	4.1	1996	2.0
1971	4.4	1984	3.8	1997	2.6
1972	4.5	1985	4.0	1998	6.8
1973	3.9	1986	3.8	1999	6.3
1974	4.0	1987	3.1	2000	4.1
1975	4.1	1988	2.5	2001	3.7

Source: Korea National Statistical Office (2002), *http://kosis.nso.go.kr/cgi-bin/html_out.cgi?F*

Despite Korea's remarkable economic achievements, the labour market also has a dark side, epitomized by long working hours and a high incidence of industrial accidents. Although working hours in Korea have decreased substantially since the mid-1980s, they are still longer than most other countries for which relevant data are reported in the ILO Yearbook (47.5 hours per week in 2000). Although the number of persons losing work time through injury fell from 142,100 in 1986 to 69,100 in 2000, the number of deaths from fatal injuries actually increased from 1,660 in 1986 to 2,528 in 1998. In addition, the number of workdays lost due to occupational injuries slightly increased during 1986-2000 (from 38,171,000 days in 1986 to 44,090,000 days in 2000) (see Table 2.5).

Table 2.5   Wages and working conditions in Korea

Year	Changes in real wage (%) [a]	Weekly actual working hours (all industries) [b]	Persons injured with lost work time (1,000 persons) [a]	Deaths from occupational injuries (persons) [a]	Workdays lost due to occupational injuries (days) [a]
1986	5.3	52.5	142.1	1,660	38,171
1987	6.9	51.9	142.6	1,761	42,010
1988	7.8	51.1	142.3	1,925	38,566
1989	14.6	49.2	134.1	1,724	37,513
1990	9.4	48.2	132.9	2,236	43,588
1991	7.5	47.9	128.2	2,299	46,245
1992	8.4	47.5	107.4	2,429	50,574
1993	7.0	47.5	90.3	2,210	46,835
1994	6.1	47.4	85.9	2,678	52,676
1995	6.4	47.7	78.0	2,662	55,332
1996	6.6	47.3	71.5	2,670	44,082
1997	2.5	46.7	66.8	2,742	46,634
1998	-9.3	45.9	51.5	2,212	41,511
1999	11.1	47.9	55.4	2,912	39,398
2000	5.6	47.5	69.0	2,528	44,090
2001	1.5	-	-	-	-

Sources:
[a]   Korea Labour Institute (2002), *KLI Labour Statistics.*
[b]   Korea National Statistical Office (2002), *http://www.nso.go.kr/cgi-bin/sws_999.cgi.*

Government Policy on Employment and ER

Traditionally, Korea has been characterized as an anti-Communist developmentalist state in which the government has long given pre-eminence to two fundamental, substantive goals: national security under the threat of Communist North Korea and rapid economic growth. Specific policies have been legitimized by the demonstration of their contribution to one or both of these goals. Consequently, the state has played a dominant role in the labour relations process as well as in other policy areas, not by applying formal laws and regulations but by intervening to promote two key policy objectives: (1) building a productive labour force and (2) maintaining tight labour control and low labour costs.

Firstly, in the early stages of industrial development, in the absence of natural resources Korea achieved economic competitiveness in the international market through abundant, cheap and productive labour. The major goal of employment policy was to provide labour market and labour relations conditions that would promote rapid economic growth. This strategy was characterized by the term 'developmentalism' (Kim, 1993; Rodgers, 1990). Economic growth was accompanied by extensive investment in human resources and education: the ratio of government expenditure on education to the total government budget reached 17.4 per cent in 1994. This was greater than that of most major countries except Singapore (e.g., 10.8 per cent in Japan; 11.4 in the U.K.; 14.1 in the U.S.; 23.4 in Singapore) (Korea Labour Institute, 1998). The cultural value placed on education, influenced by Confucianism, was also instrumental in building a relatively high-quality labour force during the early period of economic growth. Approximately one-fifth of the adult Korean population has a college degree, the highest figure among OECD member countries after the United States and the Netherlands (OECD, 2000).

Secondly, during the period of economic growth, the maintenance of an unchallenging labour movement and low-waged labour force was believed to attract foreign investment, accomplish cost competitiveness for Korean products in overseas markets and consequently to promote continued growth. The government suppressed any independent labour movement for most of the post-war period, with only the government-controlled Federation of Korean Trade Unions (FKTU) recognized as a legal union federation until 1997. The state used the threat from the Communist North Korea as an excuse to justify its authoritarian labour policy. Under these circumstances, the independent labour movement was isolated from the existing social order and collective bargaining was not recognized as a mechanism by which to determine economic issues in industrial relations.

The process of political democratization since the late 1980s, however, has been accompanied by a surge of workforce militancy and violent labour disputes. Since the labour movement had been suppressed by successive governments, workers saw democratization as an opportunity to remove the vestiges of past labour suppression. Their demands were not confined solely to improved wages and working conditions: they sought political liberalization, the right to form and control their own unions and intervention in certain management prerogatives. Thus, since the late 1980s, Korea has been widely known for an aggressive and dynamic labour movement. Confronting unprecedented workforce militancy during this period, the state has increasingly lost control over the labour market as well as the trade unions (Kim, Bae and Lee, 2000).

The financial crisis in November 1997, however, resulted in a crisis consciousness among the three actors, and led them to form the Tripartite Commission, which would not otherwise have been possible due to their traditionally hostile relationships. In the past, the Korean government had considered labour to be an obstacle to economic development, subordinated official labour unions to the state and suppressed any independent labour movement. The creation of the Tripartite Commission implied that the Korean government regarded labour at least as a legitimate party (actor) to the political structure.

Within a month of the formation of the Tripartite Commission in January 1998, in the midst of the financial crisis, the Commission produced the first autonomous tripartite agreement in Korean labour history: the Social Compact. There was no doubt that the Social Compact improved the government's crisis management capacity and helped the country overcome the credit crunch. However, the Commission has not produced any significant agreement since then and its operation was effectively paralysed after the withdrawal of a key labour participant, the Korean Confederation of Trade Unions (KCTU), in February 1999. Although the government's effort to create a more consensual system of conflict resolution was noteworthy, the outcome has yet to be proved successful.

Labour Laws

As shown in Table 2.6, the legal system in the area of labour comprises three sources: the constitution, labour laws addressing individual issues and labour laws addressing collective issues. The new constitution in 1948 guaranteed the right to organize, the right to bargain collectively and the right to strike (Park, 1979). Subsequently in 1953, American-style labour laws were enacted to guarantee full-fledged trade union rights. However, throughout the 1960s and 1970s these laws were frequently revised so as to substantially restrict union activities. For example, an amendment in 1972 suppressed unions, and strikes were prohibited until 1980.

Since the late 1980s, there have been further revisions of labour laws, in the reverse direction (i.e., to provide more freedom). However, the current labour law, revised in 1998, still contains some restrictions on the labour movement, such as a prohibition of union activities for public employees and university professors and emergency arbitration of labour disputes in some industries by the Ministry of Labour. In the same context, Korea has not yet ratified any of the ILO's core human rights conventions (e.g., freedom of association and the recognition of the right to collective bargaining [conventions 87 and 98], the elimination of all forms of forced or compulsory labour [conventions 29 and 105], the abolition of child labour [convention 138] and the elimination of discrimination in respect of employment and occupation [convention 111]) (Kwon, 2000).

Table 2.6   Major labour laws in Korea

Classifications	Laws and articles
Constitution	1. Article 32 (Right to work)
	2. Article 33 (Right to bargain and right to act collectively)
Labour laws addressing individual issues	1. Labour standards act
	2. Minimum wage act
	3. Gender equality act
	4. Industrial safety and health act
	5. Basic employment policy act
	6. Employment security act
	7. Workers compensation act
	8. Basic vocational training act
Labour laws addressing collective issues	1. Trade union and arbitration act
	2. Labour relations commission act
	3. Act concerning the promotion of worker participation and cooperation

On the other hand, during the period of rapid economic growth, the Korean government formulated legal frameworks for individual labour rights. Although the collective rights of workers (i.e., the right to organize and to strike) were severely circumvented by successive governments, the rights of individuals were protected by detailed legislative measures. The underlying purpose of this imbalance seemed to be to discourage collective actions by providing individual-level protection. Korean laws and regulations covering individual workers' rights were, in some respects, more extensive than those of Western countries. For example, establishments with five or more employees could not lay off workers without just cause, courts recognized layoffs only if there was no other way of solving business problems and fair criteria were to be used to select the workers to be laid off. However, these protections were not always strictly enforced and did not enable the improvement of labour standards to keep pace with the speed of economic growth. Consequently, until the 1990s, labour standards for Korean workers were characterized by long working hours, low wages and a high incidence of occupational injuries in both absolute and relative terms.

Employers and Employment Practices

Economic growth in Korea has been led by large, indigenous, private organizations, receiving guidance and support (e.g., low-interest, long-term bank loans) from the state. Unlike Singapore and Taiwan, foreign direct investment has never played a central role in economic development, although since the 1997-1998 financial crisis it has become more influential. The Korean economy has been heavily dependent upon *chaebols*, such as Samsung, Hyundai, LG and SK. In the 1990s, the top 50 *chaebols* accounted for nearly 20 per cent of gross national product (GNP) and employment, and 40 per cent of sales in manufacturing.

Most private companies in Korea are still dominated by the founding father's family members (i.e., sons and grandsons). The style of management is generally considered to be authoritarian or paternalistic, although there is a substantial minority of companies with a participative or progressive management culture and style. Tayloristic management systems have been a dominant method of production, especially in manufacturing facilities, although a few more progressive employers have experimented with lean production (e.g., Samsung Electronics, Daewoo Motor Company) or team production (e.g., LG Electronics).

Since the late 1980s, most Korean employers have been uneasy about dealing with the newly formed and aggressive unions, tending to try to suppress them rather than to acknowledge their existence and legitimacy. Although the responses of employers to the emergence of militant unionism have varied, the main approach since 1987 has been to adopt hard-line methods of suppression (e.g., dismissal of union activists, blacklisting), rather than more accommodative means (Wilkinson, 1994). However, there are well-known exceptions where an ER system based upon the principle of the high performance work organization (HPWO) has been implemented, such as LG Electronics.

Employment practices in Korea have been characterized by the principles of the seniority-based wage and long-term employment. Under the traditional, long-term employment system, a company usually hired recent graduates. After joining the firm, workers received training, performed various jobs through rotations and transfers and were paid based upon the length of service. Traditionally there was no formal layoff system comparable to that of the US or European countries, and companies generally did not dismiss permanent employees. Until the 1990s, even when certain departments were over-staffed (because of business downturns), companies tried not to dismiss workers against their will. Instead, they retained them for as long as possible by reallocating them to different roles, reducing overtime and delivering paid off-the-job training sessions. Thus employment was, in principle, guaranteed until a certain age. Although this age varied in each company and industry, it was generally between 50 and 60. Although lifetime employment systems were limited mainly to regular, particularly male, workers in large companies, there was little doubt that they were the norm. Furthermore, the normative influence of these practices extended to smaller companies and even peripheral groups, such as part-time workers.

Since the 1997 economic crisis, however, the lifetime employment principle has almost broken down. Korean employers have been eager to adopt alternative employment principles to deal with the economic crisis. Korean government officials believed that securing labour market flexibility was a promising approach to improving the economic competitiveness of Korean firms, and encouraged private firms to implement bold restructuring programs, including massive layoffs. During the financial crisis, there were many incidents of workers being dismissed against their will using honorary retirement programs. Consequently, the unemployment rate in Korea rose sharply from 2.1 per cent in October 1997 to almost nine per cent in the early part of 1999. Reflecting the increasing use of contingent labour, outsourcing and employment restructuring, companies providing temporary workers, employee leasing and outplacement services have boomed since the late 1990s.

Since the financial crisis, Korean human resource management (HRM) has become increasingly Americanized. 360 degree appraisal has been introduced in an increasing number of firms; hiring decisions have been decentralized; the selection process puts more importance on interviews than traditional paper-and-pencil tests; training and education programs focus more on technical knowledge and skills than on loyalty and commitment to the company; and companies publicly announce that they do not provide employment security but rather employability. There had already been a tendency to adopt American-style HRM practices before the financial crisis, but it seemed to accelerate the trend (Kim and Yu, 2000).

The Labour Movement and Union Relations in Korea

After the breakdown by force of the Communist labour movement in 1949, the government recognized the Federation of Korean Trade Unions (FKTU) as the only legal, national-level union federation. The FKTU, established in

1960, received financial support from the government, and its policies and activities were generally subordinate to the state. Economic success, substantial wage increases and the military threat from North Korea were used by successive governments to justify their authoritarian labour policies, which contributed at least partially to the relatively low unionization ratio in Korea (lower than 20 per cent over the last two decades: see Table 2.7).

However, the policy of suppressing the labour movement and maintaining low labour costs was aligned with the interests of one side, namely employers, and in conflict with the interests of labour (Kim, 1993; Rodgers, 1990). Industrial growth, the emergence of a middle-class and rising levels of education all helped to strengthen workers' political base. From the late 1970s onward, a strong labour movement emerged separately from the formal union organization. This movement was characterized by a proliferation of wildcat strikes in the late 1970s and 1980s, and disputes over management-controlled company unions. The late 1980s saw a particular turning point. The 'Democratization Declaration' by President Rho Tae-Woo in June 1987 led to the greatest labour turmoil in Korean history, known as the 'Great Labour Struggle'. There were 3,749 strikes in 1987, a 13-fold increase over the previous year (see Table 2.7). Along with this unprecedented amount of labour unrest, the union movement has expanded. Union membership increased during the 1986-89 period from 16.8 to 19.8 per cent of employment. In the early 1990s, a militant – and illegal – national federation was organized, the Korea Confederation of Trade Unions (KCTU). After the largest general strike in Korean history in early 1997, the Trade Union Law was revised to allow the KCTU to become a legitimate union federation.

Most Korean unions are organized at the level of the individual enterprise. Members of enterprise unions are full-time, blue-collar and some white-collar workers (excluding temporary or part-time employees). While collective bargaining was circumscribed by the government until the late 1980s, since the Great Labour Struggle of 1987 it has become an increasingly important method of wage determination. In the unionized sector, wages and working hours are determined by collective bargaining between enterprise unions and individual employers, while there are multi-employer bargaining practices in the transportation, mining and textile industries.

Korean labour laws restrict collective activities to such an extent that many union activities in labour disputes are technically illegal. The government has not hesitated to break up illegal strikes with police troops and to arrest union leaders who have violated the substantive or procedural terms of the labour laws. For example, union members have been detained for participating in general strikes to protest against unpopular government labour policies (violation of substantive terms), or for beginning work stoppages despite being ordered by the Labour Relations Commission to bargain further (violation of procedural terms). At the bargaining table, unions will often demand the release of jailed union leaders and members who have been arrested in the last round for technically illegal activities. In several well-known cases, these legal issues, which are beyond the reach of individual employers, have become substantial obstacles to negotiation, resulting in impasse and further illegal strikes. This kind of vicious circle has been repeated a number of times. In this sense, the main problem in Korean labour relations is not labour-management disputes, but labour-state disputes. One task for the parties to ER may be to identify practical ways to minimize state intervention and maximize the space for voluntary and autonomous negotiation to take place between employers and employees.

Table 2.7   Industrial relations indicators in Korea

Year	Number of union members	Union membership ratio (%)	Number of strikes and lockouts	Workers involved in strikes and lockouts	Workdays lost due to strikes and lockouts
1981	966,738	20.8	186	34,586	30,948
1982	984,136	20.2	88	8,967	11,504
1983	1,009,881	19.4	98	11,100	8,671
1984	1,010,522	18.1	113	16,400	19,900
1985	1,004,398	16.9	265	28,700	64,300
1986	1,035,890	16.8	276	46,941	72,025
1987	1,267,457	18.5	3749	1,262,285	6,946,935
1988	1,707,456	19.5	1873	293,455	5,400,837
1989	1,932,415	19.8	1616	409,134	6,351,443
1990	1,886,884	18.4	322	133,916	4,487,151
1991	1,803,408	17.2	234	175,089	3,271,334
1992	1,734,598	16.4	235	105,034	1,527,612
1993	1,667,373	15.6	144	108,577	1,308,326
1994	1,659,011	14.5	121	104,339	1,484,368
1995	1,614,800	13.8	88	49,717	392,581
1996	1,598,558	13.3	85	79,495	892,987
1997	1,484,194	12.2	78	43,991	444,720
1998	1,401,940	12.6	129	146,065	1,452,096
1999	1,480,666	11.9	198	92,026	1,366,281
2000	1,526,955	12.0	250	177,969	1,893,563

Source: Korea National Statistical Office (2002), *http://kosis.nso.go.kr/cgi-bin.*

As the conflicts surrounding employment restructuring intensified after the 1997-1998 financial crisis, all aspects of strike activities also increased. As shown in Table 2.7, the number of strikes increased from 78 in 1997 to 250 in 2000. The number of workers involved in strikes rose from 43,991 employees in 1997 to 177,969 in 2000, and the number of working days lost due to strikes jumped from 444,720 days in 1997 to 1,893,563 in 2000. Interestingly, the number of strikes called to protest about employment and working conditions accounted for almost two-thirds of the total strike activities in the late 1990s (much greater than that of strikes due to wage issues). Thus, employment-related issues have been more important bargaining subjects than wage issues.

Chapter Summary

Since the early 1990s, Korea has been under heightened competitive pressures as a result of the challenges of the rapidly developing countries such as China, Thailand, Indonesia, Vietnam and Malaysia. These countries have begun to compete successfully with Korea in the low value-added manufacturing industries, mainly due to cheaper labour costs. Indeed, Korean economic competitiveness reached a near-crisis in the early 1990s, because Korean products were priced higher than those of low-wage competitors (i.e., China, Vietnam, Thailand and Malaysia), and their quality was known to be inferior to those of high value-added competitors (i.e., Europe, Japan and the U.S.). The slowdown of the Korean economy had already begun in the early 1990s, and the 1997-1998 financial crisis seemed to be a culmination of the decline in competitiveness. Although the subsequent recovery weakened the crisis consciousness among the Korean people, the task of improving economic competitiveness remains. Since the financial crisis, Korean policymakers have attempted to upgrade the economy by finding niche markets and developing the information technology (IT) and biotechnology (BT) industries.

Both the state and employers in Korea have seen their authoritarian regimes challenged by the labour movement in the wake of the democratization process. While there have been efforts to seek out a new model of industrial relations which will be conducive to a more democratic society, they have so far failed to embrace the newly emerging militant segments of labour (Wilkinson, 1994). The need for a new model of industrial relations is more urgent in the era of restructuring and downsizing. Although the state did put notable efforts into the creation of the Tripartite Commission, at this point its effectiveness is questionable.

Without embracing labour in the policy-making process, states may experience serious conflicts in the implementation of economic restructuring programs. Indeed, when the ruling party (the New Korean Party) passed the January 1997 labour law that enhanced flexibility in the utilization of human resources and gave employers substantial freedom to lay off employees against their will, labour (both the KCTU and the FKTU) responded with the biggest general strike in Korean history, involving more than two million participants. In this sense, the future of the Korean economy and its ER system depends in part on the development of an overarching ideology and a set of congruent rules that can accommodate the interests of all three parties in the era of restructuring.

References

ILO (1999), *The Social Impact of Globalization in the Republic of Korea*, ILO, Geneva.

Kim, D.-O. (1993), 'An analysis of Labor Disputes in Korea and Japan: The Search for an Alternative Model', *European Sociological Review*, vol.9, no.2, pp.139-154.

Kim, D.-O., Bae, J. and Lee, C. (2000), 'Globalization and Labor Rights: The Case of Korea', *Asia Pacific Business Review*, vol.6, no.3/4, pp.133-153.

Kim, D.-O. and Yu, G.-C. (2000), 'Emerging Patterns of Human Resource Management in Korea: Evidence from Large Korean Firms', in *Proceedings of the 12th World Congress of the International Industrial Relations Association*, May 29 – June 2, International Industrial Relations Association, Tokyo, pp.195-206.

Korea Labour Institute (1998), *Overseas Labour Statistics*, Korea Labour Institute, Seoul. (In Korean.)

Korea Labour Institute (2001), *KLI Labour Statistics* Korea Labour Institute, Seoul. (In Korean.)

Korea Labour Institute (2000), *Overseas Labour Statistics*, Korea Labour Institute, Seoul. (In Korean.)

Korea National Statistical Office (2002), *http://kosis.nso.go.kr/cgi-bin/sws_999.cgi*.

Kwon, J. D. (2000), *ILO and International Labor Standards*, Joong Ang KyungJe, Seoul. (In Korean.)

National Statistical Office (Various Years), *Yearbook of Economically Active Population Survey*, Korea Labour Institute, Seoul. (In Korean.)

OECD (2000), *Pushing Ahead with Reform in Korea Labor Market and Social Safety-net Policies*, OECD, Paris.

Park, Y.-B. and Lee, M.B. (1995), 'Economic Development, Globalization, and Practices in Industrial Relations and Human Resource Management in Korea', in A. Verma, T.A. Kochan and R.D. Lansbury (eds), *Employment Relations in the Growing Asian Economies*, Routledge, New York, pp.27-61.

Park, Y.-K. (1979), *Labor and Industrial Relations in Korea: System and Practice*, Sogang University Press, Seoul.

Rodgers, R.A. (1990), 'An Exclusive Labor Regime under Pressure: The Changes in Labor Relations in the Republic of Korea since Mid-1987', *UCLA Pacific Basin Law Journal*, vol.8, pp.91-161.

Seoul Economic Daily (2001), *International Trade and Korea*, May 17.

Wilkinson, B. (1994), *Labor and Industry in the Asia-Pacific: Lessons from the Newly-Industrialized Countries*, Walter de Gruyter. New York.

3 Cultural Background and Organizational Strategy

This chapter introduces the environment of social and organizational culture that underpins Korean ER/HRM systems, before explaining key organizational strategic issues as further background. As other organizational and managerial factors have changed, shared values and norms of society and its organizations have also shifted. Accordingly, it is necessary to analyse these aspects of culture in order to better understand Korean ER/HRM systems.

National Culture

Confucian Heritage

Korea's religious and philosophical beliefs are rooted not just in Confucianism, but also Buddhism and the Taoist traditions of holism, which are shared with its Asian neighbours (Morden and Bowles, 1998). Buddhism was the national religion during both the *Silla* (BC 57 ~ AD 935) period and the era of *Koryo* (AD 918-1392), the ancient Korean states. The Bulguksa Temple and the Sokkuram stone cave shrine were built in Kyongju, the capital of Silla. Korean Buddhist thought is closely related to the philosophical thinking of Chinese Buddhism. However, Korean masters, with intensive research and practice, created a distinct version, differentiated by aspects such as the holistic Buddhist practice of three approaches, meditation, studying sutras and haunting in the period of forming a new direction. The Unified Silla employed Buddhism as the fundamental socio-political ideology for the reconciliation and the integration of people, regions and social classes. Hence, the main ideology of Korean Buddhism is the pursuit of compassion, harmony and unification, which originates from Silla Master Wonhyo's thoughts. His whole philosophy is centred on the idea of reconciliation. This emphasis on compassion, taken along with traditional Confucianism, has had a long-term impact on Korean society, surfacing in such aspects of HRM as the paternalistic approach and work harmonization.

The most obvious feature of the Taoist influence on the Korean people is the search for blessings and longevity. The indelible Taoist marks put into the two Chinese characters *su* (longevity) and *bok* (bliss) appear on many everyday objects such as spoons, pillow cases and doors of wardrobes. This is evidence that Taoism has permeated the everyday life of the Korean people. The strongest imprint of its teachings can be found in the guiding principles of the Hwarang of Silla (a group of elite youths in the Silla Dynasty who excelled in beauty, bravery and military arts), namely patience, simplicity, contentment and harmony. Taoism is also related to the ideas of yin-yang and the 'Five Agents' (metal, wood, water, fire and earth). Other important features include a belief in physical immortality, alchemy, breath control and hygiene (internal alchemy).

Beyond Buddhism and Taoism, Confucianism has also been very influential in Korean history. It was the state religion during the 600-plus years of the Yi Dynasty (1392-1910). Confucianism influenced not only the values and norms, ways of thinking, attitudes and conduct of Koreans, but also affected corporate culture and management systems and practices. Therefore, some understanding of its contents and role is necessary for an informed analysis of Korean ER/HRM systems.

Since it is not an easy task to explain all the Confucianist beliefs in one chapter, we will approach it by introducing the five ethical codes governing human relations. These include: (1) filial piety to parents (or a close relationship between a father and son); (2) absolute loyalty of subjects to sovereigns (or the king); (3) obedience to one's husband and warmth toward one's wife (or separate roles for women and men); (4) precedence of the elder over the younger (or respect for elders); and (5) mutual trust among friends. These codes place an emphasis on harmony and social order. Although their influence is gradually eroding, many of these teachings have been accepted as socially desirable until relatively recently. Everyone is expected to abide by these ethical codes, and the strong social norms have led to disapproval of those who defy them.

The Confucian traditions led on the one hand to hierarchical and unequal relationships between senior and junior members of society, and between the upper class and the lower class. High priority was traditionally given to members of the upper class and more 'senior' people. There were four classes in the society of the Chosun dynasty (from 1392 to 1910): the *yangban* (ruling or upper class), the *jungin* or *seoin* (middle class), the *sangmin* or *yangin* (peasant farmers and craftsmen) and the *cheonmin* (underprivileged class). This feudal system, rigidly stratified from top to bottom, was maintained by a hierarchical and authoritarian structure (Kwon and O'Donnell, 2001). This tradition influenced leadership style, which was authoritarian and hierarchical, and brought about unequal relationships between members of different social strata. However, on the other hand, the Confucian traditions also generated some sense of equality.

Afterwards people began to disregard the ruling class or leaders during the colonial period and the subsequent authoritarian military governments. This trend was reinforced after people saw a number of political and economic leaders publicly exposed as corrupt. Under this momentum, the Korean people generated a greater sense of social equality. In addition, the Confucian tradition itself also emphasizes the obligation of senior or upper class people to take care of junior and lower class people with courtesy. Therefore, within Confucianism, equality is perhaps a necessary condition for inhwa (harmony).

In short, the Confucian tradition has had both a positive and negative impacts on the relationships among people. These social values and norms resulted in and are related to several other ideological orientations such as familism, collectivism and yongoism, to which we shall now turn.

Familism

Confucian beliefs emphasize the importance of one's family and clan. One important tradition is ancestor worship. The rite is usually held at the eldest son's house. This tradition has an impact both at family and company level.

Within a family, this tradition has resulted in such cultural features as a preference for sons over daughters, the adoption of one's brother's son and unequal inheritance in favour of the eldest son. The older generations preferred sons to daughters. In the past, many families kept on having babies until they had a boy. When a family had no son, the head of the family adopted one from his nearest relatives (usually his brother) so as to carry on the line. However, adoption from a family where no blood-based relationship existed was uncommon in Korean society. As a result, many Korean children have been internationally adopted by families from foreign countries. In addition, the eldest son usually inherited the family assets and took over his father's rights over and duties for the family.

At the company level, familism resulted in family-based management and ownership on the one hand, and a paternalistic approach to the employment relationship on the other. The aforementioned inheritance system was also applied to the business arena. Many companies had blood-based succession practices. Many *chaebol* groups were established and run by founders and scions of such families as Lee (Samsung), Chung (Hyundai) and Koo (LG). 'Clan' (chiban) has extensively influenced the organization and management of such enterprises. Even the employer-employee relationship can be seen as an extension of familism. Owner-employers usually regard their employees as extended family members. Employees have a strong loyalty and sense of belonging. This has brought about a primarily paternalistic leadership style.

Collectivism

Human relations in the five aforementioned Confucian ethical codes seem to have generated predetermined, unequal relationships. However, these did not necessarily generate one-sided misrule. Rather, the emphasis has been on harmony in human relations. In the Korean language, the plural form (e.g., we, our, or us) has normally been used to designate the single form (e.g., I, my, or me). Here we explain collectivism in Korea.

According to Hofstede (1991), collectivism refers to 'a society in which people from birth onwards are integrated into strong, cohesive in-groups, which throughout people's lifetime continue to protect them in exchange for unquestioning loyalty' (p.51.). Korea, Japan and China belong to the collectivist type of society (Hofstede, 1991; Hofstede and Bond, 1988). However, these countries take different approaches to their collectivism. Collectivism in Korea has some common features with both Chinese and Japanese, but it also has unique aspects. In Japan the concept, based on enterprise collectivism, is characterized by commitment and loyalty to the firm on the one hand, and harmony and solidity among people, groups and departments on the other (Hampden-Turner and Trompenaars, 1993). The Japanese emphasize group harmony (wa) (Cho and Yoon, 2001). Collectivism in China is characterized by loyalty and solidity to the inner circle of family, so it relies more on guanxi (relational networking) (Redding, 1990). The scope of guanxi goes beyond the group or enterprise level. In this sense, Korean collectivism is similar to Chinese, being a *yongo*-based,[1] inner circle-centred philosophy which stresses harmony within an inner circle. However, the Korean concept of harmony (inhwa) focuses on the emotional aspect of relationships, while Chinese guanxi centres on the exchange of favours (Cho and Yoon, 2001).

Collectivism in Korea, which we can term dynamic collectivism, can be characterized by in-group harmony, optimistic progressivism and the hierarchical principle (Cho and Yoon, 2001). In-group harmony generates internal cohesiveness and solidity and involves personal sacrifice for the inner circle and collective goals, and dynamic interactions and active exchanges of information and knowledge among in-group members. For the out-group, different principles are usually applied. Therefore, the harmony does not go beyond the group boundary. This limited coverage of group harmony is called bounded collectivism (Bae and Rowley, 2001). Optimistic progressivism is another feature of dynamic collectivism. Korean people have optimistic views about the future. Companies also set high performance goals and quantifiable targets (Cho and Yoon, 2001). This feature also generates in-group solidity and unity, and at the same time creates some tension and competitive relationships with out-groups. This feature is also related to the can-do spirit, *palli-palli* (literally, quickly-quickly or hurry up) culture and a climate which values hard work. Some negative implications include neglect of due process, sacrifice of personal and family life and loss of health. The final feature of dynamic collectivism is the hierarchical principle. This characteristic is related to the aforementioned Confucian ethical codes and to familism and the paternalistic style. Employers and managers take responsibility for their employees and even their employees' families, while employees in turn have a strong loyalty and commitment to their boss and group (Cho and Yoon, 2001).

All these features taken together constitute dynamic collectivism. Collectivism in Korea is dynamic in the sense that it has active dynamics within the in-group but some tension and competition among groups, which generate and some paradoxical aspects. This collectivism and in-group nature is highly related to *yongo*-based connections, to which we now turn.

Yongoism

Yongo refers to connection. *Yongo*-based relations have pervaded almost every aspect of Korean society. Three of *yongo's* different manifestations are *hyulyon* (connection by blood), *hakyon* (by education) and *jiyon* (by geography). The existence or non-existence of *yongo* will result in different outcomes in decision-making, attitude and behaviour. *Yongo* has been applied to such cases as a medical appointment in a general hospital, promotion within a company, recruitment, political campaigning and elections and the selection of partner for strategic alliances. Pivotal centres for *hyulyon*, *hakyon* and *jiyon* are clan councils (a meeting of family members with the same ancestral root), an alumni association and a hometown friendly society, respectively.

Hyulyon originates in blood- or marriage-based relations. Since Korean clans have been traditionally based on the paternal bloodline, relatives on the mother's side have low priority, as do those with a more distant relationship to the patriarch. Company succession is also related to hyulyon. According to a survey of 486 company chairmen and presidents in 1984, 124 respondents (25.5 per cent) stated that they would select their children or relatives as the successor to the company (Korea Chamber of Commerce and Industry, 1984).

Hakyon ties are usually formed among alumni of the same high school or university. Such connections are prevalent in many areas of Korean society including political parties, company executive teams and faculty members of universities. Kim and Moon (2002) analysed resumes submitted by outside directors to the Korean Listed Companies Association in 2000 and compared the data with those from owners and professional CEOs. They established the existence of high school and college ties. The data showed that 266 (10.4 per cent) out of 2549 outside directors had high school links and 121 (12.3 per cent) college links with owners, whereas 121 (5.6 per cent) had high school and 247 (25.3 per cent) college connections with professional CEOs. These results do not support the intention of government regulations intended to improve the transparency of corporate management.

In the case of college faculty composition, as of April of 2001, 96.1 per cent of faculty members of Seoul National University (SNU) had been graduated from the SNU. In the cases of Yonsei and Korea Universities, 71.8 per cent and 66.7 per cent of faculty members were graduates of their own institutions (The Dong-a Ilbo, April 1, 2002).

Jiyon denotes connection on the basis of regional origin, usually hometown or birthplace. The Korean peninsula has been physically and ideologically divided into South and North Korea for more than 50 years. South Korea has been further politically and psychologically divided into east (Yongnam district; the south-eastern part of Korea) and west (Honam district; the south-western part of Korea). Since the 1945 liberation from Japan, most presidents of Korea have come from the Yongnam district. Kim Dae-jung in 1998 was the first president to come from the Honam district. Before his election, people living in the Honam district felt politically, economically and socially victimized. Under the current government, the situation has been suddenly reversed. People are still debating whether the changes brought in are remedial measures for past discrimination or further discrimination now turned against the Yongnam district.

The distribution by hometown of people holding one of the 120 key high-ranking government posts shows some interesting results. The number of government officials from the Yongnam district decreased from 41.5 under the Kim Young-sam (from Yongnam) administration to 38.4 under Kim Dae-jung. However, the number of officials from the Honam district increased from 11 to 27.3 over the same time period (The Dong-a Ilbo, April 2, 2002). Kim and Moon's (2002) analysis also shows that township ties (jiyon) exist in companies' governance structure. In 2000, 438 (37.3 per cent) of outside directors had ties with the owner's birthplace, while 392 (41.2 per cent) of outside directors had such ties with the birthplace of professional CEOs.

In summary, while these *yongo*-based relations facilitate dynamic interactions among in-group members, they result in a high degree of exclusion of out-group members. When institutions were inefficient and not well established, *yongo*-ism actually played a facilitating role, expediting progress. This can be positively interpreted as the exercise of social capital. However, the *yongo*-based tradition also hampers the process of enhancing trust and transparency, resulting in inefficiency, corruption and selfishness. It also facilitates the practice of taking care of people who have connections rather than competencies, constituting high and strong entry barriers to, for example, a certain status.

Economic Development and National Culture

The paradoxical relationship between Confucian values and economic development has been addressed in previous research (Bae and Rowley, 2001). Before Asian countries were economically developed, Confucian values and collectivism were considered hindrances to economic progress when compared to Western values and individualism. When the 'Asian tigers' showed rapid economic development, many attributed it to such traditions (Sinha and Kao, 1988; Hofstede and Bond, 1988) but when the 1997 crisis hit, Confucian traditions were once again attacked. Triandis (1973) explains earlier economic development models by constructing a dichotomy between the attitudinal characteristics of 'traditional' and 'modern' societies. This means that economic development requires change in attitudes and values. This paradigm of development has been challenged. Sinha and Kao (1988:12) argue that Asian development and growth has been '... widely attributed to both management styles and work attitudes that are rooted in Confucian social values, familism and institutional structure that are not necessarily Euro-American'. Triandis (1988) also argues that both individualism and collectivism have had some influence on economic development and organizational effectiveness. Therefore, it might be unreasonable to assert that collectivism is not related to (or is negatively related to) economic development. However, Confucian values are not sufficient in themselves to ensure this although they may be necessary (Hofstede, 1991). Attributing the rapid industrial progress of the 'Asian tigers' to the Confucian tradition fails to explain the equally rapid industrialization of non-Confucian countries in South America and Southeast Asia (Kim, 1997).

Therefore, rapid economic development and expeditious learning at the national level cannot be solely attributed to Confucian traditions. It may make more sense to attribute rapid learning and development to such situational factors as individual commitment and entrepreneurship, discipline at the organizational level, effective mobility and networking at the societal level and particular cultural traits at the national level (Kim, 1997). The relationship between values and development is interactive rather than uni-directional, or may even be circular in the sense that social values produce economic development, which brings about cultural change, which in turn results in further development and so on (Bae and Rowley, 2001; Sinha and Kao, 1988; Triandis, 1994).

While we accept that the Confucian tradition is not the only reason for Korea's rapid economic development, there is no doubt about its contribution, made in two different ways: by improving the Korean people's general competence and by enhancing their levels of commitment. First of all, the Confucian tradition emphasized education, which in turn enhanced the general competence of workers (Bae, 1997). The existence of a well-educated and skilled workforce with a concomitant investment in human resource development was positively related to rapid industrialization and economic development. This is demonstrated by the high levels of literacy, high enrolment rate in the corresponding age group, high ratio of education and R&D expenditure to gross domestic product (GDP) and the high proportion of scientists and engineers per head of population.

For Koreans, education has been considered one of the best and quickest ways to improve social status and to achieve *jasusungga* (making one's own fortune). From the Chosun dynasty onwards, high-ranking officials have been recruited via the highest-level state examination. Passing this board or gaining a degree from a prestigious university is a way to elevate one's status. This is one reason why Koreans spend such huge amounts on their children's education. Their heavy investment is evident in both the levels of school enrolment and participation in private education. As shown in Table 3.1, several indicators of human resource development have continually improved during this century. By 1995, the gross enrolment rates for secondary and tertiary education were about 90 and 55 per cent respectively, which compares favourably with most OECD countries (World Development Report, 1998/99). The enrolment rates later increased for secondary and tertiary education (see Table 3.1). More than 70 per cent of the workforce in Korea has been graduated from high school.

In terms of the ratio of central government education expenditure to GDP, Korea spent 1.9 per cent in 1965, 2.9 per cent in 1980 and 3.6 per cent in 2000. The high level of education influenced rapid development, which along with economic growth also brought about huge investment in human capital. The recent World Development Report (1998/99: 1) also attributes the rapid increase of income per capita in Korea to its success in acquiring and utilizing knowledge. It reported that 40 years ago Ghana and Korea had virtually the same income per capita, but that by the early 1990s Korea's was six times higher. In addition to education, both governments and private firms have spent hugely on research and development (R&D). Up to the early 1980s, the government spent more than private firms, and then the ratio was reversed from the mid 1980s onwards. The number of researchers started out as only 2,135, rapidly increasing to 159,973 in 2000. The ratio of R&D expenditure to GNP was 2.89 in 1997.

Table 3.1 Human resource development in Korea

Indicator \ Year	1965	1970	1975	1980	1985	1990	1995	2000
Enrolment Percentage[a]								
Elementary School (ages 6-11)	97.7	100.7	105.0	102.9	99.9	101.7	100.1	98.5
Middle School (ages 12-14)	41.4	51.2	71.9	95.1	100.1	98.2	101.6	99.1
High School (ages 15-17)	26.4	28.1	41.0	63.5	79.5	88.0	91.8	96.4
Tertiary School[b]	7.2	8.4	9.3	15.9	35.1	37.7	55.1	80.5
No of School Students (1,000)								
Middle Schools	751	1,319	2,027	2,472	2,782	2,276	2,482	1,861
High Schools	427	590	1,123	1,697	2,153	2,284	2,158	2,071
Junior Colleges	23	33	63	165	242	324	570	913
Universities	106	146	209	403	932	1,040	1,188	1,665
No of Graduates (1,000)								
Junior College	8	8	14	52	74	87	143	223
University	36	24	34	50	119	166	181	214
No of Tertiary School Students (per 10,000 pop)	49.5	62.5	98.7	140.2	355.7	389.9	519.8	711.5
The Ratio of Education Expenditure to (%)								
GDP	1.9	2.9	2.2	2.9	3.1	2.8	3.3	3.6
Government Budget	16.2	17.6	14.4	18.9	19.9	22.3	22.8	19.8

Notes:
[a] Enrolment as a percentage of the corresponding age group.
[b] Tertiary education institution includes junior colleges, universities of education and universities.
Sources: Ministry of Education and Korean Educational Development Institute. Handbook of educational statistics, 2000. (KEDI, 2000). Ministry of Education and Human Resources Development and Korean Educational Development Institute. The profile of educational statistics. (KEDI: 2001).

All these indicators show that human resources have been developed extensively at both national and firm levels. The number of researchers per

10,000 head of population has risen from only 0.7 in 1965 to 28.5 in 1995 (see Table 3.2).

Table 3.2   Researchers and expenditures in research and development (1965-2000; billions of won)

	1965	1970	1975	1980	1985	1990	1995	2000
R&D Expenditures	2.1	10.5	42.7	282.5	1,237.1	3,349.9	9,440.6	13,848.5
Government	1.9	9.2	30.3	180.0	306.8	651.0	1,779.5	3,451.8
Private Sector	0.2	1.3	12.3	102.5	930.3	2,698.9	7,661	10,396.7
Government vs. Private	61:39	97:03	71:29	64:36	25:75	19:81	19:81	25:75
R&D/GNP	0.26	0.38	0.42	0.77	1.58	1.95	2.71	2.69[c]
R&D Expenditures (% of Sales in Mfg.)	NA	NA	0.36[b]	0.50	1.51	1.96	2.55	2.17[d]
Number of Researchers (Total)[a]	2,135	5,628	10,275	18,434	41,473	70,503	128,315	159,973
Government/ Public Institution	1,671	2,458	3,086	4,598	7,542	10,434	15,007	13,913
Universities	352	2,011	4,534	8,695	14,935	21,332	44,683	51,727
Private Sector	112	1,159	2,655	5,141	18,996	38,737	68,625	94,333
R&D Expenditure/ Researcher (W 1,000)	967	1,874	4,152	15,325	27,853	47,514	73,574	86,568
Researcher/ 10,000 Population	0.7	1.7	2,9	4.8	10.1	16.4	28.5	4.9[e]

Notes:
[a]   The figures do not include research assistants, technicians and other supporting personnel.
[b]   For 1976.
[c]   The figure represents R&D/GNI (gross national income).
[d]   The figure includes R&D expenditures of firms to external recipients too.
[e]   The figure represents 'researcher/1,000 working population'.

Sources: Ministry of Science and Technology (Korea), *Report on the Survey of Research and Development in Science and Technology* (Seoul : MOST, 1994 and 2000).

Transitions in National Culture

Recently, some scholars have asserted that the Confucian tradition in Korea had changed into 'neo-Confucianism' as a result of the influences of Western cultures and Christianity (Bae, 1997; Kim, 1997). Neo-Confucianism is a blending of East and West, and of old and new, characterized by an amalgam of familism, collectivism, and evaluation and payment based on seniority on the one hand, and pragmatism, ability orientation and individualism on the other.

In this transitional period, the Korean people have placed a high value on both tradition and the new ideas of individualism and personal achievement. Consequently, the five ethical codes of traditional Confucianism have been challenged, as have paternalistic authoritarianism, the seniority-based approach, familism, *yongo*-ism and collectivism. These changes in cultural features are summarized in Figure 3.1. The erosion of traditional values has been influenced both by domestic factors such as industrialization, democracy and labour disputes and external factors such as the adoption of Western cultures and Christianity.

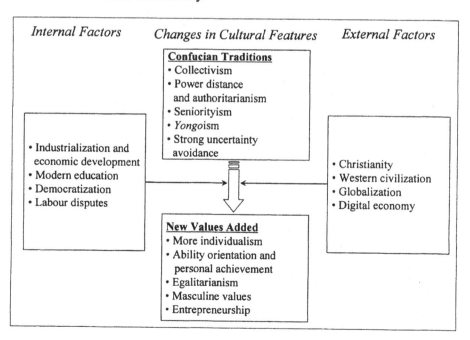

Figure 3.1   Changes in cultural features

In Korea, strikes have been strongly linked to political instability (together with social change and the development of the labour movement) rather than economic conditions. Hence, the 1987 Great Labour Struggle was a reflection of social and political turbulence. In addition, many conflicts have arisen between different groups: north and south, east and west, labour and management, rich and poor, male and female and older and younger. Some of these conflicts have been associated with changes in social values. Consequently, Korean society has experienced anomie and some of the aforementioned social values have been seriously challenged. This trend is also reflected in the changes in HRM, towards systems based more on performance/ability, in the early 1990s. These have been accelerated by the influences of globalization and the financial crisis of 1997. For example, Korean people have traditionally excluded foreign people and other countries. The reasons for this include the fact that the population is largely homogeneous in terms of ethnic group, some bad experiences of foreign countries and rulers and the tradition of a closed and passive agrarian society. However, attitudes changed enormously, both voluntarily and involuntarily, after the financial crisis. Hofstede (1991), from a cross-cultural perspective, characterizes Korean culture as having the following features: (1) a large power distance (scored 60 on the power distance index); (2) collectivism (scored 18 on the individualism index); (3) a feminine side (scored 39 on the masculinity index); (4) high uncertainty avoidance (scored 85 on the uncertainty avoidance index) and (5) a long-term orientation (scored 75 on the long-term orientation). Although here we have no concrete evidence, our general impression is that all of these dimensions are now changing toward the other ends of the continua. The more universal rather than country-specific, and peripheral rather than core, values and norms were probably first to change.

Organizational Culture

In this section, we explain some aspects of Korean companies' organizational culture. General social values and norms have had an influence on organizational values and norms. More recently, just as has been the case for the national culture, organizational cultures have been challenged and have transformed so as to adapt to globalized and turbulent environments.

Two Faces of National Culture: Positive and Negative Roles

Korean culture has two faces in terms of its role in the process of adopting employment systems. Here we must distinguish between two different levels of culture: the basic set of values themselves, and the routine practices which firms derive from them. Both underlying values and routine practices, as shown in Figure 3.2, can have dual roles, either facilitating or impeding the adoption of such approaches as high performance work systems (HPWS) (Bae and Rowley, 2001).

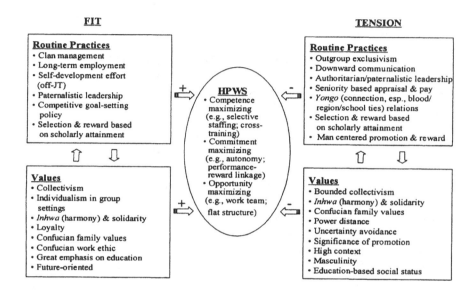

Figure 3.2   Dual roles of national culture in adoption of HPWS

Source: Reprinted from Journal of World Business, Vol.36(4), Bae, J. and Rowley, C., The impact of globalization on HRM: The case of South Korea, p.416, Copyright (2001), with permission from Elsevier.

In Figure 3.2, 'fit' refers to the facilitating role, and 'tension' the hampering role of culture in adopting HPWS. Fit and tension can occur at both the level of values and of routine practices. First of all, the Korean cultural tradition can easily support the adoption of high involvement HPWS: for example, the underlying values and norms of Korean society such as loyalty, cooperation and harmony mesh well with this (Lee and Johnson, 1998). Korea's collectivism can also align well with work teams, which are a linchpin of HPWS. However, aspects of bounded collectivism (e.g., the exclusive limitation of harmony to those within the group boundary) impede the adoption of a work team system. Furthermore, when the team leader is 'junior', this lead to considerable difficulties in demonstrating 'leadership' as seniority rules still operate. This argument has two main implications. From the macro perspective, changes to social values may generate tradeoffs, bringing some of both 'fit' and 'tension'. At the micro firm level, management needs to activate positive values whilst impeding some negative values.

Social Values and Corporate Cultural Characteristics

The five ethical codes of Confucianism and their impact on corporate cultural characteristics and management systems and practices are summarized in Table 3.3. The social values of traditional hierarchical family systems have influenced Korean companies, making them strongly hierarchical, with vertical organizational principles[2] (Bae and Rowley, 2001). In addition, a similar level of importance has been assigned to the authority and paternalism of owner managers. Among peers at work, trustworthy relations, collectivism, a strong sense of duty and *inhwa* are highly valued. They usually work hard and are devoted to the company. As depicted in the table, the traditional social values governing human relations are directly responsible for some features of HRM systems and practices, such as seniority-based systems, the paternalistic approach, long-term attachments, tenure-based promotions and job grade by cohort. As influenced by the traditional social values, Korean ER systems and practices were characterized by severe labour disputes, a strong sense of solidarity and a unitary view of ER.

A survey of 88 Korean large companies in 12 different industries conducted in the late 1980s showed evidence of these core values in their vision statements (Lee, 1997). The following concepts were obtained from the vision statements: inhwa, solidarity and cooperation (46.4 per cent); devotion and hard work (44.2 per cent); creativity and development (41.2 per cent); honesty and credibility (28.8 per cent); quality, technology and productivity (16.9 per cent); responsibility (16.9 per cent); progressiveness or enterprising spirit (14.3 per cent); national wealth through business (14.3 per cent); rational and scientific approach (10.4 per cent); and sacrifice and service, etc. (6.9 per cent).

Another survey in 2000 involving the top 10 corporate groups showed a change in the core values of Korean firms. The rank order of the values from the top was creativity, adaptability to change, challenge, teamwork, integrity and devotion, hard work, loyalty to the organization and obedience to the boss. Interestingly, while the latter four values (i.e., integrity and devotion, hardworking, loyalty to organization and obedience to boss) decreased in significance compared to 1995, the former four values (i.e., creativity, adaptability to change, challenge, teamwork) gained in relative importance. This data reflects recent changes in Korean firms' core ideology (i.e., core values and company credos) with more emphasis on creativity, competitiveness, value creation, diversity, customer satisfaction, respect for the individual and so on. Examples of core values and credos in chaebols include respect for the individual, the pursuit of technology and empowerment (Samsung); value creation for customers, respect for the individual and empowerment (LG); diligence, thriftiness, trust and affection (Hyundai); humanism, rationalism and realism (SK); trust, credibility, innovativeness and inhwa (Sangyong); and creativity, challenge and sacrifice (Daewoo) (Chung, Lee and Jung, 1997).

Table 3.3 Confucian ethical codes and corporate culture and systems

The Five Ethical Codes Governing Human Relations	Features of Corporate Culture	Features of Traditional HRM and ER Systems and Practices
Filial piety to parents; close relationship between father and son	Belongingness; kinship-based relations; *inhwa*	Employment relationship as an extension of familism; long-term attachment
Absolute loyalty of subjects to sovereigns (or to the king)	Owner manager's authority and paternalism	Personality (not ability) as recruitment criterion; severe labour disputes; unitary view of ER
Obedience to husband and warmth toward wife; separate roles for women and men	Hardworking attitude and devotion to company (esp., men)	Glass ceiling and discrimination against women
Precedence of or respect for elder over younger	Hierarchical relationship between managers and employees	Seniority-based systems; tenure-based promotions
Mutual trust among friends	Trustworthy relations among peers; camaraderie; collectivism	Job grade by cohort; strong labour solidarity

To investigate the culture of companies operating in Korea, we employed the competing values framework of a culture quadrant developed by Cameron, reported in Cameron (1978) and Quinn (1988). The cultural dimensions and items used for this framework included:

- group culture: a very personal place, like an extended family; head of the unit as mentor or sage; 'glue' is loyalty and tradition; emphasis on human resources;
- developmental culture: very dynamic and entrepreneurial place; head of unit is an innovator or risk taker; 'glue' is a commitment to innovation and development; emphasis on growth and acquiring new resources;
- rational culture: very production orientation; head of unit as producer or technician; 'glue' is tasks and goal accomplishment; emphasis on competitive actions and achievement;
- hierarchical culture: very formalized and structured place; head of unit is a coordinator or an organizer; 'glue' is the formal rules and policies; emphasis on permanence and stability.

Using this instrument, we surveyed 103 companies operating in Korea in 2000 (Rowley and Bae, 2002). The sample consisted of 41 indigenous Korean firms, 28 American, 10 Japanese and 24 European subsidiaries. Although these firms were not representative of each group, some interesting information emerged from the results (see Table 3.4). Overall, an ANOVA test for the between-country groups indicated that except for group culture, all the competing value quadrants (i.e., developmental, rational and hierarchical) were statistically significant at the conventional level ($p=0.05$). The post hoc test using the Tukey method showed that American subsidiaries, compared to Korean or Japanese, had higher values for both developmental and rational cultures. However, for hierarchical culture, Asian (Korean and Japanese) firms had higher values on average. European subsidiaries were in the middle, between oriental and American firms.

In the case of the between-value comparison, both Korean and Japanese firms had higher values for group and hierarchical values vis-à-vis developmental and rational values, while the reverse was true in American firms. All these results are consistent with the aforementioned characteristics of social and corporate values and norms in Korea.

Recent Changes in Corporate Cultures[3]

Ghoshal and Bartlett (1997) suggest that worldwide management roles are undergoing transformation in an era of high uncertainty. The changes they suggest are taking place are from 'resource allocators' to 'institutional leaders' for top-level managers, 'administrative controllers' to 'supportive coaches' for senior managers and from 'operational implementers' to 'aggressive entrepreneurs' for operating-level managers. These suggestions can also be applied to Korean firms and management. Traditional Korean culture facilitated top-down, paternalistic and authoritarian styles of leadership, similar to the pre-transformation management roles Ghoshal and Bartlett suggest (1997). Given the highly uncertain environments within the digital, global and knowledge-based economies, some transition towards the latter style of management is crucial. This transition would bring about some cultural conflict, which would then need to be resolved.

Table 3.4   Cultural differences between Korean indigenous firms and foreign subsidiaries

Cultural Dimension	Korean (N=41)	American (N=28)	Japanese (N=10)	European (N=24)	ANOVA F value	*Tukey* Test
Group	3.54	3.58	3.43	3.51	0.177	All groups no difference
Develop-mental	3.37	3.69	2.88	3.31	2.96**	American > Japanese
Rational	3.41	3.99	3.20	3.68	5.67***	American > Korean = Japanese
Hierarchical	3.48	2.91	3.60	3.25	6.65***	Japanese = Korean > American

Note: ** $p < .05$; *** $p < .001$

To elucidate the point further we can examine two examples of cultural change in Korean corporate groups: Samsung and LG. Samsung started as a trading store in 1938 before setting about business development in earnest, establishing the Cheil Sugar Manufacturing Company in 1953 and Cheil Industries in 1954. Thereafter Samsung had two distinguishable stages (Rowley and Bae, 2002). The first stage was led by Lee Byung-Chull, the founder, and lasted until the mid-1980s; the second stage, after a transition period of 1983-1992 for the change of leadership, was run by his son Lee Kun-Hee. From the beginning, Samsung emphasized a rationality-based approach and systematic processes. During Lee Byung-Chull's leadership, a typical management style could be expressed as 'look even at a stone bridge before one leaps' ('act with the utmost caution'). Samsung's core values and capabilities during the first stage included rationality, rules and regulations, thorough analysis and evaluation, low risk-taking, hard work and well-planned processes. These values and capabilities ensured high growth and solid establishment for the firm in an environment of low uncertainty.

However, Lee Kun-Hee's Frankfurt Declaration in 1993 launched the 'new management' movement through a call for radical changes of organization and culture. He once described this as 'change everything except the wife and children'. The movement sought a 'quality-oriented, global-centred, risk taking' approach. Core values during this stage included risk taking, autonomy, diversity and creativity. In a contrast to the previous approach, Lee Kun-Hee's approach could be characterized as 'leap if you see just a wooden bridge without being afraid'. The management styles, core values and orientation of the two stages were in striking contrast. The resulting cultural conflict was seen as a necessary evil, a by-product of the organization's reorientation. The previous values, which had once been Samsung's core capabilities, came to be regarded as core rigidities and signs of inertia.

Our second example is the LG group, which had similar experiences. Its earlier core values were inhwa (harmony) and solidity. Accordingly, LG valued camaraderie, trust, respect and love among members, and a sense of unity and cooperation. These values enhanced members' loyalty and devotion to the company and served as core capabilities for the company's growth. However, over time, they rendered LG people conservative, passive and easy-going in terms of their attitudes and behaviour. Respect for people and inhwa were sometimes interpreted as lenient evaluation, overlooking a person's faults and favouring long-term attachment regardless of performance. A survey of LG management and people in the late 1980s showed that about 60 per cent recognized LG as a humane and conservative organization (Lee, 1997). About 80 per cent of participants also indicated that they wanted to move toward making LG a more aggressive, proactive and competitive company. To address these rigidities the LG group launched a vision team charged with changing its core values. In February 1990, the chairman, Koo Cha-Kyung, declared two new core values: 'creating value for customers' and 'management based on esteem for human dignity'. At the same time, the group emphasized the importance of autonomy in being able to respond quickly to uncertain environments. More recently, LG have emphasized the 'first class' LG concept, to redirect their way of thinking and attitudes from an approach that was comfortable and soft to a more aggressive and tough stance. LG is now aggressively setting more challenging targets to increase its competitiveness.

Organizational Strategy

Korea's industrialization and economic growth have been attributed to various factors. Adapting Porter's (1990) diamond model of national advantage and Tushman and O'Reilly's (1997) organizational architecture model, a congruence model of industrialization and organizational architecture can be derived (Rowley, Bae and Sohn, 2001). As depicted in Figure 3.3, the congruence model contains both national-level fit (between government, markets, culture and organizations) and firm level fit (between entrepreneurship, structure/systems, culture/process and people/HRM).

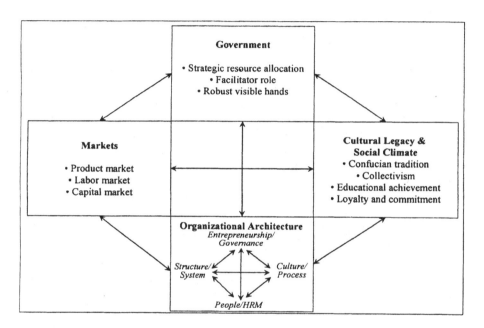

Figure 3.3 Unique institutional arrangements in a model of economic development and growth

Source: Adapted and reprinted from Asia Pacific Business Review, Vol.7(4), Rowley, C., Bae, J. and Sohn, T., Capabilities to liabilities in Korean management, p.3, Copyright (2001), with permission from Frank Cass.

More specifically, national-level fit means there is a good alignment between government and its policy (strategic resource allocation and a strong and visible influence on the planning and implementation of industrial policies), Confucian heritage and social culture (collectivism, growth-driven and can-do spirit, in-group harmony and high commitment and loyalty), chaebols and good organizational architecture and market conditions. Firm level fit means a good alignment between visionary entrepreneurs, a cheap but well-trained workforce, a goal-directed and hierarchical structure and dynamic collectivism. The closeness of these two fits made Korean industrialization and rapid economic growth possible. The national fit argument is principally based on the view that the aforementioned macro factors constitute a coherently interlocking set of institutions (Rowley, Bae and Sohn, 2001). The nature and degree of the congruence may either positively or negatively affect the process of economic development. This implies that a congruence that has brought about positive effects can also bring negative ones.

At the national level, the industrial policies of governments in the 1960s and 1970s were quite different from those in the 1980s and 1990s. Kim (1997) describes the contents and characteristics of the earlier industrial policies as export orientation, deliberate promotion of big business and the heavy and chemical industries and the repression of labour to maintain industrial peace. The growth of chaebols was strongly related to these industrial policies. Sometimes, the rank order of corporate groups changed not because of companies' capabilities, but because the government had chosen certain industrial policies (see Table 3.5 for the rank order of chaebols by year). As Hyundai was divided in 2000, both Hyundai and Hyundai Motor feature in the *chaebol* list of 2002: however, Hyundai had yielded first place to Samsung. Daewoo has now dropped off the list. Sunkyoung (SK) was 10th in 1979, but leapt to 5th in the 1980s and has remained within the top five.

The key features of industrial policies in the 1980s and 1990s included the promotion of small and medium-size enterprises, export orientation, antitrust and fair trade, trade liberalization, financial liberalization, protection for intellectual property rights and greater emphasis on the development of R&D manpower (Kim, 1997). Whilst the government played the most significant role in the industrialization which took place during 1960s and 1970s, from the 1980s onwards this was led by private companies and entrepreneurs: the ratio of R&D expenditures of government versus private in 1980 was 64 to 36 and in 1985 was 25 to 75 (see Table 3.2).

At the firm level, there are, at the risk of oversimplification, two routes to competition: producing low value-added products by using cheap and low-skilled workers or producing high value-added products with quality by using expensive but highly skilled workers (see Rowley and Lewis, 1996). Until the mid 1980s, the first strategy prevailed in Korean firms and worked fairly well. However, environmental changes such as global competition and advances in technology made it almost impossible for Korean firms to retain competitive advantage using this approach (Rowley and Bae, 1998). Price advantages based on the short-term cost-minimization approach may cause problems for companies in the long run by preventing them from building up the competence and commitment of their human assets. Hence, a strategic change toward the second route to competition, supported by employee competence and commitment, has been suggested. This can be enhanced through various HRM practices (Pfeffer, 1998) and requires firms to reconfigure their organizational architecture.

Table 3.5 The rank order of *chaebols* by year

Rank	1960	1972	1979	1987	1992	2002
1	Samsung	Samsung	Hyundai	Hyundai	Hyundai	Samsung
2	Samho	Lucky	Lucky	Samsung	Samsung	Hyundai
3	Gaepung	Hanjin	Samsung	Lucky	Daewoo	LG
4	Daehan	Shinjin	Daewoo	Daewoo	Lucky (LG)	SK
5	Lucky	Ssangyong	Hyosung	Sunkyoung	Sunkyoung (SK)	Hyundai Motor
6	TongYang	Hyundai	Kukje	Ssangyong	Hanjin	Hanjin
7	Kukdong	Daehan	Hanjin	Hanwha	Ssangyong	Posco
8	Hankuk Glass	Hanwha	Ssangyong	Hanjin	Kia Motors	Lotte
9	Donglip Industrial	Far Eastern Shipping	Hanwha	Hyosung	Hanwha	Kumho
10	Taechang Textile	Dainong	Sunkyoung	Lotte	Lotte	Hanwha

Source: Data are from Gong (1993) and Korea Fair Trade Commission.

In order to review briefly Korean industrialization and organizational strategy, we used knowledge-based theories of the firm and perspectives on organizational learning. Based on these theories, Korean industrialization can be perceived as a learning process (Kim, 1997; Bae, Rowley and Sohn, 2001) which generates knowledge that increases the competitiveness of firms and countries. A recent report from World Development (1998/99) also treats the problems of development as a knowledge issue. The Report attributes the rapid increase of income per capita in Korea to its effectiveness in generating and exploiting knowledge. It points out that 40 years ago Ghana and Korea had virtually the same income per capita, but that by the early 1990s Korea's was six times higher: 'some reckon that half of the difference is due to Korea's greater success in acquiring and using knowledge' (p.1).

Following Bae, Rowley and Sohn (2001), we also argue that Korean firms successfully went through their first learning process from the early 1960s to the mid-1980s, and that the second learning process from the mid-1980s onwards was less successful. While the first phase was characterized by single-loop learning, the second could be perceived as double-loop learning. Single-loop learning means 'instrumental learning that changes strategies of action or assumptions underlying strategies in ways that leave the values of a theory of action unchanged' (Argyris and Schön, 1996:20). This type of learning does not bring about paradigm change. March (1991:

71) conceptualizes this type of learning as exploitation, which involves 'refinement, choice, production, efficiency, selection, implementation, execution'. Double-loop learning, in contrast, is 'learning that results in a change in the values of theory-in-use, as well as in its strategies and assumptions' (Argyris and Schön, 1996:21). This brings about change in the deep structure of assumptions and requires creativity. March (1991: 71) perceives this type of learning as exploration, characterized by 'search, variation, risk taking, experimentation, play, flexibility, discovery, innovation'.

During the first learning process, good alignments existed at both national-level and firm level. These good fits brought about expeditious and successful learning until the mid-1980s. The aforementioned macro and micro factors were well meshed with the exploitation process. However, these good alignments turned into inertia and became 'misfits' that acted as liabilities in double-loop learning (for details see Bae, Rowley and Sohn, 2001). For examples, at the national level, the Korean government changed from being an effective facilitator to be more bureaucratic and inflexible, turning it into a liability. Markets (labour, product and financial) that had been less institutionalized were becoming more efficient after the mid-1980s. The most noticeable characteristics of dynamic collectivism (e.g., the emphasis on in-group harmony, optimistic progressivism and hierarchical principles) have similarly turned out to have a downside (Cho and Yoon, 2001). Some of the characteristics which did not fit well for effective double-loop learning also appeared at the micro level. The organizational architecture (i.e., entrepreneurs, HRM, structure and organizational culture) also needed to be transformed in order to be exploited.

Korean firms, therefore, were less successful in the second learning process, especially when involved in double-loop learning. However, 'unsuccessful double-loop learning' is not the final conclusion, but only a interim one. Bae et al. (2001) propose that the first learning paradigm brought about some rigidities and misfits, but at the same time laid down the potential for future learning capabilities by generating a knowledge base. An extensive knowledge base and well-trained human assets are necessary conditions for effective exploration. From the mid-1980s on, especially after 1987, Korean firms were required to be capable of double-loop learning in order to overcome environmental changes. To create another successful learning process, there are many tasks to be overcome. When we take a change management perspective, the first such task is learning to 'unlearn' (i.e., discarding the first paradigm), and the second learning to 'relearn' (i.e., taking up the second paradigm). The main goal of change management is to transform organizational inertia into effective organizational arrangements which enable high-level learning. These painful, yet fruitful, unlearning and relearning processes through effective change management are critical tasks to be resolved.

Notes

1   See the later section for more details on *yongo*.
2   This does not mean that only Confucian values generate hierarchical and vertical characteristics. In some Western countries, the aforementioned features can exist without Confucianism.
3   This part is largely reproduced from one of the authors' other work on culture and management in South Korea (Rowley and Bae, 2002).

References

Argyris, C. and Schön, D.A. (1996), *Organizational Learning II: Theory, Method, and Practice*, Addison-Wesley, Reading, MA.
Bae, J. (1997), 'Beyond Seniority-Based Systems: A Paradigm Shift in Korean HRM?', *Asia Pacific Business Review*, vol.3, no.4, pp.82-110.
Bae, J., and Rowley, C. (2001), 'The impact of globalization on HRM: The case of Korea', *Journal of World Business*, vol.36, no.4, pp.402-428.
Bae, J., Rowley, C. and Sohn, T. (2001), 'Conclusion – Knowledge, Learning, and Change in Korean Management', *Asia Pacific Business Review*, vol.7, no.4, pp.182-200.
Cameron, K.S. (1978), 'Measuring Organizational Effectiveness in Institutions of Higher Education', *Administrative Science Quarterly*, vol.23, pp.604-632.
Cho, Y. and Yoon, J. (2001), 'The origin and function of dynamic collectivism: An analysis of Korean corporate culture', in C. Rowley, T. Sohn and J. Bae (eds), *Managing Korean business: Organization, culture, human resources, and change*, London: Frank Cass, pp.70-88.
Chung, K.-H., Lee, H.-K. and Jung, K.-H. (1997), *Korean Management: Global Strategy and Cultural Transformation*, Walter de Gruyter, Berlin.
Ghoshal, S. and Bartlett, C.A. (1997), *The Individualized Corporation: A Fundamentally New Approach to Management*, NY: HarperCollins.
Gong, B.H. (1993), *Hankuk Giup Hungmangsa* (History of the rise and fall of Korean enterprises), Myungjin, Seoul.
Hampden-Turner, C. and Trompenaars, A. (1993), *The seven cultures of capitalism: Value systems for creating wealth in the United States, Japan, Germany, France, Britain, Sweden and the Netherlands*, Doubleday, New York.
Hofstede, G. (1991), *Cultures and organizations: Software of the mind*, McGraw-Hill, New York.
Hofstede, G. and Bond, M.H. (1988), 'Confucius and economic growth: New trends in culture's consequences', *Organizational Dynamics*, vol.16, no.4, pp.4-21.
Kim, L. (1997), *Imitation to Innovation: The Dynamics of Korea's Technological Learning*, Harvard Business School Press, Boston, MA.
Kim, Y. and Moon, H.-K. (2002), 'Ties among owners, CEOs, and outside directors in Korea', paper presented at the 2002 International Conference of the Korean Academy of Management on *Asian Management: Converging or Diverging?*, Hanyang University, Seoul, March 29, 2002.

Korea Chamber of Commerce and Industry (1984), *A survey report on the patterns of perceptions of top management in Korean companies*, Korea Chamber of Commerce and Industry, Seoul.

Kwon, S. and O'Donnell, M. (2001), *The Chaebol and Labour in Korea: The Development of Management Strategy in Hyundai*, Routledge, London.

Lee, H. K. (1997), *Cultural Characteristics of Korean Firms and New Culture Development*, Bakyungsa, Seoul. (In Korean.)

Lee, M.B. and Johnson, N.B. (1998), 'Business environment, high-involvement management, and firm performance in Korea', *Advances in Industrial and Labor Relations*, vol.8, pp.67-87.

March, J.C. (1991), 'Exploration and Exploitation in Organizational Learning', *Organization Science*, vol.2, no.1, pp.71-87.

Morden, T. and Bowles, D. (1998), 'Management in South Korea: A Review', *Management Decision*, vol.36, no.5, pp.316-330.

Pfeffer, J. (1998), *The Human Equation: Building Profits by Putting People First*, Harvard Business School Press, Boston, MA.

Porter, M.E. (1990), *The Competitive Advantage of Nations*, The Free Press, New York.

Quinn, R.E. (1988), *Beyond Rational Management*, Jossey-Bass, San Francisco, CA.

Rowley, C. and Bae, J. (1998), (eds), *Korean Businesses: Internal and External Industrialization*, Cass, London.

Rowley, C. and Bae, J. (2002), 'Management and Culture in South Korea', in M. Warner (ed), *Management and Culture in Asia*, Curzon Press, London.

Rowley, C., Bae, J. and Sohn, T. (2001), 'Introduction – Capabilities to Liabilities in Korean Management', *Asia Pacific Business Review*, vol.7, no.4, pp.1-21.

Rowley, C. and Lewis, M. (1996), 'Greater China at the Crossroads: Convergence, Culture and Competitiveness', *Asia Pacific Business Review*, vol.2, no.3, pp.1-22.

Sinha, D. and Kao, H.S.R. (1988), 'Introduction: Values-development congruence', in D. Sinha and H.S.R. Kao (eds), *Social Values and Development: Asian Perspectives*, Sage, New Delhi, pp.10-27.

The Dong-a Ilbo (2002), April 1, p. A10.

The Dong-a Ilbo (2002), April 2, p. A10.

Triandis, H.C. (1973), 'Subjective culture and economic development', *International Journal of Psychology*, vol.83, no.3, pp.163-180.

Triandis, H.C. (1988), 'Collectivism and development', in D. Sinha and H.S.R. Kao (eds), *Social Values and Development: Asian Perspectives*, Sage, New Delhi, pp.285-303.

Triandis, H.C. (1994), 'Cross-cultural industrial and organizational psychology', in H.C. Triandis, M. Dunnette and L. Hough (eds), *Handbook of Industrial and Organizational Psychology*, Consulting Psychologists Press, Palo Alto, CA, 2nd ed, vol.4, pp.103-172.

Tushman, M.L. and O'Reilly, C.A. III (1997), *Winning Through Innovation: A Practical Guide to Leading Organizational Change and Renewal*, Harvard Business School Press, Boston, MA.

World Development Report (1998/99), *Knowledge for Development*, Oxford University Press, Oxford and New York.

PART II
THE ORIGINS AND EVOLUTION OF KOREAN EMPLOYMENT RELATIONS

4 Employment Relations in Korea, 1890-1986: One Hundred Years of Labour Suppression

Introduction

The labour movement in Korea began with the advent of the modern wage labour system in the 1890s. This chapter discusses the labour movement and employment relations (ER) during the period of almost 100 years from 1890 to 1986. Throughout this time, the Japanese military government and successive Korean administrations continued to suppress the autonomous labour movement with some brief exceptional periods, although the nature of the labour oppression differed slightly from government to government. This chapter divides this 100-year period into 6 sub-periods mainly on the basis of the nature of the political system and the state labour policy at the time, because the state determined a large part of ER in Korea. Specifically, the sub-periods used are as follows: (1) Japanese Occupation (1890-1945); (2) the American Military Government (1946-1948); (3) the first republic (1948-1960); (4) the first half of President Park Chung-Hee's regime after the 1961 military coup (1961-1971); (5) the second half of President Park's regime (1972-1979); (6) after the 1980 military coup (1980-1986). For each sub-period, we describe the economy and the nature of the state, employers and the labour movement, as well as the interactions between the three actors and the unique features of the ER of the time.

Labour Relations under Japanese Occupation, 1890-1945

Korea was an agricultural country until the late 19th century when the wage labour system was first introduced. The advent of the labour class naturally brought about the beginning of the labour movement. As in other countries, labour organizations started out as friendly societies for mutual aid purposes, and soon became organizations seeking wage increases and reductions in

65

working hours. The Sungjin seaport labour union, founded in 1898, is known to be the first union in Korea. The early unions were usually formed in seaports and mining areas, and the first major labour dispute was led by dock and mining workers in the 1890s (Y. Kim, 1991; H. Kim, 1993). After the Japan-Korea Protection Treaty in 1905 signalled the start of forcible Japanese occupation of the Korean Peninsula, the factory system was fully introduced. The labour movement intensified as a result and spread rapidly to the manufacturing sectors, as large numbers of workers with similar concerns and complaints came together within the factories. The labour movement under Japanese occupation can be divided into three stages: (1) spontaneous and primitive (1905-1919); (2) organized (1920-1930); and (3) underground (1931-1945).

In the early period of Japanese occupation, Korean farmers were forced to leave rural areas as part of the process of land reform. Farmers separated from their land were herded to the urban areas and most became waged labourers in factories. This unlimited supply of labour from rural areas led to the formation of the labour class. For example, the number of wage labourers increased rapidly from approximately 66,000 in 1911 to 146,000 in 1915 (Y. Kim, 1991). The formation of this labour class led to a spontaneous labour movement that was not formally organized and did not have leaders. The Japanese colonial regime adopted a policy of repressing any kind of social movement in the Korean Peninsula, including the labour movement which was harshly dealt with. Despite the suppression, Korean workers were able to maintain their organizations and were often involved in scattered, but violent, strike action.

During the Japanese occupation, the majority of the manufacturing and mining industries were owned by Japanese capitalists, and there were only a small number of Korean employers. No protective labour legislation was enacted in Korea while the Japanese were present, although some such laws were passed in Japan during the same period (Y. Kim, 1991). Thus, there was no restriction on how workers could be treated. Working conditions were decided entirely by employers and foremen, and it was common for them to be extremely poor. Very low wages and long working hours were the norm rather than the exception, and the use of child labour was not unusual. Because of the unlimited labour supply from the rural areas and the existence of large numbers of unemployed, employers were able to exploit labourers through their superior bargaining power.

In these circumstances, the spontaneous labour movement aimed to address both economic and political issues. Firstly, Korean workers protested against harsh working conditions such as low wages, long working hours and authoritarian treatment in the workplace. They also demanded the abolition of discrimination against Korean workers by Japanese employers. Korean workers typically received less than 50 per cent of the wages of their Japanese counterparts doing similar work. Secondly, workers spontaneously demanded national independence: the labour movement was closely related to the anti-colonial independence movement. In fact, an explosive wave of political strikes (84 events involving 9,000 workers) coincided with the nationwide popular demonstration for the declaration of national independence on March 1, 1919.

Table 4.1   Number of labour organizations and members, 1920-1935

Year	Number of labour organizations	Number of members of labour organizations
1920	3	-
1921	90	-
1922	81	-
1923	111	-
1924	91	-
1925	128	-
1926	182	-
1927	352	-
1928	488	67,220
1929	473	61,730
1930	561	-
1931	511	-
1932	402	52,988
1933	334	41,836
1934	250	34,460
1935	207	28,211

Source: Kim, Kwak and Cheong (Forthcoming), 'Labour Movement under Japanese Occupation: 1920-1945'.

The second stage of the labour movement followed the independence movement in 1919. The aforementioned demonstration led the Japanese regime to reconsider its repressive social policy, based on suppression by the military and police forces, in the realization that it was not effective enough to silence Koreans' calls for independence. Thus, after 1919 an appeasement policy was adopted. Its underlying purpose was to accommodate to some extent the Korean population's widespread discontent with Japanese rule. The Japanese regime's labour policy was also modified to allow legitimate labour movement. Thus, various labour organizations were formed in the Korean Peninsula including the Korean Labour Mutual Aid Association the same year, the Federation of Korean Labour in 1922 and the Confederation of Korean Labour and Farmers in 1924. After the appeasement policy was brought in the number of labour organizations increased rapidly from 3 in 1920 to 128 in 1925 and 561 in 1930, and the number of members reached over 60,000 in the late 1920s (see Table 4.1).

Along with the formation of these labour organizations, workers intensified their protests against Japanese colonial rule. Between 1920-1930, the Japanese increased their efforts towards the industrialization of the Korean Peninsula in order to meet their expanding military needs. In the process, a large number of Korean workers was separated from their land and joined the urban labour class, which in turn provided the basis for an even stronger labour movement.

Meanwhile, the Japanese regime passed the Public Peace Act in 1925 to suppress socialist and union activities, prohibited union rallies and arrested union activists. Despite the passage of this Act, the Korean Communist Party was formed in 1925, led by socialists and labour activists. Four years later at Kwangju there was a large-scale student uprising for national independence, in which many labour activists were deeply involved.

Table 4.2   Strike statistics under Japanese occupation, 1918-1941

Year	Number of strikes	Number of participants	Year	Number of strikes	Number of participants
1918	50	6,105	1930	160	18,972
1919	84	9,011	1931	205	17,114
1920	81	4,599	1932	152	14,824
1921	36	3,403	1933	176	13,835
1922	46	1,799	1934	199	13,098
1923	72	6,041	1935	170	12,187
1924	45	6,751	1936	138	8,246
1925	55	5,700	1937	99	9,148
1926	81	5,984	1938	90	6,929
1927	94	10,523	1939	146	10,128
1928	119	7,759	1940	96	4,045
1929	102	8,293	1941	56	1,799

Source: Kim, Kwak and Cheong (Forthcoming), 'Labour Movement under Japanese Occupation: 1920-1945'.

The last stage of the Japanese occupation began with the worldwide depression during 1929-1933. After it was over, Japanese troops invaded China and the China-Japan War began in 1937. The Japanese military regime attempted to maximize war production, and many Korean workers were mobilized in the manufacture of electrical equipment, machinery, explosives and railroad cars (Ogle, 1990). This massive mobilization resulted in a substantial increase in the number of wage labourers, reaching more than 2,000,000 in 1944 (Y. Kim, 1991).

At the same time, the suppressive labour policy intensified, and the labour movement was banned outright. The Japanese police jailed labour leaders, dissolved labour organizations and prohibited union meetings. Instead, industrial patriotic clubs (called Sampo, a kind of mandatory labour-management council at the workplace level) were created in every workplace to encourage wartime production (Ogle, 1990). Consequently, the number of labour organizations decreased from 561 in 1930 to 207 in 1935, and their members from 67,220 in 1928 to 28,211 in 1935 (see Table 4.1). As the suppression of labour grew stronger, most labour organizations went underground until 1945, and the number of strikes decreased gradually from 205 in 1931 to 99 in 1937 and 56 in 1941 (see Table 4.2). In the 1930s and 1940s, the labour movement was mainly led by progressive intellectuals and communists, and coincided with the underground independence movement. In this period, it was seen as a kind of patriotic struggle against the Japanese occupation (H. Kim, 1993).

Throughout the period of occupation, working conditions for Korean workers remained very poor. They were severely discriminated against. Most Koreans were unskilled workers, whereas their Japanese counterparts took the skilled jobs and supervisory positions. Korean workers earned about half of the Japanese wage, and they were not entitled to any benefits. For example, the daily wage for Korean men was only 47.4 per cent of that of their Japanese counterparts in 1939 (i.e., 1.10 won for Koreans and 2.32 won for Japanese). This kind of wage discrimination was applied to all categories of worker regardless of gender and age (see Table 4.3). In the 1930s, about 46.9 per cent of Koreans worked for more than 12 hours per day, as compared with only 0.3 per cent of Japanese. Workplace safety records were also very poor especially in the mining and manufacturing industries. For example, the injury rates for mining workers in 1943 reached 10 per cent (Y. Kim, 1991).

Labour Relations during the American Military Government, 1946-1948

At the end of World War II, Koreans achieved national independence. Right after the declaration of independence, the Korean Peninsula was politically divided into two parts: North Korea, occupied by the Soviet Union, and South Korea, occupied by the U.S. Until Koreans established their own government in 1948, the American Military Government (AMG) was in charge. The factories and assets previously owned by the Japanese were handed over to Korean owners after independence was achieved.

Table 4.3   Daily wage level by gender, age and nationality, 1929-1939 (in won)

Group/Year	1929	1930	1931	1932	1933
Korean male adult	1.00	.94	.90	.92	1.10
Korean male under age	.44	.47	.49	.30	.50
Korean female adult	.59	.61	.49	.47	.55
Korean female under age	.32	.39	.30	.30	.41
Japanese male adult	2.32	1.96	1.83	1.85	2.32
Japanese male under age	.71	.63	.81	.82	1.17
Japanese female adult	1.01	1.02	1.06	1.04	1.17
Japanese female under age	.61	-	.43	.67	.76

Source: Kim, Kwak and Cheong (Forthcoming), 'Labour Movement under Japanese Occupation: 1920-1945'.

The period 1945-1948 was characterized by political turbulence and economic hardship. Although Japanese discrimination against Korean workers disappeared, working conditions barely improved. Due to the extreme political and economic uncertainties, the Korean economy did not function properly. Korean workers suffered from high unemployment and inflation, commodity shortages, and the resultant falling of real wage. For example, the unemployment rate in May 1947 was reported to be approximately 20 per cent in rural areas and 30 per cent in Seoul, and the index of real wage fell dramatically from 108.88 in June 1945 to 37.14 in December 1945 and 30.54 in December 1947 (Park and Kim, Forthcoming). Immediately after independence, the number of strikes increased to 170 in 1946 and 134 in 1947. Workers' demands varied from wage increase to complete control of production facilities (see Table 4.4).

This period was also characterized by extreme conflicts between left- and right-wing labour groups. The National Council of Korean Trade Unions

(NCKTU, Chun Pyung), led by socialist intellectuals and labour activists, was formed in November 1945. The NCKTU was composed of 16 affiliated industrial federations and more than 1,000 local unions, and the membership reached 553,408 in December 1945 (Park and Kim, Forthcoming). The NCKTU covered the entire Korean Peninsula, and received widespread support from workers. The platform of the NCKTU was considered radical by the AMG and conservative intellectuals, because it demanded the abolition of the wage system and for workers to take control of production systems (Ogle, 1990; Park and Kim, Forthcoming). The NCKTU led a series of general strikes including the violent and well-publicized railway strike in September 1946. Without question, the leftist-led NCKTU was the centre of the labour movement from 1945 to its demise in 1949.

Table 4.4   Strike statistics under the American Military Government, 1945-1947

Year	Number of strikes	Number of participants
1946	170	57,434
1947	134	35,210

Source: Park and Kim (Forthcoming), 'Labour Relations and Labour Movement under the Rule of the American Military Government'.

On the other hand, right wing, anti-communist politicians formed the Confederation of Korean Trade Unions (CKTU, Daehan Nochong) in March 1946 to fight the NCKTU. Only a small number of labour leaders were involved in the formation of the CKTU. It did not receive widespread support from workers, and was merely an anti-communist political organization formed to oppose the left-wing NCKTU. According to AMG records, in November 1946 NCKTU membership reached 246,777, whereas CKTU membership was only 57,228 (Park and Kim, Forthcoming). Over the next few years, the NCKTU and the CKTU were involved in violent attacks on each other.

The AMG, which advocated AFL-style conservative unionism, recognized the CKTU as the only legal union federation in Korea, and the AMG and other right-wing groups suppressed the Communist labour movement. In March 1947, the U.S. military government declared the NCKTU illegal, and it went underground until its dissolution in 1949. After the demise of the NCKTU, the CKTU was regarded as the only union federation representing Korean workers. However, its independence was questioned, because it was too closely aligned with the AMG and right-wing politicians and in many cases was financially supported by employers.

Although Japanese-owned facilities had been handed over to Koreans after independence, most companies remained small-scale and were engaged in primary industries producing basic necessities. The role of employers in labour relations during this period was limited, since the extreme political and economic turbulence and the rise of radical unionism prevented them from forming a stable and systematic ER policy.

ER after National Independence, 1948-1960

When the independent Korean government was established in August 1948, three basic labour rights (the right to organize, the right to bargain collectively and the right to strike) were specified in the new Constitution. However, the Constitution also prohibited union activities for government employees and employees in the defence industry. A number of major labour laws were enacted during the 1950-1953 Korean War. Specifically, the Trade Union Act, the Labour Disputes Adjustment Act, the Labour Committee Act were enacted in January 1953 and the Labour Standards Act in April 1953. These guaranteed basic rights for workers and union members, but subsequent revisions over the next three decades put various restrictions on union activities, which were not to be relaxed until the November 1987 revision (Lee, 1993).

During the lifetime of the first republic, the Korean industrial sector comprised small- and medium-sized establishments that supplied only basic products. Personnel management and labour relations policy in these employers remained primitive. Although the Labour Standards Act was passed in April 1953, few employers observed it in practice. It was considered to be a symbolic statute, and played little part in improving working conditions.

At this time, too, the CKTU was financially supported by, and openly aligned with, the ruling party, the Democratic Liberal Party. For example, the 4th president of the CKTU, Chun Jin Han, was also appointed to the Ministry of Social Affairs. The CKTU eventually became an organ of the ruling party, one of the five social organizations within it (Ogle, 1990). Many leaders of the CKTU maintained close relationships with the ruling party, and identified themselves with employers rather than the rank and file members. In this period, the CKTU did not truly represent workers' interests, but protected the political and economic interests of a small number of labour leaders. Thus, the leadership of the CKTU were regarded as the labour aristocracy and harshly criticized by ordinary members.

In 1958, the National Conference of Trade Unions (NCTU, Nohyup) was formed by a small number of union leaders who advocated the independence of the labour movement from the government. The NCTU also demanded a democratic unionism that truly represented the interests of rank and file members. However, the CKTU and the ruling party ignored the demand, and both the CKTU and the NCTU coexisted until their merger in 1960. During the period of the first republic, union membership increased steadily from 200,000 in 1955 to 250,000 in 1958. The number of strikes also rose from 9 in 1953 to 45 in 1957 and 95 in 1959 (Y. Kim, 1991). These statistics show that despite the malfunctioning of the labour centre, workers generally recognized unions as protective mechanisms and attempted to improve working conditions through industrial action.

Political corruption – specifically, the overtly fraudulent election in March 1960 – and poor economic performance under the Democratic Liberal Party led to the Student Revolution of April 1960 and the authoritarian President Rhee Syngman's resulting fall from power and exile in Hawaii. After the revolution, the Democratic Party took power. The political vacuum was perceived by workers as a golden opportunity to advance their long-suppressed agenda and achieve real change. The rank and file members called strongly for an autonomous and independent labour movement and expelled their corrupt leaders. The Student Revolution and the popular demand for union democracy eventually led to the merger of the CKTU and the NCTU and the formation of the Federation of Korean Trade Unions (FKTU, Hankook Nochong) in November 1960.

The 1960 Student Revolution ended government control of the labour movement and boosted union activities. After the Revolution membership sharply increased from 301,000 in March 1960 to 321,000 in December 1960, and 356 new unions were formed during the 9-month period from April to December 1960. The number of strikes also rose from 95 in 1959 to 227 in 1960 (Y. Kim, 1991).

ER after the 1961 Military Coup, 1961-1971

The movement toward autonomous unionism was ended suddenly by the military coup in May 1961 led by General Park Chung-Hee. The leaders of the coup argued that the severe social disorder caused by the Student Revolution in April 1960 and the incompetence of the ruling party would shortly result in another military invasion from North Korea, and so military leadership was inevitable if a serious national crisis was to be averted. Right after the coup, its leaders temporarily disbanded the FKTU in May and then allowed it to reorganize itself in August 1961. The new military government revised the Trade Union Act, and made union involvement in politics illegal. The reorganized FKTU also pledged political neutrality and financial independence from the government. More importantly, military leaders argued that labour peace was one of the most crucial conditions for attracting the foreign investment that could help build the Korean economy, and forced the transformation of union structures from an enterprise to an industrial basis to avoid excessive labour disputes at the company level. Consequently, the various enterprise unions merged into 11 industrial unions.

After the 1961 military coup, the government played a dominant role in economic development. The ruling party, the Democratic Republican Party, led by President Park Chung-Hee, adopted an economic development strategy based upon the export of low-value added products, manufactured by cheap and diligent labour, in light industries such as textiles, garments, apparel, plywood and electronics. To maintain the low wage and disciplined work force, the government discouraged the independent labour movement. The need for rapid economic development and the threat from North Korea justified such a state-led development policy.

In 1970, the Special Law Concerning Labour Unions and the Settlement of Labour Disputes in Foreign Investment Firms was passed. It severely restricted union activities and prohibited labour disputes in foreign companies operating in Korea. The Special Law provided a basically union-free environment for foreign firms coming mostly from Japan and the U.S. Although the law was eventually repealed in 1986 (Lee, 1993), it symbolized the government's efforts to attract foreign direct investments by suppressing autonomous unionism.

Table 4.5   Economic growth and union membership, 1963-1971

Year	Growth rates of GDP (%)	Average income per capita (US$)	Number of union members	Unionization ratio
1963	9.1	-	224,000	9.0
1964	8.3	-	272,000	10.8
1965	7.4	-	294,000	10.8
1966	13.4	-	337,000	11.7
1967	8.9	123	367,000	11.7
1968	13.3	138	400,000	11.6
1969	15.9	166	444,000	12.5
1970	8.9	187	469,000	12.6
1971	9.8	212	494,000	13.0

Source: Lee (Forthcoming) 'Labour Movement during the Period of Economic Growth: 1961-1987'.

On the other hand, compared with the 1970s and 1980s, the 1960s is regarded as the period in which the constitutional rights to organize, bargain and strike were relatively well respected, and collective bargaining was allowed to function. In other words, the government seemed to adopt a relatively liberal labour policy for most of the decade. Indeed, collective bargaining took place in various industries such as communications, railroads, electric power, seaport, transportation, metal and chemicals (Ogle, 1981: 504; Park, 1993). Due to the government's liberal labour policy and workers' desire for trade unionism, union membership grew steadily. The number of union members more than doubled from 224,000 in 1963 to 494,000 in 1971, and the unionization ratio rose almost every year from 9.0 per cent in 1963 to 13.0 per cent in 1971 (see Table 4.5). The number of strikes during the 1963-1971 period was relatively stable, averaging approximately 102 and ranging from 70 in 1969 to 126 in 1964 (see Table 4.6).

Meanwhile, the Korean economy recorded a remarkable level of growth in the 1960s. The growth rate of GDP during the period 1963-1971 averaged 10.6 per cent, ranging from 7.4 per cent in 1965 to 15.9 per cent in 1969: largely due to the success of the first (i.e., 1962-1966) and second (i.e., 1967-1971) five-year economic development plans (see Table 4.5).

Table 4.6   Strike statistics, 1963-1971

Year	Number of strikes	Number of participants
1963	89	168,843
1964	126	207,406
1965	113	103,707
1966	117	145,168
1967	105	150,535
1968	112	205,941
1969	70	108,248
1970	88	182,802
1971	101	115,934

Source: Lee (Forthcoming) 'Labour Movement during the Period of Economic Growth: 1961-1987'.

Despite the double-digit growth in GDP and the rise of unionism and collective bargaining, the living standards of the working population remained very poor until the early 1970s. That is, national income per capita was only US$123 in 1967 and had only gone up to US$212 by 1971 (see Table 4.5). In particular, the unlimited labour supply from rural areas and a large number of unemployed in urban ghettos made the bargaining power of workers much weaker than that of employers, which resulted in very poor working conditions (i.e., low wages and long hours). Spontaneous protests against extremely poor working conditions were not uncommon. For example, Chun Tai-Il, a labour leader in the clothing industry, burned himself to death in 1970 in a protest against miserable working conditions and as a demand to employers to observe the Labour Standards Act.

ER under Labour Suppression, 1972-1979

In December 1971, President Park Chung-Hee declared a state of emergency and enacted the Special Act for National Security. Over the next year, the Yushin Constitution was passed to justify the ruling party's authoritarian regime and to guarantee Park's lifetime presidency. The establishment of the dictatorial state in 1972 was accompanied by very harsh repression of the labour movement. The Special Act for National Security Act limited collective bargaining activities and prohibited all kinds of collective actions. Under the Act, unions needed to obtain government permission to conduct collective bargaining, and strikes and lockouts were prohibited until 1981 when the Special Act was lifted. Due to this legal obstruction, collective bargaining was not widely practiced during 1972-1979 (Ogle, 1990).

There were economic rationales for the suppressive labour policy in the early 1970s. The Lewis-type turning point from unlimited labour supply to limited labour supply occurred in Korea in the early- or mid-1970s (Park, 1993),[1] and the government needed to intervene in labour relations to create labour market conditions that was best fit to the low-price production system and the attraction of foreign investments. The government argued that the repression of independent labour movement was the most effective way to maintain low wages, long working hours and disciplined work force.

The early 1970s is regarded as the beginning of the Korean version of authoritarian corporatism. This was composed of two components: (1) subordination and complete control of union leadership; and (2) the widespread use of police and intelligence agencies (i.e., the Korean Central Intelligence Agency, KCIA) to suppress autonomous labour movement by arresting, torturing and jailing labour activists. Labour activists were treated as a social enemy that might obstruct rapid economic development and jeopardize national security. In many cases, the KCIA overtly supported its own handpicked candidate for a position in the FKTU (Ogle, 1990). The uniqueness of the Korean version of authoritarian corporatism lies in the fact that the state never allowed its subordinated labour leaders to genuinely participate in the process of economic policymaking. The ruling elite group did not feel the need to obtain the agreement of labour leaders even when adopting an unpopular labour policy. Indeed, the corrupt and subordinated labour leaders were not truly supported by rank and file members, and were largely separated from their wider constituents.

On the other hand, the government initiated the New Factory Movement in 1973 to promote the spirit of cooperative labour relations and paternalistic management. The slogan of the New Factory Movement was 'home-like factory, family-like employees'. Five hundred factories were selected as prime examples of the New Factory Movement by the Department of Commerce and Industry in 1974. At the government's behest, the Movement spread to various factories throughout the 1970s. Despite the efforts of the state, the effects were limited largely due to the lack of interest and commitment from workers.

During the period 1972-1979, the FKTU was unable and unwilling to represent the interests of rank and file members who were suffering from extremely poor working conditions. The FKTU was under the complete control of the police and intelligence agencies, and was continually manipulated by them. Thus, spontaneous and violent worker protests and stoppages occurred in many cases without the involvement of the formal union organization. Many wildcat strikes or worker riots occurred during this period, such as those at the Korean Air Lines (KAL) building in 1971, the Hyundai Shipbuilding in 1971, the Se-jong Hotel in 1975, the Dong-Il Textile Company in 1976 and the Y.H. Trade Company in 1979.

In the 1970s, despite government suppression, progressive intellectuals belonging to the Urban Industrial Mission, the Young Christian Workers, labour education institutes in Korea University and Sogang University educated labour activists and helped workers to organize themselves. Because formal unions were unable to function, various intellectual groups such as religious organizations and university professors assumed the role.

Despite the overt suppression of the independent labour movement, union membership rose from 505,000 in 1972 to 1,094,000 in 1979 (see Table 4.7), and the unionization ratio also continued to increase, from 12.4 per cent in 1972 to 16.8 per cent in 1979. Considering the extreme nature of the suppression and subordination of labour and its leaders in this period, this uninterrupted growth is remarkable. It resulted from the rapid expansion of the employed labour force in the industrial sector and the workers' desire to be represented by protective organizations.

Rapid economic growth was again recorded in the period 1972-1979. The growth rate of GDP averaged 8.6 per cent, and income per capita also showed a more than five-fold jump, from US$316 in 1972 to US$1,636 in 1979 (see Table 4.7). From the mid-1970s on, the government attempted to shift its policy focus from light industries (i.e., textile, apparel, electronics) to heavy and chemical industries (i.e., automobile, shipbuilding, steel, chemical and construction). In the process it deliberately supported *chaebol* companies by using various preferential tax policies and providing cheap loans. Indeed, several *chaebol* companies belonging to the Samsung, Hyundai, Hanjin, Goldstar, Korea Explosives and Daewoo groups expanded rapidly during the 1970s.

Table 4.7   Union membership, unionization ratio and strike statistics, 1972-1979

Year	Growth rates of GDP (%)[a]	Average income per capita[b]	Number of union members[c]	Unionization ratio[c]	Number of strikes[c]
1972	4.9	316	505,000	12.4	346
1973	12.3	394	531,000	12.6	367
1974	7.4	540	642,000	14.2	655
1975	6.5	592	712,000	14.8	133
1976	11.2	799	823,000	15.8	110
1977	10.0	1,009	916,000	15.9	96
1978	9.0	1,399	1,017,000	16.2	102
1979	7.1	1,636	1,094,000	16.8	105

Sources:
[a]   Bank of Korea (2002), *http://dbsrv.bok.or.kr/20020320175625.xls*
[b]   Korea National Statistical Office (2002), *http://kosis.nso.go.kr/cgi-bin/html_out.cgi*
[c]   Lee (Forthcoming), 'Labour Movement during the Period of Economic Growth: 1961-1987'.

The export-oriented industrial strategy of the 1970s was based mainly on the price competitiveness of Korean products in overseas markets. Typical work organizations followed the Tayloristic production system relying on low value-added products and a low-skilled labour force. Thus, skill formation and employee commitment were not important to most companies, and employers did not recognize the need to develop systematic human resource management (HRM) (Lee, 1993). They relied on an authoritarian and paternalistic management style, and few companies experimented with any kind of workplace innovations. Most blue-collar workers had few opportunities for promotion, and high turnover rates among this group were common. On the other hand, by the late 1970s these *chaebol* companies recognized the need to systematize their management system after years of fast expansion and to encourage the long-term employment of their supervisory, technical and professional staff. Thus, an internal labour market for white-collar workers began to emerge in large *chaebol* companies from the late 1970s onward. Throughout the 1970s, most employers, except for a few progressive companies, had an adversarial attitude toward labour unions and cooperated with the government in preventing the rise of radical unionism.

Employment Relations after the 1980 Military Coup, 1980-1986

A period of severe economic depression and a series of democratization rallies by students in the Pusan and Masan areas were followed by President Park's sudden assassination by the head of the KCIA in October 1979. This ended 18 years of uncompromising rule and led to extreme political instability. This brief period of freedom from a dictatorial state, known as the 'Spring of Seoul', led to violent labour disputes such as the strikes at the Sabuk Coal Mine and the Dongkuk Steel Company in spring 1980.

General Chun Doo-Hwan stepped into the political vacuum by initiating another military coup in December 1979, and the fifth republic started in 1980. The new military government's labour policy closely resembled that of President Park, and attempted to suppress the independent labour movement even further by revising the labour laws. The amended statutes aimed to circumvent union activities and weaken the basis of the labour movement.

The details of labour law revisions in December 1980 are as follows: Firstly, the union shop became illegal. Secondly, all unions were to be organized on an enterprise basis, and other forms of organization such as regional and industrial unionism were illegal. Thirdly, third-party involvement in labour-management relations was prohibited. Thus, even union federations, church groups and domestic and foreign civil rights groups were not allowed to assist workers in union organizing, collective bargaining and labour disputes. Fourthly, a labour–management council became mandatory for all companies with more than 100 employees. At such a council, management was expected to discuss with employee representatives topics such as productivity improvement, employee welfare, education and training and grievance handling. The underlying intention behind this clause might have been to weaken the power of unions by depriving them of their grievance-handling function.

Indeed, all of the above-listed clauses were intended to weaken the labour movement in Korea, and they succeeded in doing so. In the transition from regional and industrial unions to legally mandated enterprise unions, many regional and industrial unions (e.g., the bus and taxi drivers unions) were dissolved and the leaders lost their positions (H. Kim, 1993). The banning of the union shop and third party support also immediately weakened the potential political power base of the labour movement. A more important consequence was the devastating effect on the unionization ratio. Its uninterrupted increase since 1960 was reversed for the first time after the 1980 revision, and continued to decrease in the 1980s from 14.7 per cent in 1980 to 12.3 per cent in 1986 (see Table 4.8).

Table 4.8   Union membership, unionization ratio and strike statistics, 1980-1986

Year	Growth rates of GDP (%)[a]	Average income per capita[b]	Number of union members[b]	Unionization ratio[c]	Number of strikes and lockouts[b]
1980	-2.1	1,598	948,000	14.7	407
1981	6.5	1,749	967,000	14.6	186
1982	7.2	1,847	984,000	14.4	88
1983	10.7	2,020	1,010,000	14.1	98
1984	8.2	2,190	1,011,000	13.2	113
1985	6.5	2,229	1,004,000	12.4	265
1986	11.0	2,550	1,036,000	12.3	276

Sources:
[a]   Bank of Korea (2002), *http://dbsrv.bok.or.kr/20020320175625.xls*
[b]   Korea National Statistical Office (2002), *http://kosis.nso.go.kr/cgi-bin/html_out.cgi.*
[c]   Korea Labour Institute (1996), *Overseas Labour Statistics.*

During the fifth republic (1980-1988), the fundamental characteristics of the labour suppression policy were no different from that of the previous government. Basically, it was a continuation of authoritarian corporatism. The state did not allow labour involvement in national policymaking, and attempted to control the labour movement via the police and intelligence agencies. The military government was not interested in institutionalizing labour disputes and resolving industrial conflicts through a self-regulating mechanism, but believed that they could eliminate all labour disputes and accomplish complete industrial peace by weakening trade unionism. The government used the formidable threat from North Korea as an excuse for not allowing genuine trade unionism to exist in South Korea (Park, 1993).

Chaebol companies, such as Samsung, Daewoo, Hyundai, LG, Ssangyong and SK, grew rapidly in the 1980s, and their influence spread to the banking and insurance industries. By the end of the 1980s typical *chaebol* companies owned dozens of branch companies in various industries such as automobile, shipbuilding, electronics, construction, oil refining, insurance and banking. The Korean economy's dependency on *chaebol* companies increased in the 1980s. Work organization in this decade was characterized by a top-down command system, and management style was paternalistic and authoritarian. Tayloristic and Fordist production systems were widely introduced in large manufacturing facilities during the 1980s, but workplace innovations were virtually unknown to Korean manufacturing companies (Park and Lee, 1995). Most employers treated unions in a hostile and adversarial manner, and union involvement in managerial decision-making was practiced by only a handful of progressive companies.

Under President Chun Doo-Hwan's regime, the formal labour centre, the FKTU, was not regarded as an autonomous union federation truly representing its members' interests. The police and intelligence agencies such as the KCIA openly intervened in the election of union leaders and the administration of internal union affairs. The leaders of the FKTU were believed to be subordinated to the state, did not pay attention to the voices of the rank and file members and discouraged the independent labour movement. This malfunctioning of the formal union federation might be another reason for the decline in the unionization ratio under the fifth republic.

Despite the oppressive labour policy and the inactivity of the FKTU, the number of labour disputes increased steadily from 88 in 1982 to 276 in 1986 (see Table 4.8). Because institutionalized mechanisms of dispute resolution did not work, rank and file members expressed their discontent by violent and technically illegal labour disputes. Examples include the labour disputes at Control Data, Wonpoong Wool Company and Taegu Taxi companies in the early 1980s.

A unique characteristic of the labour movement in the 1980s was the appearance of 'disguised' workers. Disguised workers were radical and militant college students who voluntarily worked at factories by disguising their status, and attempted to educate, organize and agitate factory workers. If police or employers found out that they were really college students and not 'pure' workers, they were fired immediately and their names put on a black list. Disguised workers first appeared in the late 1970s and the practice remained popular among student activists until the late 1980s. The exact number of disguised workers in the 1980s is not known, but more than a thousand students are believed to have worked in the Inchon, Kuro, Ulsan, Masan, Changwon and Kumi areas. Because legitimate institutional channels such as the FKTU were not effective in improving working conditions and resolving labour disputes, outside groups such as students became involved in labour relations. This is a clear symbol of the dysfunctional ER in the 1980s.

In contrast to its policy of labour suppression, the government made impressive efforts during this period to develop education and vocational training. Whereas the previous government had already made substantial investments in the primary and secondary education systems in the 1960s and 1970s, the quality of education at the technical college level was the focus of efforts in the 1980s. The government designed a vocational training system by imitating the German apprentice system, and created the Korean Manpower Agency in 1982 to take the central role in improving vocational and technical skills to enable workers to contribute to the newly developing chemical and heavy industries (Park and Lee, 1995).

Along with these heavy investments in formal and vocational education, the Korean economy continued to grow rapidly. Although the growth rate of GDP was negative in 1980 (i.e., -2.1 per cent) largely due to poor performance in the newly introduced chemical and heavy industries and the political turmoil in 1979 and 1980, the economy resumed its rapid expansion during the 1981-1986 period, showing an average 8.4 per cent growth in GDP (see Table 4.8).

Chapter Summary

Since the capitalist class was almost nonexistent in the early stages of the development process, the state assumed a key role in directing and coordinating economic activities. The lack of natural resources and capital and the relatively small size of the domestic market forced governments to pursue an exported-oriented strategy based on foreign investments, overseas natural resources and cheap labour (Verma, Kochan and Lansbury, 1995). Consequently, Korean economic development began by creating labour market conditions conducive to this export-oriented strategy. These conditions are characterized by low wages, a disciplined labour force and a subordinated labour movement. All of these helped attract foreign investment. In particular, the heavy commitment to investment in human capital in Korea led to a relatively high-quality workforce, which facilitated economic development in the early stages. These labour market conditions attracted foreign investment and provided comparative advantages in relatively low-price, low-quality markets, and led to growth.

Indeed, the economy showed a trend towards rapid expansion from the early 1960s onward. Economic growth since this period has been remarkable by any international standard. The GDP growth rate during the 1963-1986 period averaged approximately 8.8 per cent. Consequently, the average income per capita, an indication of living standards for the Korean population, increased from US$123 in 1967 to US$2,550 in 1986, a 20-fold increase in 20 years!

However, living standards for ordinary workers remained poor until the mid-1980s, because subordinated unions with low density were unable to act to improve pay and working conditions. For example, hourly compensation costs for manufacturing workers were still only US$1.31 in 1986. Also, Korean workers worked on average 52.5 hours per week in 1986, longer than in any other major economy (see Table 3.5).

Independent trade unionism was suppressed by the state during the greater part of the period from the late 19th century (when the labour movement began) up to 1986, although a laissez-faire labour policy was adopted during the brief periods between regimes such as immediately after national independence (i.e., 1945-1946), and after the student revolution (i.e., 1960-1961). The Japanese military government oppressed the labour movement to maintain social order and to prevent possible cooperation with the national independence movement. Subsequent Korean governments hindered autonomous trade unionism so as to maintain labour market conditions that would suit their strategy of low-cost industry and courting foreign investment. In particular, the regimes since 1972 adopted a hard-fisted labour policy, because the independent labour movement was considered to be a potential threat to the maintenance of the dictatorial political system. On the other hand, the state controlled official labour leaders, manipulated union elections and intervened in internal union affairs by using the police and intelligence agencies.

Despite this pattern of suppression, union membership showed a steady growth until 1979. The unionization ratio rose from less than 10 per cent in the early 1960s to almost 17 per cent in 1986, indicating that workers had a deep-rooted desire to be represented by protective organizations. However, the labour law revision which came about after the 1980 military coup was the most damaging obstacle to union growth, resulting in the unionized sector falling to 12.3 per cent in 1986.

Overall, the unionization ratio in Korea appears to have been relatively low. Before 1960, it was estimated at below 10 per cent, and the highest point until the mid-1980s was only 16.8 per cent (in 1979). This is lower than that of most major economies such as the U.S., the U.K., Germany, Japan, Australia, Singapore and Taiwan. Among the various reasons for this, the most important might be the prolonged suppression of unions brought about by the labour policies of successive governments.

During the Japanese occupation, most employers were Japanese and discrimination against Korean workers was an important reason for labour protests. In the 1950s and 1960s, the economy was mainly led by small and medium-sized employers. After the 1970s, *chaebol* companies grew rapidly and soon dominated the Korean economy, since the government deliberately supported them in the process of building the heavy and chemical industries. Tayloristic and Fordist production systems were in widespread use, and until the mid-1980s, most Korean employers were unaware of workplace innovations. The authoritarian and paternalistic management style was most popular in all but a handful of progressive companies.

After national independence, successive governments suppressed the labour movement and the role of employers in the labour relations area was marginal. Korean employers are believed to have a strong sense of property rights and they were generally adversarial in their attitude toward unions. However, most employers did not have to confront militant unionism at the enterprise level until the late 1980s. Formal labour organizations such as the FKTU had been largely tamed, and the government effectively prevented the rise of the militant segment of the labour movement. However, the late 1980s witnessed the explosive expression of workers' pent-up grievances and the sudden advent of militant labour movement, which turned out to be a new challenge for employers.

Note

1   According to the seminal work by Lewis (1954), in developing economies an unlimited supply of labour from the agricultural, petty trade, domestic service sectors is available at a subsistence wage, which is the principal source for economic development. He further argues that the speed of capital formation exceeds that of population growth, the surplus labour dries up and the price of labour (i.e., wage) begin to rise. Thus, the Lewis-type turning point indicates the point when the initial unlimited labour supply is replaced by limited labour supply in the subsequent period.

References

Kim, H.-J. (1993), 'The Korean Union Movement in Transition', in S. Frenkel (ed), *Organized Labor in the Asia-Pacific Region*, ILR Press, Ithaca, pp.133-161.

Kim, K.I., Kwak, K.H. and Cheong, H.K. (Forthcoming), 'Labor Movement under Japanese Occupation, 1920-1945', in Y.H. Kim (ed), *History of Labor Movement in Korea*, Institute of Labor Education and Research, Korea University, Seoul. (In Korean.)

Kim, Y.H. (1991), 'Labor Movement in the Era of Democratization', *Daily Economic Newspaper*, Seoul. (In Korean.)

Lee, M.B. (1993), 'Korea', in D.R. Briscoe, M. Rothman and R.C.D. Nacamulli (eds), *Industrial Relations around the World: Labor Relations for Multinational Companies*, Walter de Gruyter, New York, pp.245-269.

Lee, W.B. (Forthcoming), 'Labor Movement during the Period of Economic Growth: 1961-1987', in Y.H. Kim (ed), *History of Labor Movement in Korea*, Institute of Labor Education and Research, Korea University, Seoul. (In Korean.)

Lewis, W.A. (1954), 'Economic Development with Unlimited Supplies of Labor', *The Manchester School of Economic Studies*, May, pp.139-191.

Ogle, G. (1981), 'South Korea', in A. A. Blum (ed), *International Handbook of Industrial Relations*, Greenwood Press, Westport, Connecticut, pp.499-514.

Ogle, G. (1990), *South Korea: Dissent within the Economic Miracle*, Zed Books, London.

Park, Y.K. and Kim, J.H. (Forthcoming), 'Labor Relations and Labor Movement under the Rule of the American Military Government', in Y.H. Kim (ed), *History of Labor Movement in Korea*, Institute of Labor Education and Research, Korea University, Seoul. (In Korean.)

Park, Y.-B., and Lee, M. B. (1995), 'Economic Development, Globalization, and Practices in

Industrial Relations and Human Resource Management in Korea', in A. Verma, T.A. Kochan and R.D. Lansbury (eds), *Employment Relations in the Growing Asian Economies,* Routledge, New York, pp.27-61.

Park, S.-I. (1993), 'The Role of the State in Industrial Relations: The Case of Korea', *Comparative Labor Law Journal,* vol.14, pp.321-338.

Verma, A., Kochan, T.A. and Lansbury, R.D. (1995), 'Lessons from the Asian Experience: a Summary', in A. Verma, T.A. Kochan and R.D. Lansbury (eds), *Employment Relations in the Growing Asian Economies*, Routledge, New York, pp.337-358.

5 Korean Employment Relations, 1987-1996: Experiments with Pluralism and Tripartism

Introduction

After a hundred years of labour suppression, Korean labour relations encountered an incident that resulted in a fundamental transformation of industrial relations. Ironically, the very factors that had previously made rapid economic growth possible accelerated the decline of the existing political and industrial order (Verma, Kochan and Lansbury, 1995). That is, as economic growth continued, the newly formed middle-class noticed the imbalance between the rapid pace of such growth and the slow development of political and industrial democracy in society as a whole. This highly educated middle class became capable of challenging the old system. Since the mid-1980s, there had been pressure for the equal distribution of wealth and growing demands for political and industrial democracy expressed in the form of autonomous unionism, adversarial collective bargaining and aggressive labour disputes. Thus, the late-1980s witnessed the demise of the old industrial order and a search for a new one. We start this chapter by describing the Great Labour Struggle of 1987.

The Great Labour Struggle, 1987-1989

Precedents

Labour disputes in Korea have generally been strongly associated with period of political turbulence, and the 1987 Great Labour Struggle is no exception. It has been argued that strikes in Korea have always served as a device through which popular dissatisfaction with the government and political climate of the day has been manifested. Research has shown that strike waves, rather than being stimulated by the economic environment, had coincided with political instability (Bognanno, 1988; D. Kim, 1993; Park, 1985). Indeed, labour disputes in Korea during the post-war period show a very clear and consistent pattern: industrial peace during periods of social and political stability, and waves of strike action in periods of social and political turbulence.

While there were fewer than one hundred strike incidents in the whole country for each of the years 1963, 1969, 1970, 1982 and 1983, 3,749 labour disputes occurred in 1987 alone. The number of labour disputes peaked in 1919, 1929, 1945, 1960-1961 and 1980-1981. All of these periods were characterized, without exception, by political instability and social disorder: 1) the nationwide demonstration for independence from Japan in 1919; 2) the 1929 Student Uprising against Japanese authority in Kwangju; 3) the 1945 Liberation of Korea from Japanese Military rule; 4) the Student Uprisings in April 1960 against malpractice by the ruling party in national elections, leading to the authoritarian President Rhee's fall from power; and 4) President Park's assassination by the head of the Korean Central Intelligence Agency (KCIA) in October 1979, ending 18 years of uncompromising rule and extreme political instability.

An obvious question is why the disputes in the late 1980s were so much more severe than those in earlier periods of crisis? Indeed, the statement of the ruling party's presidential candidate in June 1987, promising direct elections and respect for human rights, ignited a workers' revolt of a magnitude that has seldom been seen anywhere else in the world. Within a few months, over 3,000 disputes had erupted, and more than 1,300 new unions had been organized.

The relative deprivation theory, which was developed in the 1960s, provides a tool by which to account for the unprecedented magnitude of labour disputes in Korea in 1987. According to these theorists, collective violence is explained as a response to a gap between expectations and achievements, the violence itself serving as evidence of unrealized expectations among the population. In particular, Gurr (1968, 1970) argues that a psychological variable, relative deprivation, is the basic precondition for civil strife, and the more widespread and intense the deprivation, the greater the magnitude of that strife. This proposition bears striking parallels with the situation in Korea in the late 1980s, a period when there was a huge gap between workers' expectations and achievements.

During the post-war period, the Korean economy expanded continuously at record-breaking rates, a phenomenon known as the 'economic miracle of Korea'. Per capita gross national product (GNP) increased from $87 in 1962 to $2,550 in 1986. The average annual growth in GNP reached almost 10 per cent in 1970s and 1980s. As a result of this continuous economic growth, a new middle class was formed, members of which became increasingly critical of the authoritarian political system and unequal distribution of wealth. The emerging middle class was the product of economic success, but it was also the most formidable group challenging the way the government had accomplished this growth.

The quarter century of uninterrupted economic growth had given Korean workers rising expectations of better living standards and working conditions. Also, Rho Tae-Woo's promise of political democracy in 1987 was considered to be a concession to the explosive citizens' protests held in major Korean cities against the authoritarian government of President Chun Doo-Hwan. Korean workers viewed the statement as a golden opportunity to take steps toward industrial as well as political democracy, a concept that had been suppressed by previous governments. The significantly raised expectations amongst workers for a fair distribution of resources and democratic reform of the political and social structure contributed to the significant shift in expectations among Korean workers (D. Kim, 1993).

Despite their rising expectations, Korean workers' living standards and working conditions remained stagnant and in some areas worsened during the 1980s. The working week in Korea was among the longest in the world: 54.0 hours for manufacturing workers in 1987 compared with 41.0 hours in the U.S., 41.3 in Japan and 48.1 in Taiwan. Furthermore, the number of working hours increased continuously from the mid-1970s to 1986. The average number of hours worked per month was 217.0 in 1975, 223.9 in 1980 and 227.8 in 1986. The number of injuries in occupational accidents also showed a striking increase, from 37,752 persons in 1970 to 142,088 in 1986 (an increase of 280 per cent). This took place at a time when the size of the labour force had grown by only 60 per cent (from 10.1 million in 1970 to 16.1 million workers in 1986). In addition, the increase in real wage of 140 per cent between 1975 and 1986 was far less than the 240 per cent increase in labour productivity (Korea Labour Institute, 1990). Thus, despite 'record-breaking economic growth', the wages of Korean workers remained low in comparison to the increase in productivity, the number of hours of work was among the highest in the world, and dangerous working conditions were the norm. Consequently, the gap between expectations and achievements was extremely wide among Korean workers in the late 1980s and resulted in an explosion of labour disputes in 1987 and 1988 on a scale that has seldom been seen anywhere else in the world (D. Kim, 1993).

The Great Labour Struggle, July-August 1987

Street demonstrations by students and citizens, protesting against the authoritarian regime and unequal distribution of wealth in Korean society, began in June 1987 and peaked on the 26th of that month. The state eventually acceded to popular demand by promising democratic reforms, including direct presidential elections and respect for human rights. Thus did Rho Tae-Woo, presidential candidate of the ruling party at the time, make the June 29th Political Declaration of Democratization in 1987. Although the

Declaration was not directly related to the improvement of labour rights in Korea, workers perceived this as an opportunity to achieve this and to obtain independence for the unions. Indeed, the Declaration was interpreted as a promise of political democratization and the relaxation of authoritarian labour policy. Before the June 29th Declaration, the demonstrations had been mainly led by students and citizens, not by workers. However, the Declaration lit the flame for an explosive, nationwide labour movement in the years that followed.

Within a few months (i.e., mainly June-August 1987), over 3,000 disputes had erupted involving more than 1.2 million workers and the loss of almost 7 million days (see Table 5.1). The waves of strikes were initiated by workers in the heavy industries in the Masan, Changwon and Ulsan areas, and then spread nationally. Transportation workers initiated general strikes in the early part of the Great Labour Struggle, and employees in almost all industries eventually joined in. Of the 3,235 strikes that took place in June-August 1987, 1,740 were conducted in the manufacturing industry, 1,186 took place in the transportation industry, and 118 in the mining industry. The strikers' main demands included wage increases, improvement of working conditions, unionization of non-union establishments and the elimination of company unions.

Table 5.1   Strike statistics, 1987-1996

Year	Number of strikes and lockouts[a]	Workers involved in strikes and lockouts[a]	Workdays lost due to strikes and lockouts (1,000 days)[a]	Number of arrested workers[b]
1987	3,749	1,262,000	6,947	N.A.
1988	1,873	293,000	5,401	63
1989	1,616	409,000	6,351	534
1990	322	134,000	4,487	474
1991	234	175,000	3,271	451
1992	235	105,000	1,528	77
1993	144	109,000	1,308	23
1994	121	104,000	1,484	142
1995	88	50,000	393	113
1996	85	79,000	893	N.A.

Sources:
[a]   Korea Labour Institute (1996, 2000) *Overseas Labour Statistics.*
[b]   Choi, Kim, Cho and Yu (2001), *Korean Labour Movement Since 1987.*

One notable characteristic was that many labour disputes during this period were conducted without the assistance or guidance of official labour organizations. Indeed, workers did not consult with the FKTU, because it was perceived as an administrative arm of the authoritarian government. A substantial portion of establishments involved in strikes was also non-union. Among 4,170 such establishments, 2,498 (approximately 60 per cent) were unionized, whereas 1,672 (approximately 40 per cent) were non-union. In 1,162 of these non-union establishments, unions were formed after strikes had taken place (Choi, et al., 2001).

Another noteworthy point is that most of these strikes were technically illegal. The majority did not meet the legal requirements specified in the labour law such as the observation of a 30-day cooling-off period before a dispute began. Consequently, only 5.9 per cent of strikes were classified as legal, whereas 94.1 per cent of strikes were technically illegal (Choi et al., 2001). Despite this, the police did not attempt to break up strikes in the early period of unrest, because Rho's Declaration was perceived as a promise that the state would not intervene in labour relations in the private sector. The absence of state intervention in labour disputes was one reason why so many strikes were able to take place during the Great Labour Struggle.

Consequences of the Great Labour Struggle: An Experiment with Pluralism

Without question, the Great Labour Struggle in 1987 was an important turning point in Korean labour history. It led to a fundamental transformation of Korean labour relations. Specifically, the Great Labour struggle had a tremendous impact on the following areas.

Firstly, the unprecedented strike waves in 1987 led the state to question the effectiveness of its traditional labour policy and reconsider the strategy of authoritarian corporatism. Also, the strong demands for political and industrial democracy from citizens and workers in that period made it almost impossible to maintain the policy of labour suppression. After the Great Labour Struggle, the state experimented with pluralism for the first time in Korean history. Between 1987-1989, it adopted a laissez-faire labour policy, which meant no state intervention in private labour relations: the government, including the police and intelligence agencies, did not intervene in collective bargaining and labour disputes throughout this period. It also maintained a neutral stance between labour and management by applying strict rules to employers' unfair labour practices. Thus, unions in the private sector enjoyed freedom to organize, bargain collectively and engage in labour disputes. This laissez-faire policy is believed to have prompted the subsequent expansion of the labour movement.

Secondly, the Great Labour Struggle was followed by an increase in union membership and labour disputes during the period 1987-1989. In many cases, strikes occurred without unions, which were then formed as a result of recognition strikes. Consequently, as shown in Table 5.2, the number of unions increased rapidly from 2,742 in June 1987 to 4,103 in December 1987. The number of union members also jumped by 21 per cent from 1,050,000 members in June 1987 to 1,267,000 members in December 1987, and the unionization ratio rose from 11.7 per cent to 13.8 per cent during the same period. The expansion of the labour movement continued through 1988 and 1989. Thus, the unionization ratio reached its peak, 18.6 per cent in 1989 with 7,883 unions and over 1.9 million members. The expansion of labour was accompanied by a large number of strike activities in 1988 (i.e., 1,873 strikes and lockouts) and 1989 (i.e., 1,616 strikes and lockouts), as shown in Table 5.1.

Table 5.2   Union statistics, 1987-1996

Year	Number of unions	Number of union members (1,000 persons)	Unionization ratio
Jun. 1987	2,742	1,050	11.7
Dec. 1987	4,103	1,267	13.8
1988	6,164	1,707	17.8
1989	7,883	1,932	18.6
1990	7,698	1,887	17.2
1991	7,656	1,803	15.8
1992	7,527	1,735	14.9
1993	7,147	1,667	14.1
1994	7,025	1,659	13.5
1995	6,606	1,615	12.6
1996	6,424	1,599	12.2

Source: Korea Labour Institute (2002) *KLI Labour Statistics.*

Thirdly, the Great Labour Struggle not only increased union density, but also changed the nature of the labour movement. The main participants in the labour movement before 1987 were female workers in smaller establishments in the light industries such as textiles, toys and electronics. After 1987, male employees in larger (sometimes *chaebol*) companies in the heavy industries such as steel, metal fabrication and chemicals in the Masan, Changwon and Ulsan industrial areas became a core group of the labour movement. Also, white-collar workers including professional, technical, clerical and sales employees in the banking, mass communication, insurance, finance and research sectors began to participate.

Fourthly, collective bargaining became institutionalized in the post-1987 period. Before then, it was practiced only in a limited number of establishments, and even in unionized firms wages were often determined unilaterally by management without genuine collective bargaining. After 1987, it became the most important wage-setting mechanism. The widespread practice of collective bargaining along with the strengthened negotiating power of labour resulted in rapid wage increases in the period immediately following the disputes.

Finally, after 1987 a more independent and autonomous labour movement began to emerge. In the past, typical Korean unions had been dominated by employers at the workplace level, and the union federation such as the FKTU largely subordinated to the state. However, the Great Labour Struggle changed these relationships. Korean unions became more aggressive, autonomous and independent from the state and employers. Furthermore, in order to strengthen the bargaining power of enterprise unions, the Struggle led to the formation of joint union councils encompassing all enterprise unions in a particular region, industry, or conglomerates. Examples include the Council of Hyundai Group Unions, the Council of Democratic Publication and Press Unions, the Council of Seoul Regional Unions and the Council of Masan and Changwon Regional Unions. By the end of 1989, 11 regional union councils, 11 industrial union councils and 1 conglomerate union council had been formed (Choi, et al., 2001).

Most importantly, after the Great Labour Struggle various attempts were made to create a second national union federation to compete with the conservative FKTU. The most notable example was the formation of the National Alliance of Trade Unions (NATU, Chun No Hyup) in January 1990. Membership of NATU accounted for 8 per cent of all unions and 16 per cent of all union members (H. Kim, 1993). NATU eventually turned into the second union federation in Korea, the KCTU, in November 1995.

Another consequence of the Great Labour Struggle was the expanded role of employers' associations. Although the Korea Employers Federation (KEF) had been established in 1971 as a counterpart of the FKTU, it only played a minimal role in dealing with the labour movement because the state dominance of labour relations did not provide enough room for there to be autonomous interactions between the two. However, after the Great Labour Struggle, the state recognized the importance of direct communication between labour and management, and the KEF became the most important channel representing employers at the informal bargaining table alongside the newly emerging labour movement. As well as the KEF, the Federation of

Korean Industries and the Korean Chamber of Commerce also represented their members in the area of labour relations.

Toward a New Industrial Order, 1990-1996

Rising Labour Costs and Income Policy

One direct consequence of the Great Labour Struggle was the increased bargaining power of the labour movement, which led to unprecedented wage increases. As shown in Table 5.3, the growth rate of wages in non-agricultural activities reached 15.5 per cent in 1988, 21.1 per cent in 1989, 18.8 per cent in 1990 and 17.5 per cent in 1991. The average annual growth rate of wages during the 1988-1994 period (i.e., 16.1 per cent) was much greater than that of labour productivity during the same period (i.e., 12.6 per cent), which eventually weakened the price competitiveness of Korean products.

Table 5.3   Economic indicators, 1987-1996

Year	Growth rates of GDP (%)[a]	Trade balances (in million US$)[b]	Growth rates of wages in non-agricultural activities (%)[b]	Growth rates of labour productivity (%)[a]
1987	11.0	11,058	10.1	10.2
1988	10.5	14,505	15.5	14.7
1989	6.1	5,360	21.1	7.4
1990	9.0	-2,003	18.8	15.2
1991	9.2	-8,317	17.5	17.0
1992	5.4	-3,943	15.2	11.3
1993	5.5	990	12.2	10.6
1994	8.3	-3,867	12.7	12.1
1995	8.9	-8,508	11.2	12.7
1996	6.8	-23,005	11.9	7.9

Sources:
[a]   Korea Labour Institute (2002) *KLI Labour Statistics.*
[b]   Korea Labour Institute (1996, 2000) *Overseas Labour Statistics.*

Rising labour costs resulted in an increase in the number of foreign workers. They were mainly imported from neighbouring Asian countries such as China, Bangladesh, Malaysia, Indonesia and the Philippines. The number of foreign workers reached almost 250,000 in the mid-1990s. Foreign workers were typically employed in 3D (i.e., dangerous, dirty, difficult) jobs which Korean workers were reluctant to do, receiving substantially lower wages. At the same time, many Korean firms relocated their plants to countries with cheaper labour such as China, Vietnam and Indonesia. For example, the level of outward foreign direct investment increased from approximately US$ 0.5 billion in 1986 to 5.8 billion in 1997, a more than 11-fold increase (Kim, Bae and Lee, 2001).

More importantly, successive wage increases in excess of corresponding productivity increases led to a deterioration of Korea's economic competitiveness. Because the Korean economy had relied heavily on medium- or low-quality products with cheap prices sold in the international market, rising labour costs led to poor performance. For example, the growth rate of GDP fell from 10.5 per cent in 1988 to 6.1 per cent in 1989 and remained lower than 10 per cent thereafter. The trade balance sheet showed a deficit in 1990 for the first time since 1985, which was repeated every year during 1991-1996 except for 1993 (See Table 5.3).

The government responded to this crisis by introducing an income policy, which attempted to check rising wages in the private sector by adopting a series of guidelines over the period 1989-1992. By bringing in the 'one-digit wage increase policy' in 1990 and the 'total wage system' in 1992, the government forced public corporations and large pattern-setting corporations to restrict wage increases within a 10-per cent limit. However, even with the help of the official wage guidelines, employers were not able to effectively restrain demand for high wage increases. Consequently, the actual rate of increases turned out to be much higher than the government target rate: 21.1 per cent in 1989, 18.8 per cent in 1990, 17.5 per cent in 1991 and 15.2 per cent in 1992 (see Table 6.3). Because the unilateral wage guideline had not produced the desired outcomes, the government now turned to a multilateral wage-control mechanism, namely central wage bargaining.

Central wage bargaining was practiced for the first time in Korean labour history under the Kim Young-Sam government. Urged on by the state, central wage agreements were made between the FKTU and KEF in 1993 and 1994. The 1993 agreement suggested an increase of 4.7 – 8.9 per cent, whereas the 1994 agreement recommended an increase of 5.0 – 8.7 per cent for the constituents of the FKTU and the KEF. These agreements, however, did not seem to influence wage bargaining at the enterprise level, because the nominal wage increase reached 12.2 per cent in 1993 and 12.7 in 1994 for the entire economy (see Table 5.3).

Indeed, independent unions who were not involved in the central wage agreement harshly criticized the FKTU for its participation in the process. More than 1,400 enterprise unions (representing 600,000 members) withdrew from the FKTU as a protest (Choi, et al., 2001). Thus, in November 1994, the FKTU announced that it would no longer participate in the central wage agreement. Overall, the failure of the income policy indicated that the state had increasingly lost control over the labour market as well as trade unions after the Great Labour Struggle.

The Decline of the Labour Movement, 1989-1996

The expansion of trade unionism prompted labour to pursue the institutionalization of the labour movement and the improvement of basic rights in the political arena. Firstly, a legislative bill to allow teachers and public sector employees to form unions was actively supported by both the FKTU and the independent labour circle. The resulting reform bill was passed in the National Assembly in 1988, but eventually vetoed by President Rho. Secondly, the independent labour circle attempted to participate in politics by forming a political party. The People's Party (Minjung-Dang) was established in November 1990. In the 1992 general election, the People's Party received only 1.5 per cent of the total popular votes (i.e., 319,000 votes,), and did not win a single National Assembly seat (Choi, et al., 2001). Although this experiment with politics turned out to be less than satisfactory, the People's Party was the first political party in Korean political history to be genuinely supported by rank and file union members.

The extent of trade unionism in Korea expanded significantly for a short period from 11.7 per cent in June 1987 to 18.6 per cent in 1989, an increase of 59 per cent, largely due to the influence of the Great Labour Struggle. However, the unionization ratio declined steadily after 1989. Union density eventually fell to 12.2 per cent in 1996, the same as before the Great Labour Struggle. In the following section, three main reasons for this decline will be discussed.

Firstly, both the government and employers had responded to the newly emerging labour movement by introducing hard-line measures. Rising labour costs and the resulting decline in economic competitiveness led the state to reconsider the laissez-faire labour policy that it had adopted right after the Great Labour Struggle. In fact, the government returned to its traditional suppressive and interventionist labour policy in the second half of 1989. Specifically, it tried to weaken the newly formed NATU that represented the aggressive, independent labour movement. The government strictly applied labour laws in the collective bargaining and labour dispute processes, and did not hesitate to arrest union leaders and members. The police intervened in large-scale strikes (e.g., in Hyundai Heavy Industries, Seoul Subway Corporation and Poongsan Metal Corporation in 1989), broke up strike events and arrested leaders. Consequently, the number of workers arrested for participating in union activities increased from 63 in 1988 to 534 in 1989, 474 in 1990 and 451 in 1991 (see Table 5.1).

In 1993, President Kim Young-Sam succeeded his predecessor, President Rho Tae-Woo (1988-1993). Although prior to his inauguration President Kim had been known as a advocate of political and industrial democracy, his labour policy was not very different from that of his predecessors. President Kim's government also pursued a traditional authoritarian labour policy to control and circumvent the militant labour movement. Without doubt, the suppressive labour policy contributed to the decline of unionism after 1987.

Secondly, after the Great Labour Struggle, Korean employers had difficulty dealing with the newly emerging militant unionism. During the period of authoritarian corporatism, most employers had not needed to directly confront unions. Instead, the government, with the help of police troops and intelligence agencies, had intervened in labour relations in the private sector, and maintained industrial harmony. After the Great Labour Struggle, some progressive employers recognized unions as business partners, whereas most others did not accept them. Apparently, most employers did not favour the path of participation and cooperation, preferring to try to weaken or eliminate the newly emerging militant unions through various legal and illegal means. For example, some employers adopted the 'New Personnel Policy' and 'Corporate Culture Movement' to minimize union influence in the workplace and strengthen management prerogatives. To avoid the aggression of the labour movement, a number of small- and medium-sized establishments closed plants and moved their operations to neighbouring countries such as China, Vietnam and Indonesia. Employers' strong opposition to unionism and a general avoidance strategy also contributed to the decline of union density.

Finally, like other market economies such as the U.S., the U.K. and France, changes in industrial structure and labour market led to a steady decline in trade unionism in Korea. For example, the ratio of workers in the manufacturing industry (in which union density was relatively high) to the total labour force decreased from 27.8 per cent in 1989 to 22.5 per cent in 1996 (Korea Labour Institute, 2000). Also, the number of female workers (who were relatively unlikely to be members) rose from 4,511,000 in 1986 to 7,206,000 in 1997 (Korea Labour Institute, 2002). Both these trends contributed to the steady decline of union density.

Despite the continuous and steady decline of trade unionism, the independent labour circle was successful in forming a second national union federation to compete with the official FKTU. The Korean Confederation of Trade Unions (KCTU) was formed in November 1995. It members mainly included employees of large *chaebol* companies and white-collar workers, whereas the FKTU was mostly blue-collar workers working in small- and medium-sized establishments. Unlike the docile FKTU, the KCTU was independent, militant and supported by rank and file members. The KCTU started with 600 enterprise unions, 200,000 union members, 14 regional union councils and 2 industrial union councils (Choi, et al., 2001).

International Pressures and Experiments with Tripartism

As the Korean economy became increasingly globalized in terms of trade and investment, from time to time the authoritarian labour policy and lack of rights were challenged by international organizations. Indeed, one dimension of globalization is the widespread adoption of internationally accepted labour standards (Kim and Kim, forthcoming). Specifically, since the early 1990s various international organizations have played important roles in improving labour standards in Korea.

Firstly, economic- and labour-related international organizations such as the ILO and the OECD have influenced Korean worker rights. Korea joined the ILO in December 1991 and the OECD in December 1996. Since 1991, successive governments have experienced international pressure to adopt ILO conventions. Korea has ratified only 11 (including three 'core' conventions), while on average other OECD members have ratified 64 (Kwon, 2000). Aware of growing international concern about labour standards in Korea, the ruling party, the National Congress for New Politics, made the ratification of ILO conventions one of the Top 100 Government Tasks in 1997.

In the process of joining the OECD, the Korean government made a commitment to reform existing laws and regulations on employment relations (ER) in line with internationally accepted standards such as freedom of association and collective bargaining. Consequently, the OECD Council instructed the OECD's Employment, Labour and Social Affairs (ELSA) Committee to monitor closely the progress made on labour law reforms in Korea.

The OECD ELSA Committee along with the ILO Committee on Freedom of Association has paid close attention to issues where Korean labour laws and actual practices seemed to be inconsistent with internationally accepted standards. These included the establishment of multiple unions in a single workplace, third-party intervention in collective bargaining, the right to organize public employees and teachers, the right to strike in the public sector, trade union membership of dismissed or unemployed workers, the payment by companies of full-time union officials and the imprisonment of unionists for activities that would be regarded as legitimate and legal in other member countries (OECD, 2000).

The pressure from international organizations has been insistent. The ILO has issued 7 official recommendations to allow and legalize teachers' unions in Korea since 1991, and the OECD has raised the issue of Korean labour standards five times at international forums (Korea Ministry of Labour, 2000). In the 1990s, members of the ELSA Committee and the ILO Committee on Freedom of Association visited Korea annually to examine progress on the ILO recommendations and to discuss future plans with Korean government officials.

Secondly, the movement toward linking labour standards to trade and investment decisions has put further pressure on newly industrialized countries (NICs) like Korea. With the advent of the WTO in January 1995, there have been voices (mainly from the U.S. and EU countries) advocating a link between international labour standards and the liberalization of international trade (called the 'blue round'). Indeed, this was a highly controversial issue at the 1996 Singapore Ministerial Conference. The rationale behind the proposal is that countries violating international labour standards take unfair advantage of labour exploitation, and it could be a ground for invoking trade sanctions. The labour standards referred to as the 'core' ILO standards are the right to freedom of association, the right to bargain collectively, the prohibition of forced labour, non-discrimination in employment and the minimum wage. At the Conference, delegates from the developing countries argued that linking labour standards to trade is a disguised instrument of protectionism which seeks to raise labour costs in developing countries in order to reduce their international competitiveness (WTO, 1999 and 2001). Although the idea was not realized at the Conference due to the opposition of the developing countries, the movement was a formidable threat to countries like Korea whose labour provisions are believed to be inferior to international standards (Kim and Kim, forthcoming).

Another example is the report of the Overseas Private Investment Corporation (OPIC). In July 1991 the OPIC, an independent US government agency set up to assist US companies investing in some 140 emerging economies around the world, suspended its program in Korea as the country had failed to take steps to adopt and implement internationally recognized worker rights. Consequently, government officials and employer groups in Korea paid close attention to the OPIC report on 'internationally recognized worker rights in Korea'. In June 1998, OPIC determined that Korea now satisfied the eligibility criteria and resumed its service (Kim, Bae and Lee, 2001). In summary, the positions taken by these international and private organizations have prompted the Korean government to reconsider its traditional authoritarian labour policy and to take action to confirm global labour standards.

Although the main government policy toward labour movement in the early 1990s was to suppress it, the state simultaneously pursued more accommodative means to improve the 'labour problems' (Wilkinson, 1994) in Korea. Of course, the aforementioned pressure from international organizations played some part in encouraging the Korean government to adopt this approach. These accommodative means were expressed in the form of experiments with tripartite systems including: (1) the Citizens' Economic and Social Council in 1990 and (2) the Presidential Commission on Industrial Relations Reform in 1996.

Firstly, the Citizens' Economic and Social Council was formed in May 1990 by the government's initiative. The Council was composed of 30 members including 10 labour representatives, 10 employer representatives and 10 people representing general public interests. The Council discussed various issues such as employment security, income distribution, the social security and welfare system, human resource development, finance and taxation, and issued several recommendations to the government. Although the Council did not have any participants from the government nor any decision-making authority, it helped improve the legitimacy of the state's labour policy.

A more autonomous and significant discussion among ER actors in Korea took place in 1996 under the Presidency of Kim Young-Sam. In May 1996, the tripartite actors in the ER system began to set up a new institutional arena, the Presidential Commission on Industrial Relations Reform, in which important labour issues could be formally discussed. One of the purposes of the Commission was to improve labour standards up to the level required by international organizations.

The Commission, comprising representatives of labour (5 persons), management (5 persons) and the public (20 persons), held a six-month series of public hearings and expert panels in order to reach a consensus on the labour issues in question. Despite these efforts, the Commission was unable to reach a complete consensus by November 1996.

The ruling party (then the New Korea Party) hastily decided to revise the labour law by the end of the year 1996 despite the absence of consensus in the Commission. The Ministry of Labour prepared a draft that mainly reflected employers' interests and it was passed by the ruling party in a sudden National Assembly Meeting held in the middle of the night of December 26, 1996. The National Assembly members of the opposing parties were not present. This sudden and unfair action induced the biggest ever general strike in Korea, lasting from Dec. 26, 1996 to February 28, 1997, involving 2 million participants. Both the FKTU and the KCTU participated. Influenced by the unprecedented magnitude of the opposition to the law, the ruling and opposing parties agreed to revise it again on February 17, 1997. After some conflicts among the tripartite actors, the revision was completed on March 10, 1997. The fact that the changes were forced upon the government was a clear signal that it had lost its authority in the area of labour relations.

Among the major contents of the revision, there was a significant development in basic rights. The 1997 revision aimed to improve labour standards by strengthening basic labour rights, whilst also strengthening firm competitiveness by enhancing labour market flexibility. In return for the legalization of multiple unions in a single workplace, layoffs (with a two-year reservation for implementation) and flexible working hours were legalized in turn (Kim and Kim, forthcoming).

To sum up, the experiments with tripartite systems did not turn out to be entirely successful. The influence of the Citizens' Economic and Social Council in 1990 was largely nominal, and the efforts of the Presidential Commission on Industrial Relations Reform did not generate a consensus among actors of ER and ended with the biggest general strike in Korean labour history. However, the general strike in 1997 and the subsequent revision of the law eventually resulted in substantial improvements in labour rights. There is no doubt that continued international pressure played an important role in such positive outcomes.

Chapter Summary

Due to the fact that the capitalist class was all but nonexistent in the early development process in Korea, the state assumed a key role in directing and coordinating economic activities. The lack of natural resources and capital and the relatively small size of the domestic market forced the state to pursue an exported-oriented strategy based on foreign investment, overseas natural resources and cheap labour. Consequently, economic development in Korea began with the creation of some initial conditions conducive to this exported-oriented strategy. These were characterized by low wages, a disciplined labour force and a subordinated labour movement, all of which helped attract foreign investment. In particular, Korea's heavy commitment to investment in human capital produced a relatively high-quality workforce, which facilitated the early stages of economic development. These initial labour market conditions attracted foreign investment and provided comparative advantages in relatively low-price, low-quality international markets, and led to continued growth during the period from the early 1960s to the mid-1980s. As growth continued, however, the factors that had previously made it possible actually accelerated the decline of the initial conditions (Verma, Kochan and Lansbury, 1995).

As a highly educated working class became more capable of challenging the old industrial order, from the mid-1980s on, the basis of past economic growth was increasingly being diminished. There were continuing demands for wage increases and industrial democracy in the form of militant unions, adversarial collective bargaining and chronic labour disputes. The result of these developments in the labour market reduced the initial advantage that had provided price competitiveness and attracted new investment. The culmination of the ongoing conflict between the old, authoritarian industrial order and the radical demands from the newly emerging working class was the Great Labour Struggle in 1987.

After the short-term (just two years) experiment with pluralism, the state returned to the traditional, authoritarian labour policy. Rapidly rising labour costs and the deteriorating price competitiveness of Korean products led the government and employers to adopt a strategy which would recreate or maintain the initial conditions, by undertaking a series of measures such as wage controls and subordination and/or the suppression of unions and collective bargaining. This retrospective strategy was attractive in the short run, but was not sustainable over a long period. Even though the state could successfully suppress militant labour by the use of force, the Korean economy might not have been able to overcome the challenges from neighbouring countries that could compete in the same low-quality consumer product markets but with far cheaper labour (i.e., China, Vietnam).

At this stage, the ideal path would have been to develop a new accord between the state, capital and labour under the new industrial order. The state might have incorporated unions into the national policy-making process, or enabled them to enjoy greater freedom and autonomy (Wilkinson, 1994). At the same time, the state and employers might have adopted more progressive policy options such as a radical upgrading of the economic structure by enhancing productivity through greater investment in human resources, improving the flexibility of human resources utilization and developing advanced technology and high value-added products. A movement toward a high value-added economy seemed to begin in the mid-1990s, but it did not embrace labour. While there were efforts to seek a new model of industrial relations conducive to a more democratic society (such as the experiments with tripartite systems in the early 1990s), they have yet failed to embrace the newly emerging militant segments of the labour force.

Indeed, the state intended to apply the concept of tripartism in the form of the Citizens' Economic and Social Council in 1990 and also the efforts of the Presidential Commission on Industrial Relations Reform in 1996. However, when the ruling party (the New Korea Party) passed the 1996 labour law that enhanced flexibility in the utilization of human resources and gave employers substantial freedom to lay off employees against their will, labour itself (both KTUC and FKTU) responded with the biggest general strike in Korean history in January 1997, involving more than two million participants. The general strike clearly showed the practical difficulty of applying tripartism in Korea where the tradition of an authoritarian labour policy and adversarial ER has been so long-standing and deeply entrenched.

Overall, after the Great Labour Struggle in 1987, the state increasingly realized the limitations of the traditional, authoritarian labour policy, and made an effort to seek an alternative paradigm. These efforts resulted in experiments with pluralism during the 1987-1989 period, with income policy and central wage bargaining in 1993 and 1994, and with tripartism in 1990 and 1996. However, all these experiments turned out to be short-lived or otherwise unsuccessful. The reasons for this might include: (1) the unprecedented aggressiveness of labour that could not be controlled or restrained by the state or employers and (2) the hostile relationships and lack of trust among the employment relation actors. The Korean industrial relations system had not yet developed an over-arching ideology and a set of congruent rules that could accommodate the interests of all three parties when the financial crisis took place in 1997. All parties experienced serious conflicts and hardships, as we will see in the next chapter.

References

Bognanno, M.F. (1988), *Korea's Industrial Relations at the Turning Point*, Korea Development Institute, Seoul.

Bognanno, M.F. and Kim, S. (1982), 'Collective Bargaining in Korea', in *Proceedings of the Thirty-Fourth Annual Meeting of the Industrial Relations Research Association*, January, Industrial Relations Research Association, Madison, WI, pp.193-201.

Choi, Y.K., Kim, J., Cho, H.R. and Yu, B.S. (2001), *Korean Labor Movement Since 1987*, Korea Labour Institute, Seoul. (In Korean.)

Gurr, T.R. (1968), 'A Causal Model of Civil Strife: a Comparative Analysis Using New Indices', *American Political Science Review*, vol.62, pp.1104-1124.

Gurr, T.R. (1970), 'Sources of Rebellion in Western Societies: Some Quantitative Evidence', *American Academy of Political and Social Science*, vol.391, pp.128-244.

Kang, S.H. (1998), *Korean Labour Movement: Changes for 10 Years after 1987*, Korea Labour Institute, Seoul. (In Korean.)

Kim, D.-O. (1993), 'Analysis of Labour Disputes in Korea and Japan: The Search for an Alternative Model', *European Sociological Review*, vol.9, no.2, pp.139-154.

Kim, D.-O., Bae, J. and Lee, C. (2000), 'Globalization and Labour Rights: The Case of Korea', *Asia Pacific Business Review*, vol.6, no.3/4, pp.133-153.

Kim, D.-O. and Kim, S. (forthcoming), 'Globalization, Financial Crisis, and Industrial Relations: The Case of Korea', *Industrial Relations*, vol.41, no.3.

Kim, H.-J. (1993), 'The Korean Union Movement in Transition', in S. Frenkel (ed), *Organized Labour in the Asia-Pacific Region*, ILR Press, Ithaca, New York, pp.133-161.

Korea Labour Institute (1990), *Statistics about Wages*, Seoul. (In Korean.)

Korea Labour Institute (1996), *Overseas Labour Statistics*, Seoul. (In Korean.)

Korea Labour Institute (2000), *Overseas Labour Statistics*, Seoul. (In Korean.)

Korea Labour Institute (2002), *KLI Labour Statistics*, Seoul. (In Korean.)

Korea Ministry of Labour (2000), *'99 White Paper on Labour*, Seoul. (In Korean.)

Kwon, J.D. (2000), *ILO and International Labour Standards*, JoongAng KyungJe, Seoul. (In Korean.)

OECD (2000), *Pushing Ahead with Reform in Korea – Labour Market and Social Safety-net Policies*, OECD, Paris.

Ogle, G. (1990), *South Korea: Dissent within the Economic Miracle*, Zed Books, London.

Park, S.-I. (1993), 'The Role of the State in Industrial Relations: The Case of Korea', *Comparative Labour Law Journal*, vol.14, pp.321-338.

Verma, A., Kochan, T.A. and Lansbury, R.D. (1995), 'Lessons from the Asian Experience: a Summary', in A. Verma, T.A. Kochan and R.D. Lansbury (eds), *Employment Relations in the Growing Asian Economies*, Routledge, New York, pp.337-358.

Wilkinson, B. (1994), *Labour And Industry In The Asia-Pacific: Lessons From The Newly-Industrialized Countries*, Walter de Gruyter, New York.

WTO (1999), http://www.wto.org/english/thewto_e/whatis_e/tif_e/bey7_e.htm

WTO (2001), http://www.wto.org/english/thewto_e/minist_e/min96_e/lab stand.htm

6 Changing Employment Relations in the Era of Financial Crisis and Organizational Restructuring

Introduction

After almost 30 years of rapid economic progress, the Korean economy encountered an unprecedented economic emergency in the late 1990s. For most Koreans, it has been the most formidable crisis since the Korean War in 1953. It has exerted a significant, long-lasting impact on the overall economy, the labour market, employment practices, the labour movement and the interactions between the three employment relations (ER) actors. On the other hand, it has also provided an opportunity for government officials, labour and employers to rethink their traditional policies and to formulate new strategies in the era of organizational restructuring. This chapter begins by discussing the background to the 1997-1998 financial crisis.

The 1997-1998 Financial Crisis

During the period of rapid economic growth, the comparative advantage of the Korean economy lay in its price competitiveness in the manufacturing industry. This was based upon its cheap, relatively well-educated and diligent labour force. The advent of political democratization and the strength of the labour movement since the late 1980s, however, led to an unprecedented increase in real wage (and labour costs), which caused this price advantage to vanish.

Tables 7.1 and 7.2 illustrate the declining competitiveness of the Korean economy during the period 1986-1996. The hourly compensation costs for production workers in manufacturing rose from only US$1.31 in 1986 to US$8.22 in 1996, a more than six-fold increase in 10 years. Until 1990, labour costs in Korea were the lowest of the three Asian tigers (i.e., Korea, Taiwan and Singapore). However, this position had been reversed by the early 1990s (see Table 6.1). Despite the unprecedented increase in labour costs, the labour productivity index rose from 42 in 1986 to 112.2 in 1996 (1995=100), an increase of less than three-fold in 10 years. Although the labour productivity index in Korea during 1986-1996 grew faster than that in Taiwan (from 55.2 in 1986 to 100.0 in 1996), Japan (from 75.6 in 1986 to 103.2 in 1996) and the U.S. (from 86.9 in 1986 to 113.8 in 1996), it did not catch up with the skyrocketing increase in labour costs. Without doubt, these developments resulted in the declining competitiveness of the Korean manufacturing industry.

Table 6.1   Hourly compensation costs for production workers in manufacturing (US$)

Year	Korea	Taiwan	Singapore	Japan	Germany	U.S.
1986	1.31	1.73	2.23	9.22	13.34	13.26
1987	1.59	2.26	2.31	10.79	16.91	13.52
1988	2.20	2.81	2.67	12.63	18.16	13.91
1989	3.17	3.52	3.15	12.53	17.66	14.32
1990	3.71	3.93	3.78	12.80	21.88	14.91
1991	4.61	4.36	4.35	14.67	22.63	15.58
1992	5.22	5.09	4.95	16.38	25.38	16.09
1993	5.64	5.24	5.25	19.21	24.44	16.51
1994	6.40	5.56	6.29	21.35	25.86	16.87
1995	7.29	5.94	7.33	23.82	30.65	17.19
1996	8.22	5.95	8.32	21.01	30.26	17.70
1997	7.86	5.90	8.24	19.54	26.84	18.27
1998	5.39	5.27	7.77	18.29	26.76	18.66
1999	6.71	5.62	7.18	20.89	26.18	19.20

Source: Korea Labour Institute (2000) *Overseas Labour Statistics*.

It was widely known in the 1990s that Korean products were priced more highly than those from low-wage competitors (i.e., China, Thailand, Vietnam and Malaysia), but were of inferior quality to that of high value-added competitors (i.e., Japan, the EU and the U.S.). Thus, Korean products were not attractive to either the low-end or high-end markets. The declining competitiveness led to the slowdown of the Korean economy from the early 1990s: the 1997-1998 crisis was believed to be an end result of a gradual fall in competitiveness throughout the 1990s.

When the newly elected Korean President, Kim Dae-Jung, turned in desperation to the IMF for a rescue package in November 1997, the financial and economic indexes deteriorated rapidly. For example, the foreign exchange rate (won/US$) depreciated from 921.85 in October 1997 to 1,706.8 in January 1998. In other words, the value of the Korean won fell by about 80 per cent against the US dollar in just three months, and the average value of stock in the Korean stock market dropped by approximately 60 per cent during the same period (Park, 1998).

Table 6.2   Labour productivity trends in manufacturing

Year	Korea (1995=100)	Taiwan (1996=100)	Japan (1995=100)	U.S. (1992=100)
1986	42.0	55.2	75.6	86.9
1987	45.2	59.0	79.9	89.2
1988	49.8	62.0	89.1	90.7
1989	53.3	67.7	94.4	90.8
1990	60.1	72.8	95.1	93.0
1991	68.5	79.7	98.0	95.1
1992	76.3	82.7	94.5	100.0
1993	82.8	85.4	93.5	102.2
1994	90.6	88.4	95.8	105.3
1995	100.0	94.9	100.0	109.4
1996	112.2	100.0	103.2	113.8
1997	128.8	107.0	108.2	119.6
1998	144.0	111.7	103.8	123.9
1999	171.7	119.6	106.9	131.6

Source: Korea Labour Institute (2001) *KLI Labour Statistics*.

There are two conflicting views on the causes of the financial crisis. Some scholars, mostly in Asian countries, attribute it to the globalization and instability of international financial markets, whereas others see domestic and policy factors as the primary cause. For the former camp, the sudden financial crisis is best understood as a consequence of the liberalization and instability of international financial markets. According to this theory, in the globalized financial market there are virtually no effective instruments for restraining and checking a large and sudden increase in capital inflows and outflows such as that which occurred before and during the crisis. The susceptibility of international financial markets to monetary speculation and the resultant self-fulfilling panic can lead to a sudden shift from boom to bust and vice versa.

The latter perspective, which is popular among economists who favour free-market economies, argues that a defective Asian model of development resulted in the crisis. This flawed model can be characterized by a deviation from the principles of free market economics such as widespread political interference with market processes, moral hazards and deeply embedded corruption. That is, the financial crisis symbolizes the fragility of the Asian development model. However, the general agreement seems to be that the Asian financial crisis was caused by the interaction of several factors including the two discussed above (Lee, 1998).

The IMF decided to provide a bailout program in November 1997. It included a comprehensive financing package of about US$65Bn on both a multilateral and bilateral basis. In return, the Korean government was asked to contain inflationary pressure through tight monetary and fiscal policies, to fundamentally restructure the banking and financial sector and to find a way to reduce corporations' excessive reliance on short-term financing. More important, the IMF emphasized their view that the Korean labour market was too rigid and the government needed to take the necessary steps to improve its flexibility.

Even without this pressure from the IMF, Korean government officials already believed that improving labour market flexibility was the only approach to improving the economic competitiveness of Korean firms, and strongly encouraged private and public corporations to implement bold restructuring moves including massive layoffs, outsourcing and early retirement programs. Faced with the sudden credit crunch, Korean employers also actively pursued numerical and external flexibility through layoffs, outsourcing and the replacement of regular workers with contingent labour. Some employers perceived the financial crisis as an opportunity to eliminate redundant aspects of the labour force without encountering strong resistance. Consequently, despite some opposition from the labour force, employment adjustment programs (e.g., downsizing, restructuring, exchange of business units among chaebols, mergers and acquisitions and intra- and inter-firm ventures) were pursued by many firms.

The Impact on the Labour Market

Right after the IMF bailout program in November 1997, all sectors of the Korean economy experienced employment restructuring on an unprecedented scale. In the first 16 months of the financial crisis, the number of unemployed increased by approximately 1.3 million. Consequently, the unemployment rate in Korea increased sharply from 2.1 per cent in October 1997 to 8.6 per cent in February 1999 (see Table 6.3).

The sudden increase in unemployment resulted from (1) employment restructuring programs and (2) the bankruptcy of firms that had suffered most from the credit crunch arising from tightened control of loans by a banking sector under heavy scrutiny. Among the newly unemployed people with some work experience in 1998, 56.9 per cent were identified as victims of employment adjustment programs, and 13.6 per cent as having become unemployed due to bankruptcy (National Statistical Office, February-December 1998).

Although the National Assembly passed the Unemployment Insurance Act and made it effective in July 1995, its coverage was shallow and limited. Consequently, the unemployment insurance program did not cover a substantial portion of affected workers, and most jobless people and their families suffered severe economic hardship (Kim and Kim, forthcoming).

Since downsizing had been implemented in almost all sectors of the Korean economy, collective bargaining for wage increases was displaced by the need to improve employment security. Consequently, while some unions were able to secure employment guarantee agreements with employers, concession bargaining was widespread during the financial crisis. Wage levels for most workers fell and the growth rate of real wages was −9.3 per cent in 1999.

Table 6.3   Unemployment rates around the period of the financial crisis

Month	Unemployment rate in 1997	Unemployment rate in 1998	Unemployment rate in 1999	Unemployment rate in 2000
January	2.6	4.5	8.5	5.3
February	3.2	5.9	8.6	5.3
March	3.4	6.5	8.0	4.7
April	2.8	6.7	7.1	4.1
May	2.5	6.9	6.4	3.6
June	2.3	7.0	6.2	3.6
July	2.2	7.6	6.2	3.6
August	2.1	7.4	5.7	3.7
September	2.2	7.3	4.8	3.6
October	2.1	7.1	4.6	3.4
November	2.6	7.3	4.4	3.6
December	3.1	7.9	4.8	4.1

Source: National Statistical Office (Various Issues) *Monthly Employment Trend*.

The use of contingent labour such as part-timers, temporary workers and leased workers became widespread after the financial crisis. As the size of the contingent labour force sharply rose, the Law on Protecting Dispatched Workers was enacted in February 1998 to regulate and control the sector. The ratio of contingent workers to the total employed population increased from 46 per cent in 1997 to 53 per cent in 2000 (National Statistical Office, Various Issues).[1] Contingent workers usually took the jobs of regular, full-time workers, and assumed the same level of responsibility. Their wage level, however, was approximately two-thirds of regular workers. Also, the social safety net for contingent workers was thinner than that for regular workers, since employers often failed to pay their premiums for medical insurance, unemployment insurance, social security and workers' compensation.

An organization hires contingent workers either because it wants to protect core workers in business downturns, or because it intends to replace core workers permanently to save costs and improve flexibility. In the former situation, the number of contingent workers will theoretically fall during economic downturns because contingent workers will be laid off in preference to regular workers. In the latter, the reverse is true because contingent workers replace core workers permanently. The Korean firms seem to have followed the latter path during the financial crisis, because the proportion of contingent workers to the total employed population reached a higher level during the financial crisis (Kim and Kim, forthcoming).

The increase of the contingent labour force and the weakened bargaining power of labour seemed to worsen the income distribution in Korean society. After the financial crisis, income inequalities widened. Over the period 1997-1999, although the average income of the richest 20 per cent of urban households increased by 5.2 per cent (from 4,254,800 won to 4,475,000 won per month), the average income of the poorest 20 per cent of urban households declined by 13.4 per cent (from 947,100 won to 815,600 won per month). During the same two-year period, the Gini coefficient increased from .283 in 1997 to .320 in 1999, indicating a deterioration in income distribution (Korean Ministry of Labour, 2000).

The Impact of the Financial Crisis on Employment Practices

Traditional Korean employment practices cultivated employees' loyalty and commitment through long-term employment and seniority-based pay. As economic competition intensified throughout the 1990s, these rigid practices were challenged by the need for the more flexible use of human resources. American-style employment practices focusing on relatively short-term, performance-based and market-oriented methods of managing human resources began to spread, and the legacy of lifetime employment was greatly weakened in most private companies.

The seniority-based pay system is still a dominant form of remuneration in Korea, since approximately 90 per cent of Korean firms still use length of service as one of the most important factors in determining pay. However, a wage system emphasizing individual ability and performance (a type of merit-pay system) has gained in popularity in recent years (Kim and Park, 1997). A recent survey of almost 5,000 firms by the Ministry of Labour showed that 32.3 per cent (1,612 firms of 4,998 respondents) had already adopted a merit pay system as of January 2002. This contrasts with the 1.6 per cent of Korean firms (mainly larger firms) which reported using such a system in 1996. The adoption rate has rapidly increased since then (i.e., 3.6 per cent in 1997; 15.1 per cent in 1999; 23.0 per cent in 2000; 27.1 per cent in 2001) (the Dong-a Ilbo, March 5, 2002). For most firms using a merit pay system approximately 10 per cent of employees' total compensation is believed to be at risk, whereas for the largest 50 companies the variable portion of the total compensation is around 30 per cent (the Dong-a Ilbo, January 14, 2001).

In Korea, the seniority wage approach was traditionally combined with a group bonus system. Bonuses constituted approximately 20-30 per cent of the annual earnings of workers in most companies. In principle, bonuses were supposed to be contingent on the financial performance of the company. As the bonus became regarded as a regular component of the total compensation package, however, it became more difficult to make the amount truly variable. In many cases, the terms and amount of bonuses were often determined by collective bargaining agreements or implicit agreements before the year-end performance of the company had been determined. For these reasons, there has been a widespread belief that the bonus system in Korea was not truly variable (Kim and Park, 1997). The trend in bonus payouts during the 1997-1998 financial crisis, however, greatly weakened such a belief. At this time most firms stopped paying the bonus portion of compensation or employees 'voluntarily' returned the bonus to help the company overcome the financial stress. The bonus payment resumed after the crisis. These developments show that the bonus system can respond flexibly to economic fluctuations and can be utilized as an adjustment mechanism to improve pay flexibility (Kim and Kim, forthcoming).

Since the financial crisis, Korean employment practices have become increasingly Americanized. One reason for this could be the influence of multi-national business consulting firms (i.e., McKinsey, Boston Consulting Group, Arthur Anderson, Watson Wyatt, Towers Perrin and Bain and Company). Indeed, during the financial crisis many American-based consulting firms greatly expanded their business presence in Korea, and enthusiastically disseminated the 'international standard' of employment practices. For example, 360-degree appraisal was introduced to an increasing number of firms, reducing reliance on the traditional top-down appraisal; hiring and selection decisions began to be decentralized, giving line managers more decision-making authority; the selection process placed more importance on interviews than traditional paper-and-pencil tests; training and education programs focused more on technical knowledge and skills than on loyalty and commitment to the company; and companies publicly announced that they would not provide employment security but employability. There was already a tendency to adopt American-style employment practices before the financial crisis, but it seemed to accelerate this tendency (Kim and Yu, 2000).

The Impact of the Financial Crisis on Trade Unionism and Collective Bargaining

Although trade union membership had started to decline after 1989, labour organizations experienced substantial setbacks during the early period of the crisis. Unions lost about 50,000, or 3 per cent, of their members during the first nine months of the emergency (Kim, Bae and Lee, 2000). The sudden decline was mainly due to employment restructuring and the bankruptcy of unionized companies. The dominant response of two labour centres (in particular, the KCTU) to the waves of downsizing was to oppose any employment restructuring programs by mobilizing union members, student activists and the general public and calling for a series of general strikes. Because Korean unions were trying to prevent the layoffs and refused to negotiate, they could not be involved in the process. In other words, when downsizing was inevitable, unions were not involved in the important decisions on the procedure to be taken, the choice of who would be laid off and their financial remedies (Jung, 1999).

Although the financial crisis initially appeared to be detrimental to the labour movement, it seems to have made trade unionism more active and dynamic in the long run. The latter trend was evident in the following three developments: (1) the financial crisis actually reversed the declining trend of union membership partially due to grass-roots organizing among employees in small- and medium-sized firms; (2) all dimensions of strike activities rose substantially after 1997; (3) the movement to transform traditional enterprise unions to industrial unionism was revitalized after the economic crisis.

Firstly, the financial crisis and resultant waves of massive layoffs sent mixed signals to both unionized and non-union workers. When the number of union members sharply declined due to the layoffs, it was imperative for the FKTU, which had traditionally been more cooperative with government labour policies than the KCTU, to advance its own agenda and protect its members. The FKTU had to compete with the KCTU to obtain its members' loyalty and support in the wake of employment restructuring. Thus, both the

FKTU and KCTU called a series of general strikes to stop the waves of downsizing by aggressively opposing government-initiated restructuring programs. Despite these efforts, many union members were disappointed by the failure of the organizations to protect large numbers of their members from downsizing (Jung, 1999).[2]

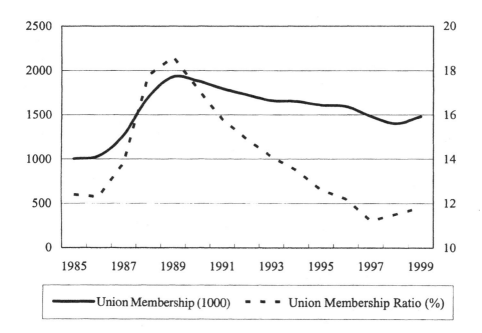

Figure 6.1   Trend of union membership in Korea

Source: Korea Labour Institute (2001) KLI Labour Statistics.

On the other hand, non-union employees increasingly felt that they too needed some protective mechanisms against the successive waves of layoffs, because it was evident that non-union employees were much more likely than unionized workers to be the victims. The non-union employees' desire for employment security led to widespread grass roots organizing. That is, it has become increasingly popular for non-union workers to organize without any help from a higher-level union organization. The KCTU's membership traditionally came from large establishments belonging to chaebols, but after the financial crisis, employees in small establishments also began to organize themselves and to approach the KCTU for affiliation. For example, during the period January 1 through May 19, 2000, 153 newly organized unions (covering 15,207 members) became affiliated with the KCTU. Most of these newly organized unions were small, averaging 99 members each (Kim and Kim, forthcoming).

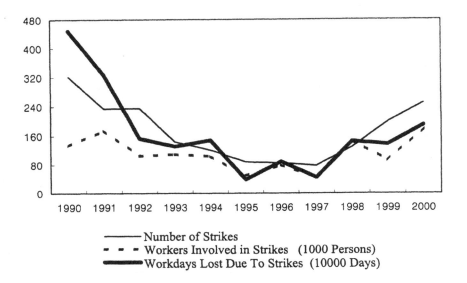

—— Number of Strikes
- - - Workers Involved in Strikes (1000 Persons)
▬▬▬Workdays Lost Due To Strikes (10000 Days)

Figure 6.2   Trend of strike activities in Korea

Source: Korea Labour Institute (2001) *KLI Labour Statistics.*

For both the FKTU and the KCTU, most of the newly affiliated unions represented white-collar and managerial employees, service workers, foreign workers and contingent labour. Indeed, many regional offices of the two union centres (i.e., the FKTU and the KCTU) experienced the same increasing trend of grass roots organizing as the non-traditional groups (Kim and Kim, forthcoming). After the unionization ratio in Korea had reached its highest level, 18.6 per cent, in 1989, the ratio declined gradually to 11.2 per cent in 1997. However, the financial crisis reversed the decline, and the unionization ratio reached 11.8 per cent in 1999. The number of unionized workers increased by about 79,000 in 1999.[3]

Secondly, all dimensions of labour conflict have increased noticeably since the financial crisis. From 1997-2000, the number of strikes increased from 78 to 250, the number of workers involved in strikes from 43,991 to 177,969 and the number of working days lost due to labour disputes from 444,720 to 1,893,563. All these numbers were more than tripled over the period. In addition, the number of unfair labour practices (ULPs) filed with Regional Labour Committees by employees in conflict with their employers rose from 495 in 1997 to 950 in 1999 (Korea Ministry of Labour, 2000). Such ULP filings have traditionally been positively correlated with the magnitude of labour disputes in Korea (Kim and Kim, forthcomiing). As shown in Table 6.4, after the financial crisis, the number of strikes due to employment and working conditions accounted for almost four-fifths of the total (i.e., 196 out of 250) in 2000, leaving strikes due to wage issues at only one-fifth of the overall strike activities (i.e., 54 out of 250). This trend was a sharp contrast to the earlier pattern, in which wage-related strikes accounted for approximately or sometimes more than half of the total number of disputes until the mid-1990s. This clearly indicates that employment-related issues led to most of the disputes between labour and management after the financial crisis.

Table 6.4   Statistics on labour disputes in Korea

Year	Number of strikes	Reason for strikes: unpaid wages (number)	Reason for strikes: wage increase (number)	Reason for strikes: employment and working conditions (number)
1986	276	48	75	153
1987	3,749	45	2,613	1,102
1988	1,873	59	946	868
1989	1,616	59	742	815
1990	332	10	167	145
1991	234	5	132	97
1992	235	27	134	74
1993	144	11	66	67
1994	121	6	51	64
1995	88	0	33	55
1996	85	1	19	65
1997	78	3	18	57
1998	129	23	28	78
1999	198	22	40	136
2000	250	7	47	196

Source: Korea Labour Institute (2001) *KLI Labour Statistics*.

Finally, the movement toward industrial unionism intensified after the financial crisis. Enterprise unionism was one of the traditional characteristics of Korean trade unionism. The massive layoffs led union leaders to realize it had inherent limitations. Enterprise-based unions could not respond effectively to industrial- and national-level employment issues, such as industry-level restructuring plans forced through by the government. The movement towards industrial unionism had been initiated by a minority of union leaders before the financial crisis. However, Korean labour laws enforced enterprise unionism by prohibiting other forms of organization until 1987, but the two revisions in 1987 and 1997 made industrial unionism both legal and easier to establish.

Thus, both the increasing need for industrial organization and the changes in labour law accelerated the movement towards industrial unionism. For example, the formation of the Banking Employees' Industrial Union was a direct response to the first round of banking industry restructuring in 1998, which led to layoffs of approximately 40 per cent of employees in the sector. The most important goal of the transformation of existing banking enterprise unions into one industrial union (i.e., the Banking Employees' Industrial Union) was to protect the job security of the remaining employees against an imminent second round of employment restructuring. Employees in the banking industry believed that a single, large-scale industrial union would be more effective than scattered enterprise unions in preventing the government and employers from implementing unpopular employment restructuring programs.

The transformation from enterprise unionism to industrial unionism was decisive and swift. In the two-year period from 1998 to 2000, almost 20 industrial unions were formed. Industrial unions belonging to the KCTU include the Korean Teachers and Educational Workers Union (87,000 members), the Korean Health and Medical Workers (39,000 members), the Korean Metal Workers Union (32,000 members), the Korean Press Union (18,800 members), the Korea Securities Trade Union (15,600 members) and the Korean Life Insurance Labour Union (14,400 members). Industrial unions belonging to the FKTU include the Korean Tax Workers Union (98,000 members), the Korea Financial Industry Union (50,000 members), the Korean Postal Workers Union (29,000 members), the Korean Union of Teaching and Educational Workers (28,000 members), the Korean Railroad Workers' Union (27,600 members) and the Korean National Electrical Workers' Union (25,000 members). Most of these industrial unions were formed by merging existing individual enterprise unions. The combined membership of these industrial unions reached 32.8 per cent of total union membership in Korea (502,310 industrial union members out of 1,529,560 total union members) as of July 2001 (Kim and Kim, forthcoming).

So far, however, industry-level bargaining has only been conducted in a handful of sectors such as education, hospitals and banking mainly due to the refusal of employers in other sectors to participate. It may be expected to become more popular in the future, at least where industrial unions exist. However, we would not expect all enterprise unions to transform themselves into industrial unions, for various reasons such as the refusal of their leaders to give up their vested rights. Thus, future trade unionism in Korea is most likely to be a mixture of enterprise and industrial unions.

In the long run, the movement toward industrial unionism would be expected to improve the organizing potential of Korean labour unions. As the number of union members in the manufacturing sector decreases due to downsizing, plant closing and bankruptcy, it has become more important to organize the expanding sectors of the economy such as the service and information technology sectors and contingent labour force. Enterprise unions have only limited incentives and resources to organize workers in other enterprises. Indeed, organizing employees outside the enterprise does not help strengthen its power (Freeman and Rebick, 1989). In contrast, industrial unions would be expected to be more interested in organizing employees in these sectors than enterprise unions, since organizing efforts directly strengthen their power.

The Experiment with Democratic Corporatism

The Early Success of the Tripartite Commission

The financial crisis in November 1997 resulted in a crisis consciousness among the three actors, leading them to form the Tripartite Commission, which otherwise would not have been possible due to their hostile relationships. The resistance which was anticipated from labour and international pressure prevented the Korean government from relying on its traditional, authoritarian and oppressive labour policy when it imposed its economic restructuring agenda. As a result, it had to resort to a more consensual system of ER. In the past, the Korean government had considered labour to be an obstacle to economic development and had tried to subordinate official labour unions to the state and to suppress any independent organizing. The creation of the Tripartite Commission implied that the Korean government at least now regarded labour as a legitimate actor in a political structure.

As shown in Table 6.5, on January 20, 1998, all parties to the Tripartite Commission announced the first Tripartite Joint Statement and identified the shared goal of economic reform and the principle of fair sharing of burdens. After two weeks of heated debates, on February 9, 1998 the Tripartite Commission agreed upon 90 major items and declared its Social Compact to the public. In return for accepting the immediate implementation of layoffs of redundant labour, unions and workers gained the legalization of basic labour rights. This point has been regarded as the main content of the Social Compact. Among the 90 agreed-upon issues, the most important items included:

- to allow immediate implementation of layoffs of redundant labour force (However, all other measures should be sought to solve business problems before finally resorting to layoffs; layoffs should be carried out only in the case of business crisis; fair criteria should be applied to select the workers to be laid off; advance notice should be given to affected employees);
- to improve income security programs for the unemployed;
- to provide government employees with the right to organize;
- to guarantee teachers the right to organize trade unions from July 1999;
- to guarantee political activities of trade unions by revising the Elections Act and the Political Funds Act during the first half of 1998;
- to recognize unemployed workers' right to join trade unions organized on the trans-enterprise level from 1999.

Although the FKTU ratified the Social Compact in the Executive Committee meeting, the rank and file members of the KCTU challenged it. During the negotiations, KCTU members demanded some kind of job/wage bargaining (e.g., saving jobs in exchange for lowering wages or reducing working hours), but the agreement, which focused on the implementation of the legal layoff system and improvement of basic labour rights, disappointed them. Consequently, 'the Great Compromise' of the Tripartite Commission in February 1998 was rejected by a big margin (88:184) at the ratification vote by delegates from KCTU-affiliated enterprise unions. The leaders of the KCTU, including the Chairman, resigned immediately afterwards. Although the legality of the agreement was questioned by some observers due to the failure of the KCTU's ratification process, the government ignored the opposition of the KCTU members and the layoff system was swiftly enacted.

Despite the KCTU's failure in the ratification vote, the public welcomed the agreement, because the 'Great Compromise' was the first genuine agreement in Korea to have been made autonomously by labour, management and the state. Indeed, the positive impacts of the Tripartite Commission cannot be overemphasized. There is no doubt that the Social Compact greatly improved the credibility of the Korean economy, highlighted the government's crisis management capacity, and helped the country overcome the credit crunch.[4]

Table 6.5   The chronicles of the Tripartite Commission

Dates	Activities
Jan. 15, 1998	The First Tripartite Commission was launched with Mr. Han Kwang-ok as Chairperson and held its first session
Jan. 20, 1998	The Tripartite Commission adopted 'Tripartite Joint Statement on Fair Burden Sharing in the Process of Overcoming Economic Crisis' at its 4th session
Feb. 6, 1998	The Tripartite Commission held the 6th session and adopted Social Compact to Overcome the Economic Crisis (Agreed upon 90 items including consolidation of employment adjustment-related laws, recognition of eligibility of the unemployed for the membership of non-enterprise-based trade unions and legalization of teachers' trade unions)
Mar. 28, 1998	Regulations on the Tripartite Commission were proclaimed (Presidential Decree No. 15746)
June 3, 1998	The Second Tripartite Commission was launched with Mr. Kim One-ki as Chairperson and held its first session
Feb. 24, 1999	The KCTU withdrew from the Tripartite Commission
May 24, 1999	The Act on Establishment, Operation of the Tripartite Commission (Legislation No. 5,990) was enacted and proclaimed
Sep. 1, 1999	The Third Tripartite Commission was launched with Mr. Kim Ho-jin as Chairperson and held its first plenary session
Aug. 8, 2000	The Fourth Tripartite Commission was launched with Mr. Chang Young-chul as Chairperson
Aug. 9, 2002	The Fifth Tripartite Commission was launched with Mr. Shin Hong as Chairperson

The Subsequent Malfunctioning of the Tripartite Commission

Nevertheless, repeated withdrawals from the Tripartite Commission by both labour and business representatives after the Social Compact in February 1998 made its future uncertain. The newly elected KCTU leadership refused to join. Consequently, the Second Tripartite Commission was formed without the participation of the KCTU on June 3, 1998. In an attempt to persuade the KCTU to join in, the government made an exclusive agreement with it that the Commission would discuss the following agenda items: restriction of layoff and worker dispatch systems, reduction of working hours and strict prohibition of employers' unfair labour practices. After the agreement, the KCTU joined the Second Tripartite Commission.

In July 1998, however, the government, without any consultation with the Tripartite Commission, announced restructuring plans for the banking and public sectors, which were likely to involve large-scale layoffs. This announcement was considered a violation of the spirit of the Tripartite Commission. Thus, the FKTU and the KCTU decided not to join in, and the KCTU called a general strike. The government had to make another agreement with the FKTU and the KCTU on July 25, 1998 promising public hearings on the financial crisis, prohibition of employers' unfair labour practices and prior consultation with labour in the case of public sector restructuring. The two labour centres then agreed to rejoin the Commission on July 27, 1998. At this time, the KEF defied the state-labour agreement, and withdrew from the Commission. However, the government succeeded in persuading the KEF to reverse this decision.

In August 1998, the government again announced the unilateral restructuring of the banking industry and the restructuring and privatization of public enterprises. This announcement was a direct violation of the agreement of July 27, 1998. As a result, labour leaders grew increasingly suspicious of the authority and credibility of the Tripartite Commission, and publicly described it as a 'rubber stamp' of the government's liberal economic and employment policy. The KCTU eventually withdrew from the Commission on February 24, 1999, with a general strike, and has not returned since.

The Commission has not functioned effectively since February 1999 because both the FKTU and the KEF have repeatedly withdrawn from and rejoined it. As a result, the Tripartite Commission has failed to produce any significant agreements. For example, it was not able to reach agreements on the following issues: the right to organize government employees and the reduction of legal working hours from 48 to 44 hours per week. Thus, in September 2002, the Ministry of Labour attempted to enact laws in these issues without a consensus from the Tripartite Commission.

Chapter Summary

Overall, the financial crisis in the late 1990s strongly influenced labour market outcomes, ER and employment practices in Korea. Some of the impacts, however, were found to be temporary, and showed a V-shaped form: that is, a deep and sharp recession was followed by an equally steep recovery in some dimensions. As the Korean economy recovered, real wages showed an 11.1 per cent increase in 1999. The unemployment rate also decreased from 8.6 per cent in February 1999 to 3.4 per cent in October 2000. Right after the financial crisis, the bargaining power of unions was weakened significantly, and concession bargaining was the norm. After the 1997-1998 financial crisis, however, the bargaining power of unions bounced back and 'give-back' bargaining became widespread, which led to wage increases of over 10 per cent in 1999. Also, the ratio of employee compensation to GDP, which indicates the overall bargaining power of labour in a given society, decreased from 64.2 per cent in 1996 to 59.0 per cent in 1998, but reached 59.8 per cent in 1999 implying that labour had recovered some power in Korean society (Bank of Korea, 2000).

Other effects seem to be more fundamental and may have a lasting impact on ER. Although the unemployment rate returned to normal levels in 2000, the financial crisis fundamentally changed the nature of unemployment. That is, the proportion of long-term unemployed (longer than one-year) to the total number of unemployed rose from 4.2 per cent in 1996 to 15.5 per cent in 1999. The ratio of unemployed in their 40s and 50s to the total increased from 13 per cent in September 1997 to 20 per cent in June 2000 (National Statistical Office, Various Issues). The ratio of discouraged unemployment to total unemployment is estimated to be about 20 per cent. All these statistics show that the unemployment post-1977 has become a more chronic, entrenched social problem than previously (Kim and Kim, forthcoming).

The new trends in employment practices, focusing on increasing flexibility and short-term efficiency, now seem to be the dominant method of managing human resources. The increase of the contingent labour force could weaken the solidarity of labour and worsen the income distribution in Korean society. Indeed, income inequalities have already started to widen. The problems of long-term unemployment, middle-age unemployment and discouraged unemployment were exacerbated by the financial crisis. Thus, for the first time since the 1960s, unemployment became a chronic problem in Korean society (Kim and Kim, forthcoming).

The financial crisis led ER actors to form an unprecedented institutional arena, the Tripartite Commission. The early success and subsequent malfunctioning of the Tripartite Commission have some interesting implications. Previous theoretical models listing conditions for successful corporatism have mainly emphasized environmental and structural elements. These elements are a small and open economy (Katzenstein, 1985); high union density and centralized peak organizations of union and employers (Lash, 1985; Streeck, 1985); oligarchic leadership of union federations (Schmitter, 1974; Streeck, 1988) or internal union democracy (Baccaro, 2000) and the existence of a social democratic or labour party (Lash, 1985).

The Korean case, however, lacks most of these structural and environmental conditions, since ER in Korea can be characterized by divided labour movement, low union density, weak employers' federation and a nonexistent social democratic or labour party. Instead of the above environmental and structural factors, the crisis consciousness shared by ER actors and their resulting strategic choices seems to have played a vital role in initiating democratic corporatism and leading to the early success of the Commission. In this sense, the Korean case indicates the need to re-examine the validity of previous literature stressing structural and environmental conditions for the success of democratic corporatism.

However, the lack of a social partnership ideology and mutual trust, together with differences in expectations, were the factors most detrimental to the effective functioning of the Tripartite Commission in the long run. There has been a clear difference of expectations between labour and the state regarding the true nature of the Tripartite Commission. Whereas labour believed that the Commission represented the philosophy of democratic corporatism, the state did not share that belief but implicitly considered it a weaker and extended version of its traditional authoritarian corporatism. When labour, especially the KCTU, realized this and withdrew from the Commission, it became more or less paralysed. Taken as a whole, the case of the Tripartite Commission provides a research setting through which to examine how various factors (e.g., structural and environmental factors, crisis consciousness, strategic choices, social partnership ideology, mutual trust and differences in expectations) influence the performance of democratic corporatism at various stages.

Overall, it is noteworthy that ER actors were able to transform Korean ER from authoritarian corporatism to democratic corporatism in the wake of such a financial crisis. However, the continuing effectiveness of the Commission is questionable at time of writing. Its early success and subsequent malfunctioning reflects the current nature of ER in Korea. Vestiges of authoritarian corporatism, an overly aggressive labour movement and deeply entrenched hostility from employers all seem to be obstacles to the transformation of the current Korean model to a more consensual model of ER.

One clear lesson from the financial crisis in terms of industrial policy is that the Korean economy urgently needs to identify core competencies and niche markets that neighbouring competitors cannot easily imitate. Without question, price competitiveness is no longer an advantage for Korean industry. After China joined the WTO in 2001, this issue became even more acute. For example, in the electronics industry, labour costs in China are approximately one-eighth of those in Korea but Chinese production workers show a roughly similar level of labour productivity to their Korean counterparts.

Efforts to upgrade the Korean economy has intensified since the financial crisis, and the government and industry leaders have made enormous investments in information technology (IT), biotechnology (BT) and nanotechnology (NT) industries. For example, the government planned to induce approximately US$ 9.9 billion of investment in the IT industry in 2002 (the Dong-a Ilbo, January 21, 2002), which was equivalent to about one-ninth of the total government expenditure the same year. Similar plans to bring about approximately US$ 10 billion investment in the BT industry during the 2002-2007 period were also announced. The government also planned to spend 17 per cent of its total R&D budget in the BT area by 2007 (the Dong-a Ilbo, December 13, 2001). The financial crisis seems to have caused the Korean economy to move its focus from traditional manufacturing industries to technology- and knowledge-intensive IT and BT industries.

Notes

1   The concept of contingent workers as defined by the National Statistical Office is believed to be rather wide, because it includes all employees with employment contracts of less than one year and employees who have stayed on the job longer than one year but are ineligible for some benefits (such as lump-sum severance pay). If one uses an alternative estimation using a narrower definition, which includes only employees with less than one year's service, contract and non-standard employees such as part timers, leased employees and employees from temporary help agencies, the proportion of contingent workers to employed population was approximately 29.3 per cent in 2000 (Jung, 2000).

2   The first author of this book conducted semi-structured interviews in June and July 2000 with representatives of the Korean Employers Federation, the Federation of Korean Trade Unions, the Korean Confederation of Trade Unions, the Daily Labour News and the Korea Labour & Society Institute. The comments of these interviewees have been selectively cited. Interviewees from the Daily Labour News and the Korea Labour and Society Institute explicitly mentioned that since the financial crisis and the resultant employment reductions the number of union members attending union meetings (especially among white-collar workers) had been noticeably lower. The interviewees interpreted this trend as an indication of union members' disappointment at the powerlessness of their unions during the downsizing drives. In the same context, an interviewee from the FKTU mentioned that since the financial crisis, rank-and-file union members' interest in the company's financial situation had been greatly increased, which reflected their concern for employment security. In particular, union members' interests in employee stock ownership programs (ESOP) had increased, because they believed that they might change major management decisions such as restructuring and employment reduction through their influence as stockholders (Kim and Kim, forthcoming).

3   Another reason for the increased unionization ratio in 1999 was the legalization of teachers' unionism in Korea. Approximately 17,000 teachers joined teachers' unions for the first time in 1999.

4   An interview participant from the Tripartite Commission and the Korea Employers Federation (KEF) mentioned that the Social Compact might have been one of the most symbolic incidents that helped the country overcome the 1997-1998 financial crisis.

References

Baccaro, L. (2000), 'Centralized Collective Bargaining and the Problem of 'Compliance': Lessons from the Italian Experience', *Industrial and Labor Relations Review*, vol.53, no.4, pp.579-601.

Bank of Korea (2000), http://www.bok.or.kr/bokis/bokis/m_statis_disp_main

Dong-a Ilbo (2001), *Organizational DNAs Are Changing*, January 14. (In Korean.)

Dong-a Ilbo (2001), *US$10 Billions Will Be Invested in BT Area by 2007*, December 13. (In Korean.)

Dong-a Ilbo (2002), *IT Will Induce US$10 Billion Investment*, January 21. (In Korean.)

Dong-a Ilbo (2002), *32% of Companies Operating the Merit-pay System*, March 5. (In Korean.)

Freeman, R.B. and Rebick, M.E. (1989), 'Crumbling Pillar? Declining Union Density in Japan', *Journal of the Japanese and International Economics*, vol.3, pp.578-605.

Jung, E.H. (1999), *Economic Crisis and Industrial Relations in Korea*, Korea Labour and Society Institute and Friedrich Ebert Stiftung, Seoul. (In Korean.)

Jung, J.-H. (2000), 'Diversification of Employment Patterns and Recent Compensation Practices', *Quarterly Labor Review*, vol.13, no.4, pp.54-69. (In Korean.)

Katzenstein, P. J. (1985), *Small States in World Market*, Cornell University Press, New York.

Kim, D.-O., Bae, J. and Lee C. (2000), 'Globalization and Labour Rights: The Case of Korea', *Asia Pacific Business Review*, vol.6, no.3/4, pp.133-153.

Kim, D.-O. and Kim, S. (forthcoming), 'Globalization, Financial Crisis, and Industrial Relations: The Case of Korea', *Industrial Relations*, vol.41, no.3.

Kim, D.-O. and Park, S. (1997), 'Changing Patterns of Pay Systems in Japan and Korea: From Seniority to Performance', *International Journal of Employment Studies*, vol.5, no.2, pp.117-134.

Kim, D.-O. and Yu, G.-C. (2000), 'Emerging Patterns of Human Resource Management in Korea: Evidence from Large Korean Firms', in *Proceedings of the 12th World Congress of the International Industrial Relations Association*, May 29 – June 2, International Industrial Relations Association, Tokyo, vol.5, pp.195-206.

Korea Labour Institute (2000), *Overseas Labour Statistics*, Seoul. (In Korean.)

Korea Labour Institute (2001), *KLI Labour Statistics*, Seoul. (In Korean.)

Korea Ministry of Labour (2000), *'99 White Paper on Labour*, Korea Ministry of Labour, Seoul. (In Korean.)

Lash, S. (1985), 'The End of Neo-corporatism?: The Breakdown of Centralized Bargaining in Sweden', *British Journal of Industrial Relations*, vol.23, no.2, pp.215-239.

Lee, E. (1998), *The Asian Financial Crisis: The Challenge for Social Policy*, International Labour Organization, Geneva.

National Statistical Office (1998), *Monthly Report on the Economically Active Population Survey*, National Statistical Office, Seoul, February-December. (In Korean.)

National Statistical Office (Various Years), *Yearbook of Economically Active Population Survey*, National Statistical Office, Seoul. (In Korean.)

Park, Y.-B. (1998), 'The Financial Crisis in Korea: The Industrial Relations Connection', *Perspectives on Work: The Magazine of the IRRA*, vol.2, no.2, pp.37-41.

Schmitter, P. (1974), 'Still The Century of Corporatism?', *Review of Politics*, vol.36, pp.85-131.

Streeck, W. (1985), 'Neo-corporatist industrial relations and the economic crisis in West Germany', in J. Goldthorpe (ed), *Order and Conflict in Contemporary Capitalism*, Clarendon Press, Oxford, pp.291-314.

Streeck, W. (1988), 'Editorial Introduction to Special Issue on Organizational Democracy of Trade Unions', *Economic and Industrial Democracy*, vol.9, no.3, pp.307-318.

PART III
KOREAN HRM SYSTEMS:
PAST AND PRESENT

7 The Origins and Evolution of HRM, 1910-1987: A Historical Sketch

Introduction

This chapter outlines a historical sketch of the Korean human resource management (HRM) system from the Japanese colonial period up to 1987. In order to delineate this historical trajectory, we have divided it into three different periods: (1) the Japanese colonial period (1910-1945); (2) the transitional and rebuilding period after national independence (1945-1961); and (3) industrialization (1962-1987).

HRM during Japanese Colonial Period: 1910 to 1945

While enterprises in Korea had started out in business in the late nineteenth and the early twentieth centuries, during the Japanese colonial period their activities were restricted. In this section, the general economic context and the establishment of early companies are explained, then the characteristics of HRM during the colonial period introduced.

The General Economic Situation and the Establishment of Early Companies

The colonial period was characterized by the distinction between Korean and Japanese capital and firms. During the period 1911-1919, companies owned by Koreans increased by 36 (27 to 63), whilst firms owned by Japanese increased by 180 (109 to 289). Similarly, the level of paid-in capital to companies owned by Japanese increased at a great rate (see Table 7.1).

Before we explain HRM during the Japanese colonial period, we will provide some brief company information as background. Some examples of the predecessors of current Korean chaebols include Doosan, LG and Samsung. The Doosan Group began when Park Seung-jik started a tiny store in Baeogae, Seoul in 1896. In 1905, he established Kwangjang & Co., the first stock company, to manage the Dongdaemun (the East Gate) market. Koo

In-hwoi started the Guin store in 1931, converting it to a stock company in 1940. This was the beginning of the LG group. Lee Byung-Chull, the late founding Chairman of Samsung, started a business with that name in Taegu in 1938, then, 10 years later, Samsung Moolsan was established.

Table 7.1   Number of firms and paid-in capital by nation during 1910s (unit: 1,000 won)

Year	Owned by Korean		Owned by Japanese	
	No of Firms	Paid-in Capital	No of Firms	Paid-in Capital
1911	27	2,742	109	5,063
1913	39	4,906	132	7,046
1915	39	5,066	144	8,807
1917	37	5,871	177	38,019
1919	63	11,404	289	83,376

Source: Adapted from Hwang, 1999, p.111.

There were other prominent companies (e.g., Kyungbang, YuHan and Hwasin as well as the predecessors of the current chaebols. These corporations were not only major companies for those times but were also large enough to have personnel practices. Kyungsung Spinning (or Kyungbang) Co., Ltd. was established in 1919 by Kim Songsu, a Korean nationalist entrepreneur. This company became the first modern textile factory and the first national company to have genuine national capital. It grew rapidly in the 1930s and became one of the major Korean companies of the time. Although Kyungsung Spinning started its business with 250,000 won of paid-in capital in 1919, the capital dramatically increased to 2,000,000 won in 1935, to 5,000,000 won in 1940 and to 10,500,000 in 1944. Over the same period, the number of spinning and weaving machines in the factory increased from 100 in 1922 through 672 in 1933 to 1,086 in 1943 (Kyungsung Spinning, 1969). In 1939, Kyungsung Spinning established a factory in Manchuria, China. As of 2002, Kyungbang has eight affiliated firms with about 1,500 employees.

Dr. New Ilhan founded YuHan Corporation in 1926 for the importation, exportation and sales of pharmaceutical products. It then became incorporated and grew by building branch offices in Southeast Asia throughout 1936. With Korean independence in 1945, YuHan lost its branch offices in North Korea and Manchuria. YuHan has always been well known for its philosophy, 'profits of a company should be returned to society'. It has also emphasized integrity, as exemplified by the passage 'the life of a company depends upon its integrity' suggested by Dr. New. Another example is Hwasin Corporation. Park Hungsik established the Sunil Paper Corp. in 1926, then bought up Hwasin Store to found the Hwasin Trading Co. in 1931 (renamed to Hwasin Corporation in 1934). In the 1930s, other affiliated firms were established, especially in commerce and trading. The Hwasin chain stores improved the distribution structure through the establishment of nationwide multiple shops (Hwasin Corporation, 1977).

HRM Practices during the Colonial Period[1]

The major tasks of personnel units during this period were to ensure discipline and control: personnel affairs were used as a mechanism for rule-observance (Lee, 1998).

During this period, personnel-related units started to be established in major companies. Personnel affairs were generally dealt with by a General Affairs Subsection (gye) (e.g., Commercial Bank in 1917 and Dong Wha Pharmaceutical in 1939) or a Personnel Subsection (Hwasin in 1937 and YuHan in 1947) under the control of the General Affairs Section (gwa). Later these subsections were upgraded to Personnel Sections (see Table 7.2). In the case of Kyungbang, a Labour Subsection was established in 1944, then upgraded to HR Section in 1949. Compared to the manufacturing or sales unit, and accounting systems, personnel-related units were adopted relatively late on. The Chosun Shipping and Transportation Co. had a General Administration Subsection under a General Administration Section. About one third of its 17 tasks were related to personnel, including (1) workforce management (i.e., number of employees and recruitment), (2) employee retirement and transfer, (3) duty and reward/punishment, (4) compensation and (5) mutual aid and ceremonial occasions (Chosun Shipping and Transportation, 1940). In 1937, the company established Personnel and Welfare Subsections under the control of the General Administration Section.

During the earlier stages of the firm, Kyungbang had not needed a job-ranking system. However, it adopted a job-ranking system in the late 1930s as the size of the workforce increased. All jobs were divided into two different job classes, and each job class had three job grades. For example, when high school graduates were employed, they were entitled to a post on the third job grade of the lower job class. In 1944, the system was changed to include a single job class with eight job grades. YuHan also adopted the job-ranking system in the 1930s. Job levels comprised president, executive director, department manager, section chief, subsection chief and staff member. Hwasin had an interesting approach to job assignment. When new employees joined, they were assigned to work in the shops even though they were college graduates. This was intended to enhance their field knowledge and awareness of the company's activities and services.

The predominant approach to recruitment in those times was hiring through personal connections and referrals. At Kyungbang, the number of workers rapidly increased to about 3,500 in the 1940s. As the company needed more workers, it employed recruiters from various provinces, who visited their hometowns to recruit women. In addition, it recruited at any time on demand. When workers were employed, they were contracted for three years, and all of them lived in a factory boarding-house. These practices continued until the late 1950s.

YuHan had similar recruitment practices. During its early stages, the company relied on personal referrals. When it needed more workers, from 1936 on, YuHan also employed recruiters. Job applicants were screened through the examining of papers and interview. Since YuHan was more westernized and traded with foreign countries, it gave preferential treatment to those who had graduated from a college-level institution and spoke good English. Graduates from Posung College (the predecessor of Korea University) and Yonhi College (of Yonsei University) were targeted by YuHan as promising employees. Hwasin tried to eliminate favouritism based on school, blood and region by setting up procedures to recruit based on individual personality and competence. However, it gave preferential treatment to descendants of deceased patriots or patriotic young adults. Employee education and training programs were also developed in Kyungbang. Interestingly, most education programs were implemented in the factory boarding-house, where more than 90 per cent of the workers lived. The curriculum included character building, technology and science. In the case of YuHan, English proficiency was a critical factor for successful performance on the job. At that time, YuHan imported pharmaceuticals from the USA and sold them in Korea, so their business documents were written in English. YuHan therefore offered their staff classes in language skills and pharmaceutical knowledge twice a month. Hwasin also provided basic educational programs intended to raise employees' cultural level and health of body and mind.

Looking at compensation, the average starting monthly pay during Kyungbang's pioneer days was about 20 won. When newly employed, workers served an apprenticeship for six months on lower pay followed by normal employment with higher pay. Since the pay system during the colonial period was controlled by the Japanese government-general, pay increases were not allowed. Pay was therefore composed of basic pay and various special allowances, presumably to find a way to increase the total level of compensation without increasing the basic wage.

At YuHan, while female workers were on a daily wage, a monthly salary system was firstly adopted for regular male workers from about 1937 on. A bonus system was also employed. From the same period, YuHan paid bonuses once a year amounting to 200-600 per cent of monthly salary. A special bonus system was applied to sales people. Like Kyungbang, YuHan also had various allowances. Surprisingly, YuHan granted 1,070 (7.13 per cent) out of 15,000 shares to its employees in 1937. Hwasin guaranteed its employees' living with a higher pay level.

With regard to welfare, the factory boarding-house had annexed facilities for education, health care and recreation and sports. In addition, there was a mess hall, public bathhouse, washhouse and store. The health care facilities consisted of a medical room with professionals and assistants available for consultation. YuHan also had annexed facilities including a boarding-house, assembly hall and swimming pool, and had medical facilities.

In sum, although major companies had adopted personnel administration practices during this period, they were not yet systematically institutionalized. The level of HRM was primitive and each individual function (e.g., recruitment, training, compensation and work system) had not been fully developed. Therefore, the HRM system of this period can be described as primitive personnel management.

HRM during the Transitional and Rebuilding Period: 1945 to 1961

During this period, Korea was in turmoil and suffered some violent and turbulent times. The Korean people had to survive a range of difficult situations from national independence and the tragic division of the peninsula (1945), the Korean War (1950-1953), the student revolt (1960) and the military coup (1961). The resultant social upheaval generated threats but also provided opportunities for some. Personnel administration during this period was strongly related to observing the ordinances enacted by the US military government (Lee, 1998). In this section, a discussion of general situations is followed by explanations of specific HRM practices.

General Issues

After independence in 1945, the American military administration defined companies owned by Japanese as enemy property, and confiscated 6,881 firms. From mid-1950s, the term *chaebol* started to be well known in society (Lee, 1999). In 1955, the rank order of the top five enterprises on the basis of assets was: Samyang Co., Korea Coal Corp., Korea Development Bank, Lucky Chemical Industrial Co. (the predecessor of today's LG Chemical) and Kumsung Textile Co. (of Ssangyong Corp.).

In 1960, the top 10 Korean chaebols were Samsung, Samho, Gaepung, Dae Han, Lucky, Tongyang, Kukdong, Hankuk Glass, Donglip Industrial and

Taechang Textile. This order has changed since then (see Table 3.5). How did these chaebols form so rapidly? Some of the reasons include (Lee, 1999): (a) the assignment of import quota and import permits, insulating firms from competition; (b) purchase of enemy property at cheap prices; (c) selective allocation of aid and goods; (d) privileged bank loans with low interest; and (e) preferential treatment in contracts with the Korean government and the US military for reconstruction after the war. Political connections were critical in ensuring individuals' rapid capital formation.

In the case of Samsung, several affiliated firms were established during the early 1950s: Samsung Corporation (a trading company) in 1951, Cheil Sugar Manufacturing Co. (now an independent company no longer affiliated with Samsung) in 1953 and Cheil Industries Inc. in 1954. By 1960, it had 19 affiliates. In the case of LG, the founder and chairman Koo In-hwoi established the Lucky Chemical Industrial Co. (now LG Chemical) in 1947, heralding the beginning of the modern LG. By 1960, Lucky had four affiliated firms. Samho and Gaepung also had seven affiliated firms each, and Dae Han six, by 1960.

Meanwhile, President Rhee Syngman's administration had begun laying some of the critical foundations for future economic development by formulating a land reform policy for the more equitable distribution of income, investing in education for human resource development and implementing the development of import-substitution industries for domestic consumption (Chung et al., 1997; Mason et al., 1980). The general level of education, in particular, increased considerably during this period. This laid the groundwork for the utilization of a skilled workforce during the industrialization process.

HRM Practices after Independence

The establishment of a Korean government in 1948 and the Korean War helped to enhance the importance of personnel affairs (Lee, 1998). Firstly, Korean firms had the chance to learn from the advanced personnel administration practices of the US during the economic aid and reconstruction process. In addition, the US military's approach to logistics, personnel and administration were transferred to private organizations. However, HRM practices did not develop significantly during this period. The enactment of various labour laws in 1953 provided a basis for the formation of personnel administrations.

Table 7.2   The establishment of HRM-related units in major companies

Company (Year)	HRM-Related Unit	Year
Dong Wha Pharm. (1897)	• General Affairs Subsection	1939
Commercial Bank of Korea (1899)	• General Affairs Subsection	1917
	• HR Section	1942
Kyungsung Spinning Co., Ltd. (1919)	• Labour Subsection, Labour Section	1944
	• Labour/Welfare Section, General Affairs Dept.	1946
	• Upgraded to HR Section, General Affairs Dept.	1949
YuHan Corp. (1926)	• HR Subsection, General Affairs Section	1941
	• Upgraded to HR Section, General Affairs Dept.	1967
Hwasin Corp. (1926)	• HR Subsection, General Affairs Section	1937
Dong-A Pharmaceutical Co., Ltd. (1932)	• HR Section	1968
	• Upgraded to HR Section, HR Dept.	1978
	• Labour Section	1978
Cheil Sugar Mfg Co. (1953)	• HR Section, General Affairs Dept.	1978
	• Upgraded to HR Dept.	1982
Dong-il Textile (1955)	• HR Section	1969
Tong Yang Cement Corp. (1957)	• HR Subsection, General Affairs Section	1967
Kolon (1958)	• HR Section (1969)	1969
Goldstar Co., Ltd. (LG Electronics) (1958)	• HR Section, General Affairs Dept.	1969
	• HRD Section, General Affairs Dept.	1972
	• Upgraded to HRM Dept.	1974
	• HRM Division	1978
Hansung (Seoul) Electric Co. (KEPCO) (1898)	• HR Section, Secretary's Office	1952
	• HR Section, General Affairs Dept.	1961
	• Upgraded to HR Dept.	1966
	• Education and Training Dept.	1977
Hanil Cement Corp. (1961)	• HR Subsection, General Affairs Section	1964
	• Upgraded to HR Section, General Affairs Dept.	1978
Korea Oil Corp. (SK Corp.) (1962)	• Labour Dept.	1965
	• Renamed to HR Dept.	1971
Honam Oil Refinery Co. (LG-Caltex Oil Corp.) (1967)	• HR Section, General Affairs Dept.	1968
	• Welfare Dept.	1974
	• Upgraded to HR Dept.	1977
Pohang Iron and Steel Co., Ltd. (POSCO) (1968)	• HR & HRD Sections, General Affairs Dept.	1969
	• HR, Labour, Recruitment, & Safety Sections, HR Dept.	1973
	• Divided into HR Dept. (for education, training and administration) and HR Office (for HR practices, labour and manpower)	1974

Source: Adapted from Ahn (1989) and Ahn et al. (2002).

The formalization of HRM and the adoption of various personnel functions were actively implemented only after the economic development plan of 1962 had been launched. Therefore, the features of personnel units were not so different from those of the preceding colonial period: personnel-related units were established, changed, or upgraded in major corporations (see Table 7.2). Kyungsung Spinning Co. established a Labour Subsection in 1944, then changed it to a Labour & Welfare Section under the control of a General Affairs Dept. in 1946, before upgrading it to an HR Section in 1949. Hansung (Seoul) Electric Company (the predecessor of the current Korea Electric Power Corporation, KEPCO) formed the HR Section under the Secretary's Office in 1952.

During this period, one major change was the adoption of a public recruitment process, inviting applicants from the general public rather than by personal referrals. YuHan became one of the first corporations to adopt the system in the late fifties. Samsung and Kia also did so in 1957. From the 1960s, Kyungbang took the approach of inviting applications from the public. In small companies, however, people were still usually employed based on their connections.

Lee Byung-Chull of Samsung placed a high priority on human assets, and interviewed and selected job applicants personally. The key success factors of Samsung Moolsan were (1) the involvement of employees in investment and profit sharing, (2) the opportunities for qualification enhancement, (3) ability-based personnel management and the principle of 'rewarding for good work and punishing for bad work' and (4) the provision of economic security (Hwang, 1999, p.352). A 'human-assets first' policy was stressed in theory and practice. Samsung recruited 27 new employees through the public recruitment system in 1957, five of whom became presidents of affiliated companies. When recruited, employees were assigned to certain jobs and departments according to competence and aptitude.

Most companies' pay systems during this period were based on seniority. Chungju Chemical Fertilizer applied a salary-ladder system based on seniority from 1958. In addition, gender and level of education were also critical factors affecting pay. The wages for female workers at Kyungbang were 80 per cent that of males in 1950 (Kyungsung Spinning, 1969). The traditional Four Classes structure of society (i.e., sa-nong-gong-sang, representing aristocrats, farmers, artisans and tradesmen) emphasized the importance of education. *Sa* means a classical scholar or a learned man: this was the most respected class, made up of those who ruled society. As a result, scholarship (i.e., gaining a high level of education) was a critical factor in personnel affairs including pay. Various allowances were also paid to workers in many companies such as, for example, those granted to employees with some distinction of status or job rank in Kyungbang. Furthermore, companies also provided bonuses once or twice a year. Hwasin paid bonuses at Lunar New Year and on the Harvest Moon Day. Kyungbang gave a special bonus in December of 1945 in commemoration of national independence. To pay this it sold its total stock and gave 20 per cent of the total profits to its employees. YuHan had a similar practice, paying 200-600 per cent of employee's monthly salary as a bonus.

Other types of personnel practices also began to emerge during this period. The mandatory retirement (i.e., age-limit) system started to be established from the 1950s and became firmly institutionalized in the 1970s. Before the practice of paying a retirement allowance (i.e., pension) was generalized through the revision of the Labour Standard Law in 1961, some companies had already begun doing so. The practice was first adopted by state-owned enterprises and later spread to private companies (Ahn, 1989). A range of welfare facilities (e.g., boarding-houses, medical facilities and mess halls) was also established. Mutual-aid associations, scholarship funds and special educational programs (e.g., night classes for those who could not attend regular schools) were other examples of the welfare systems provided by several major firms.

In summary, HRM during the rebuilding period barely improved on previous practice. Various labour laws enacted in 1953 provided some guidance for personnel administration and at the same time posed some restrictions on its management. In addition, the personnel administration of the US military spread first to public then private companies. However, primitive personnel management dominated, although a certain level of personnel management was achieved in some major companies in the sense that they strengthened the institutionalization of some of their HRM functions.

HRM during Industrialization: 1962 to 1987

During the period of industrialization, HRM systems in major companies became firmly institutionalized. This was the time when the traditional Korean HRM system became formulated, characterized by seniority-based job grading and pay, lifetime employment, the use of internal labour markets and the recruitment of new graduates. This traditional version of HRM systems remained dominant until the mid-1980s.

HRM-Related Organizations

The establishment of independent HRM functions and organizations is an important indicator of the development of HRM/IR within companies. As shown in Table 7.2, most companies set up their HRM-related units during the 1960s with the exceptions of some of the older firms (e.g., Kyungbang and Yuhan). Most companies started by forming an HR Subsection (*gye*) under the control of the General Affairs Section (*gwa*). This Subsection was subsequently upgraded to a full HR Section. The most critical change in this period was the further progress of the HR-related unit, gaining full independence from the general affairs unit to become an HR Department (*bu*).[2] Accordingly, the rank of the person in charge of HRM rose from *gyejang* (subsection chief) through *gwajang* (section chief) to *bujang* (department head or general manager). In the 1990s, most large companies placed an executive member in charge of the HRM department.

The Formalization of HRM

The rules and regulations of HRM and industrial relations were formulated in large firms from the early 1960s onward. Some were compulsory and others optional. In Goldstar Co. (now LG Electronics), many rules and regulations were laid down, including; Disciplinary Standards, Promotion Standards and Performance Appraisals Operation Standards (in 1966); and Regulations for Daily Employment, Performance Evaluation Rules, Personnel Administration Regulations, Office Regulations and Employment Regulations (in 1969). In the Samyangfoods Co., Ltd., established in 1961, a similar list of rules and regulations came in during 1960s and 1970s, including: Employment Regulations and Collective Agreements (in 1965); Pay Regulations and Personnel Committee Regulations (in 1968); Personnel Administration Regulations (in 1970); Safety Supervision Rules and Job Evaluation & Performance Appraisal Regulations (in 1972); Promotion Regulations (in 1975); and Efficiency Rating Regulations (in 1980).

Other companies that formulated Personnel Administration Regulations and other related documents during this period include (Ahn, 1989): Hanil Cement (1962), Hankuk Glass (1958), Chungju Chemical Fertilizer (1958) and Dong-A Pharmaceutical Co., Ltd. (1969). In summary, the formalization of HRM/IR in Korean firms, which had begun during the late 1950s, continued through to the mid-1960s and progressed even further to encompass more specific functions in the 1970s.

Work Systems

The key features of work systems in Korean HRM were job grade systems, broadly defined jobs and dual systems. The situation in Korea was similar to that of Japan (Morishima, 1995).

The job grade system, which is person- rather than task-oriented, can be broadly defined as an employee hierarchy based on education, gender, tenure, ability, responsibility level of tasks and so on (Ahn, 1996). It formed the fundamental basis of the whole HRM system and was used to decide on promotion and salary increases. Every new employee was assigned to a certain starting job grade according to level of education, gender and work experience, from which each individual climbed the rungs of the company ladder to the higher grades (see Table 7.3). For example, as shown in Table 7.3, female high school graduates were assigned to the lower fifth job grade, and their male counterparts to the upper fifth job grade, while college graduates entered at the fourth job grade. These initial assignments represented the starting positions from which individual could then progress to higher levels of the hierarchy.

There are at least three types of job grade systems (Yang and Ahn, 1992): task-based (typical American type), competence-based (Japanese type) and person or post-based (traditional Korean type). In the first, the grade is literally based on the characteristics of the job itself (e.g., level of difficulty of the tasks involved) which is determined by job analysis and evaluation. Job grades are therefore determined by job values. The second type is based on employees' skill and knowledge development, and is found in Japanese firms (Morishima, 1995). In this case, the job grade goes together with the incumbent's competencies. The final type is the post grade system, which is typical of Korean firms. In this system, employees' job grades are based on ranks in the organization. For example, when an employee is promoted to general manager, he or she would automatically move up to the first grade, and at the same time would receive an automatic increase in salary. One issue with this system was that it operated without much consideration being given to job-related abilities and qualifications.

Until the late 1980s, job grade systems were regarded as rank systems based on seniority, in which rank and job grade were related on a one-to-one basis (Bae, 1997). This tradition originated in part from the traditional Korean cultural and institutional context handed down from the Chosun Dynasty. It was also influenced by the Japanese factory system and the military system (Park and Lee, 1995).

As shown in Table 7.3, another feature of the job grade system in Korean firms was the dual hierarchy. Managerial and administrative employees on the one hand, and production employees on the other, had different job grade ladders. While the former type of jobs typically offered about eight grades of progress, the latter had only about three or four. Therefore, production employees had fewer opportunities for promotion, lower pay and worse work conditions (Park and Lee, 1995). Korean HRM systems had broadly defined jobs and flexible job assignments. Although job descriptions existed, they were rarely used for task accomplishment.

Table 7.3   Relationship of job grade to rank in a large manufacturing firm

Job Grade	Managerial and Administrative Jobs		Production Jobs	
	Matching rank/position	Min. years someone has to stay	Matching rank/ position	Min. years someone has to stay
First Grade (A)	General Manager (*Bujang*)			
First Grade (B)	Deputy General Manager (*Chajang*)	4 years		
Second Grade (A)	Section Chief (*Gwajang*) (A)	3 years	Foreman	
Second Grade (B)	Section Chief (*Gwajang*) (B)	2 years		
Third Grade	Deputy Section Chief (*Daeri*)	3 years	Group Leader	7 years
Fourth Grade	Senior Administrative[a] (*Sawon A*)	3 year	Team Leader	7 years
	Junior Administrative[b] (*Sawon B*)	2 years		
Fifth Grade (Male) Fifth Grade (Female)	Staff Member[c] (*Sawon C*)	4 years	Team Member	10 years

Notes:
a   Assigned to 4-year university graduates
b   2-year college graduates
c   High school graduates

One basic personnel management technique used in general and work systems is job analysis. State-owned enterprises first began to perform job analysis in the early 1960s, and the technique had spread to private companies by the end of the same decade (Ahn, 1989). KEPCO (Korea Electric Power Corporation) adopted a Civilian Occupation Specification to match jobs and employees' abilities, but this was not actively utilized. As organization size increased and more systematic approach needed, KEPCO began to conduct job analysis for the first time in Korea in 1963. This job classification system became the basis for recruitment, assignment, transfer, promotion and compensation. Other companies that conducted job analysis included Korea Oil Corp. (later Yukong, then now SK Corp.) (in 1967), Pohang Iron and Steel Co. (POSCO) (in 1971), Goldstar Co. (present LG Electronics) (in 1966) and the Cheil Sugar Manufacturing Co. (in 1972) (Ahn, 1989).

Human Resource Flow

Inflow: recruitment and selection As was the case in most firms during earlier periods, recruitment in small companies and firms in rural areas continued to rely on referrals and personal connections, especially for production employees during industrialization (Koch, *et al.*, 1995). However, recruitment processes in large companies became more formal. Large Korean companies periodically hired a cohort of new school graduates once or twice a year. *Chaebols* recruited all new employees for their affiliated companies at the same time.

When Korean corporate groups placed recruitment advertisements, they clearly stated their hiring specifications. Interestingly, most ads specified an age limitation (usually around 28 years), level of education and/or major and a military service requirement (see Table 7.4). the screening process had several stages. the first round was usually a written exam to test English proficiency, general knowledge and/or knowledge of the candidate's major. This was followed by an interview testing both job-related ability and personality and a health check-up. Korean firms gave more weight to human nature (e.g., personality and attitude) than job-related competence (e.g., ability and knowledge). In addition, corporate groups also clearly stated their target number of recruits. The top 4-5 groups usually recruited a similar number of new employees each year. Graduates from the leading universities often received better treatment.

Historically, new graduates rather than experienced ones, and generalists rather than specialists, were preferred until the late 1980s (Von Glinow and Chung, 1989). While this tradition is quite different from the American system, which prefers specialists with experience, it was similar to that of Japanese firms (Morishima, 1995). In addition, both Korean employers and employees used the cohort as a reference group for the evaluation of employee progress and position in the organization.

Table 7.4   Qualifications and selection process for new employees in major groups (in 1984)

Company Group	Basic Requirements for Application	Selection Process*	Target Number
Samsung Group	- Born after 1 January 1957 - Already graduated or expect to graduate in February 1985 with specialism in designated or related majors - No evasion of military service	- 1st round: Written exam (English and major) - 2nd round: Interview and health check-up	1,600
Hyundai Group	- Born after 1 January 1956 - Already graduated or expect to graduate in February 1985 with specialism in designated or related majors - Completed military duty or exempted from it; no disqualification from travel abroad	- 1st round: Written exam (English) - 2nd round: Interview and health check-up	1,600
LG Group	- Born after 1 January 1957 - Already graduated or expect to graduate in February 1985 from the four-year-course universities - Completed military duty or exempted from it	- 1st round: Written exam (English and major) - 2nd round: Interview	1,500
Daewoo Group	- Born after 1 January 1957 and completed military duty; male only - Already graduated or expect to graduate in February 1985 - Specialism in designated or related majors from the four-year-course universities	- 1st round: Examining applicants' documents - 2nd round: Interview, then health check-up	1,600
Ssang-yong Group	- Born after 1 January 1955 - Already graduated or expect to graduate in February 1985 from the four-year-course universities - Specialism in designated majors - Completed military duty or exempted from it; no disqualification from travel abroad	- 1st round: Examining applicants' documents - 2nd round: Written exam (English and major or essay) - 3rd round: Interview and aptitude test (for computer-related jobs)	400

* Only those who passed the 1st round test eligible for 2nd round exam.
Source: Adapted from Ahn (1989).

Through flow A promotion system was adopted in Korean firms from the 1960s onwards. As shown in Table 7.3, staff were expected to remain in each job grade for a minimum period. For example, *gwa-jang* had to spend at least 9 years in post to be considered for promotion to *bujang*. This practice implies that seniority was considered more critical than abilities or performance. In the early stages of their career, most employees could predict their career prospects in the organization. Two critical factors for promotion consideration were seniority and educational attainment, which continues to be the case at least in part (Park and Lee, 1995). However, for promotion to higher-level management, performance has become a more important factor than seniority (Koch, *et al.*, 1995). In family-owned *chaebols*, *hyulyon* (family connection) was also a critical factor for reaching higher-level management (Von Glinow and Chung, 1989). However, decision making for promotion was based on various criteria including screening eligibility, education level, tenure, performance evaluation, promotion exam, minimum years in post, rank position and so on. A survey conducted by the Korea Employers' Federation in 1984 revealed the length of time (in years) it took people to achieve promotion. It took on average 3.9 years for new graduates to be promoted to *daeri* (deputy section chief), 3.5 years from *daeri* to *gwa-jang* (section chief), 3.6 years from *gwa-jang* to *chajang* (deputy general manager) and 3.5 years from *chajang* to *bujang* (general manager). Cumulatively, it took on average 14.5 years for a new employee to become *bujang*.

Outflow: termination and retirement A mandatory retirement system was adopted in Korean firms during the 1960s and 1970s. However, different companies had different age limits. Typically, a lump sum retirement payment was paid, usually amounting to one month's salary for each year of service. The majority of firms set 55 as the age limit from the late 1970s through to the 1980s. About 50 per cent of companies had a single mandatory retirement system, in which the criteria were indiscriminately applied to all employees. The rest had multiple age limits based on gender, job grade and/or job group. Even managerial and administrative employees could be terminated in their forties or fifties, because very few of them could stay until retirement age. Most college graduates could normally expect to be promoted as far as general manager. However, after that position, there was less chance of further advancement. Those who did not expect to be promoted usually left for other jobs even though the firm had not terminated them.

Korean HRM systems, compared to Japanese ones, had limited arrangements in place for lifetime employment. Large Japanese firms enhance the flexibility of staffing practices through '[the] practice of transferring employees out of the parent firm to its subsidiaries and related companies' (Morishima, 1995: 136). This practice partly allowed for the adjustment of employment levels and redundancy control with regard to older employees. However, employee redeployment and transfer issues were limited in Korean firms (Koch, et al., 1995), with some exceptions in the military, banking and public sectors.

Training and Development

Training and development in Korean firms can be classified into several categories, such as training and education for newly recruited and existing employees; in-house and external training; training and education in language proficiency, job ability, character building; and basic and advanced courses.

When new recruits joined companies, the first thing they did was to attend group-level socialization camps. From the very beginning of the new employees' career with the firm, each company pursued an indoctrination process designed to inculcate its corporate culture and business philosophy. Another purpose of such camps was to develop 'all-purpose' general skills through which to enhance team spirit, 'can-do spirit', adaptability to new environments, problem-solving abilities and so forth (Bae, 1997). This new employee orientation lasted for about 3-6 months. One of its most important goals was indoctrination of employees into the company's core values, founder and management philosophy and culture (Chung, Lee and Jung, 1997). For this, companies also used sahoon (shared values explicitly articulated), a company song and a catchphrase. During this orientation process, new employees began to become 'Samsung-man', 'Hyundai-man', 'LG-man', 'Sunkyong (SK)-man' and so on. In addition, new employees also built up feelings of belonging, loyalty and commitment. Goldstar Co. offered this kind of education program for newly recruited employees, and then extended them to existing employees.

From the 1960s on, Korean firms invited foreign engineers to work with them in order to transfer technical skills and technologies. In addition, some companies such as Cheil Industries and Goldstar sent trainees to more economically advanced countries to acquire new skills (Ahn, 1989). During the same period, managerial-level training programs focused more on moulding managers to the company's core values and philosophy rather than developing their job-related abilities and knowledge (Steers, Shin and Ungson, 1989). In addition, the programs placed more emphasis on building character and developing positive attitudes than on professional competence.

A popular way to improve job-related skills and knowledge was job rotation. However, it was less systematically applied, as was the practice of multi-skills training, both of which varied between industries (Park and Lee, 1995). Production employees were usually involved in on-the-job training to enhance job-related skills. For example, Goldstar Co. increased their investment in human capital through the 1980s. Training and education expenditure was 342 million won in 1979, increasing to 814 million won in 1982, then 2,213 million won in 1984. The number of training and education hours per employee was 37 hours in 1979, thorough 44.3 hours in 1982, to 121.8 hours in 1984 (Ahn, 1989).

Performance Appraisal and Remuneration Systems

Performance appraisal In many companies, the main purpose of the performance appraisal was administrative with only a minimal developmental component (Bae, 1997). The administrative use of the process included ranking candidates for promotion, rating employees for pay increases and examining them for job assignments. Many firms also adopted relative appraisal systems, designed to assign a certain predetermined percentage of staff to each grade.

Table 7.5   Performance evaluation factors in Goldstar's early years

Factors	Points	Components
Human Factors	300	Diligence, responsibility, cooperation, kindness, credibility, self-development, expressiveness, personality
Job Abilities	500	Swiftness, accuracy, understandability, discernment, attentiveness, planning ability, investigation ability, executive ability, negotiation, creativity
Service Record and Prospects	200	Selecting one criterion from the performance evaluation sheet

Source: Adapted from Goldstar Company (1993).

Appraisal systems largely focused on person-related attributes such as 'proper' attitudes toward the job, management and company. In most firms, only a unilateral top-down appraisal was used, and little feedback was provided to employees. In Goldstar Co., three factors were used for performance evaluation: human factors, job-related abilities and service record (task performance) and prospects (see Table 7.5). Human factors accounted for 30 per cent of the total points. In Samsung Electronic, the grade given on the evaluation of work performance determined employees' bonus level (see Table 7.6). It was a zero-sum system, in which the total amount given to high performers was equivalent to the total amount subtracted from poor performers.

Table 7.6   Bonus adjustment rates based on work performance in Samsung Electronic Company

Evaluation Grade		Adjustment Rate (A)	Adjustment Rate (B)
Superior		150% addition	100% addition
A (*Ga*)		100% addition	70% addition
	High	50% addition	30% addition
B (*Na*)	Middle	Standard rate	Standard rate
	Low	50% deduction	30% deduction
C (*Da*)		100% deduction	70% deduction
Not Qualified		150% deduction	100% deduction
Subjects for Application		Employees above 4th Grade	Employees of 5th Grade

Source: Adapted from Lee, 2000, p.30.

Remuneration systems One feature of the reward systems in Korea was the complexity of the wage structure, principally due to the various types of allowances (Bae, 1997). The three basic components of pay were basic salary, allowances and bonuses (see Table 7.7). Basic salary accounted for the largest portion and provided a central skeleton for the remuneration system. The starting level of such a basic salary was determined by educational background and experience and annual salary increases were given according to seniority. Employees were usually paid less than their contributions in the earlier stages of their career, while salary would exceed their contributions later on.

Allowances could be categorized into at least three groups: job-related, living-related and variable. Job-related allowances were usually related to the difficulty level of tasks, the duties of certain posts and the qualifications of incumbents. Living-related ones were strongly related to the necessities of life. Variable allowances were given to unusual cases. Although variable or irregular types of bonus existed, fixed or regular bonuses predominated. In many cases, the amount was fixed annually (e.g., 400 per cent or 600 per cent of a month's gross salary). Since in many companies fixed bonuses were paid to employees regardless of performance, bonus systems rarely served as motivators.

The seniority-based pay system was prevalent. As of 1979, the proportion of companies adopting it for white-collar employees was 72.4 per cent, while for production and technical jobs it was 53.9 per cent (Ahn, 1989). To summarize, the traditional HRM system in Korea during the period of industrialization can be characterized by the recruitment of new graduates, a generalist orientation, the use of indoctrination and socialization, seniority-based systems and monthly salary, complex pay components, a traditional boss-subordinate form of appraisal, rank-based job grade systems, a department or section-based structure, broadly-defined jobs and limited lifetime employment (Bae, 1997).

Table 7.7   The components of salary in Korean firms

Component	Types	Examples
Basic Pay (Salary step by job grade system)	Single-factor Type	Job, ability, age, tenure, or living cost-based basic salary
	Mixed Type	Tenure + competence, age + competence, living + competence + job and so forth
Allowances	Job-related	Service, job grade, post, qualification, technical skill and work environment allowances
	Living-related	Family, length of service, price, housing, meal, commuting allowances
	Variable	Annual or monthly leave, overtime, night duty and non-duty (or holiday work) allowances
Bonuses	Regular or Fixed	Year-end, summer, winter, festive day (the lunar New Year and Full-moon Harvest Day), founding anniversary bonuses
	Irregular or Variable	Special bonus for service, physical training bonus

Issues and Discussion

In this section, some issues are discussed in more detail in order to probe traditional Korean HRM arrangements more deeply and come to a more fundamental understanding. These issues include the changing roles of HRM, and the centralized structure of the HRM unit.

The Changing Roles of HRM

As described earlier, the HRM-related unit in Korean firms started out as just a small subsection under the general affairs section, and was then extended to become a larger independent division. Accordingly, the role of the unit changed. We will use the example of Samsung Electronic to examine the changing roles of HRM unit, as explained in Table 7.8. Since Samsung Electronic is one of the major companies in Korea, this example may provide a practical template for HRM roles in other Korean firms.

Table 7.8   The evolution of HRM and its roles in the Samsung group

Issues	I. Formation of Conventional Rules (Pre-1966)	II. Establishment and Operation of Explicit Rules (1967-1986)	III. Destruction of Old Rules and Reformation of New Rules (1987-1995)
Changes in Major HRM Practices	*Establishment of integrated management system* - Group-wide public recruitment system - Formation of group-wide single position and treatment system	*Advancement of personnel administration* - Formalization of personnel-related rules and regulations - Job analysis - Experimentation with job-ability qualification system and job-based pay	*Exploration of new rules* - Innovative welfare system - Adoption of new HRM system (*sininsa jedo*)
Role Change of HRM Unit	Stewards (or servants) of management	Administrators (or keepers) of rules	Strategic partners or business strategy implementers
Chairman's Secretary Office		- Rule formulators - Provision of solutions for problems - Reflection of management needs	- Bring up a problem - Coordinator
Affiliated Firms		- Managing and operating through rules	- Provision of solutions for problems - Harmonization of management and employee needs
Change in Major HRM Strategy	- Cost minimization	- Cost minimization - Keeping order in organizations	- Cost minimization - Keeping order in organizations - Revitalization of organizations

Source: Adapted from Lee, 2000, p.23.

The first role of HRM in Samsung was to act as the stewards of top management. During this stage, HRM staff focused on controlling people and costs, and prioritized the establishment of a group-wide single recruitment system and a single position and treatment system. During the industrialization period (1967-1986), the HRM unit became the administrators (or keepers) of explicitly articulated rules. This was the period in which HRM systems became firmly established in Samsung-affiliated companies. In the next stage, HRM people began to act as strategic partners or implementers of strategy. During this period, new HRM systems were adopted.

Table 7.9   HRM-related reporting items requiring approval from the office of the Chairman's secretary (in Samsung)

Items \ Job Grade	(Deputy) General Manager Level	Section Chief Level	3rd Grade	4th Grade	5th Grade	Technician and Special Post
Recruitment by Ad in Newspaper	⊙	⊙	⊙	⊙	⊙	⊙
Recruitment by Other Means	⊙	⊙	⊙	△	△	
Promotion in Status or Rank	⊙	⊙	△	△		
Assignment to a New Position	⊙	△				
Dismissal/ Discharge	△	△				
Reward/ Punishment	⊙	⊙	⊙	△	△	
Transference to Affiliated Firms or (Foreign) Subsidiary	⊙	⊙	⊙	⊙	⊙	⊙
Exceptional Rules for Personnel Affairs	⊙	⊙	⊙	⊙	⊙	⊙

Notes:
⊙   Prior approval needed.

△   An *ex post facto* report.

Source: Samsung Group (1985).

While the roles of HRM extended and improved over time, the roles were still reactive rather than proactive. When corporate and business strategies were formulated, HRM simply supported the planning group and top management by implementing their strategies. In addition, HRM staff rarely had education and training opportunities. Therefore, redefining the new roles of HRM and the competences of its managers are tasks that remain to be resolved.

A Single Centralized Structure

Another issue is the single centralized structure of an HRM organization in a large company. Again, we have used the example of Samsung: the items which required approval from the office of the Chairman's secretary are summarized in Table 7.9. It can be seen that a number of items needed prior approval. Other large companies had similar traditions. This approach ensured that large firms could maintain single, standardized HRM systems. As a result, they could manage and control human resources efficiently at the expense of diversity and adaptability to dynamic business environments. Centralization was actually needed during industrialization when business groups were growing in terms of both size and scope. Nowadays, these core capabilities have turned to core rigidities. Many large companies have now started to decentralize their HRM-related decision-making, empowering business divisions. Differentiating between issues which should be decentralized and those which should be integrated is now a critical issue of strategic choice.

Chapter Summary

In this chapter, we have sketched out the history of Korean HRM from the Japanese colonial period up until the 1987 6.29 Declaration. First, we delineated some of the characteristics of HRM before industrialization (during the Japanese colonial period, and from liberation until industrialization). To illustrate these we introduced some major companies established in the earlier years such as Kyungbang, YuHan and Hwasin. HRM was adopted on an ad hoc basis and not all of its functions were fully developed. However, the major firms adopted some advanced HRM practices. HRM-related units were emerging, and some formalization of HRM was achieved during this period.

We then presented an overview of traditional Korean HRM during industrialization (1962-1987) in terms of work system, human resources flow, training and development and performance appraisal and remuneration.

Traditional HRM can be characterized by the seniority-based system, limited lifetime employment, the job grade system and the recruitment of graduates. These features worked well until the mid-1980s. However, the traditional HRM systems showed some rigidities and dysfunctional factors. Hence, *sininsa* (new HRM) systems were adopted in the early 1990s. This issue is discussed in the next chapter.

Notes

1 The contents of this section came from Kyungsung Spinning (1969), YuHan Corporation (1976), Hwasin Corporation (1977) and Ahn et al. (2002).
2 The rank order of HRM-related unit from the largest to the smallest is department (bu), section (gwa), and subsection (gye).

References

Ahn, C. (1989), 'Personnel management and labor relations', in Korea Employers Federation (ed), *The Forty-Year History of Labor Economics*, Seoul.

Ahn, C., Yoo, P.,.Seo, J., Baik, K. and Choi, Y. (2002), *The new paradigm of management: The history of management in Korea*, Pakyoungsa, Seoul. (In Korean.)

Ahn, H.-T. (1996), *The Current Situations And Future Directions of New Personnel Management Systems In Korean Firms*, The Korea Employers' Federation, Seoul. (In Korean.)

Bae, J. (1997), 'Beyond seniority-based systems: A paradigm shift in Korean HRM?', *Asia Pacific Business Review*, vol.3, no.4, pp.82-110.

Chosun Shipping and Transportation (1940), *Chosun Unsong Jusikhoesa 10 Nyunsa* (Ten-year history of Chosun Shipping and Transportation), Seoul, March.

Chung, K.H., Lee, H.C. and Jung, K.H. (1997), *Korean management: Global strategy and cultural transformation*, Walter de Gruyter, Berlin and New York.

Goldstar Company (1993), *Gumsungsa 35 Nyunsa* (Thirty-five-year history of Goldstar Company), Seoul.

Hwang, M.-S. (1999), *The History of Korean Entrepreneurs*, Dankook University Press, Seoul. (In Korean.)

Hwasin Corporation (1997), *Hwasin 50 Nyunsa* (Fifty-year history of Hwasin corporation), Seoul, June 1.

Koch, M., Nam, S.H. and Steers, R.M. (1995), 'Human resource management in South Korea', in L.F. Moore and P.D. Jennings (eds), *Human Resource Management On The Pacific Rim: Institutions, Practices, And Attitudes*, Walter de Gruyter, Berlin and New York, pp.217-242.

Kyungsung Spinning Company (1969), *Kyungsung Bangjik 50 Nyunsa* (Fifty-year history of Kyungsung Spinning Company), Seoul.

Lee, B. (2000), *Personnel management and labor relations in a non-union large corporate group: Changes in human resource practices and roles of human resource department in Samsung Electronic Company*, Unpublished master's thesis, University of Tokyo.

Lee, G. (1998), 'The evolutions and methods of human resources management in Korea', *The Korean Personnel Administration Journal*, vol.22, no.2, pp.3-27. (In Korean.)

Lee, H. (1999), *The history of Korean chaebol formation*, Bibong, Seoul. (In Korean.)

Mason, E.S., Kim, M.J., Perkins, D.H., Kim, K.S. and Cole, D.C. (1980), *Economic and social modernization of the Republic of Korea*, Cambridge, MA: Harvard University Press.

Morishima, M. (1995), 'The Japanese human resource management system: a learning bureaucracy', in L.F. Moore and P.D. Jennings (eds) *Human Resource Management On The Pacific Rim: Institutions, Practices, And Attitudes*, Walter de Gruyter, Berlin and New York, pp.119-150.

Park, Y.-B. and Lee, M.B. (1995), 'Economic development, globalization, and practices in industrial relations and human resource management in Korea', in A. Verma, T.A. Kochan and R.D. Lansbury (eds), *Employment Relations In The Growing Asian Economies*, Routledge, London and New York.

Samsung Group (1985), *Personnel management manuals*.

Steers, R.M., Shin, Y.K. and Ungson, G.R. (1989), *The Chaebol: Korea's New Industrial Might*, Harper and Row, New York.

Von Glinow, M.A. and Chung, B.J. (1989), 'Comparative human resource management practices in the United States, Japan, Korea, and the People's Republic of China', in G. R. Ferris and K. M. Rowland (eds), *Research in personnel and human resources management*, JAI Press, Greenwich, CT, (Supplement), vol.1, pp.153-171.

Yang, B.-M. and Ahn, H.-T. (1992), *The Theory And Practice Of Skill Grade Systems*, KEF Institute of Labour Economics, Seoul.

YuHan Corporation (1976), *YuHan 50 Nyun* (Fifty years of YuHan). Seoul.

8   HRM Systems in Transition

Introduction

Over the past 15 years or so, human resource management (HRM) systems and practices in Korea have gone through tremendous changes. Before 1987, traditional HRM systems were characterized by long-term attachment, a seniority-based approach and an internal labour market. From the early 1990s, more performance-based systems with greater emphasis on rationality, fairness and competence came into use. Then after the financial crisis hit Asian countries in 1997, Korean companies began to prefer more flexible HRM systems, characterized by numerical flexibility, outsourcing, the use of part-time and temporary workers and merit-based pay systems. In addition, firms started to intensively train and develop HRM managers to enhance their professional competences. HRM departments have been challenged to transform their roles. All of these issues are explained and discussed in this chapter.

Transitions for Korean HRM Systems

The characteristics of traditional HRM systems and new HRM systems are quite different as Table 8.1 shows. These differences stem partly from macro environmental and institutional changes. The Korean economy required restructuring from the mid-1980s onwards and export and labour markets became less favourable for most firms. In many industries, the source of competitive advantage changed from low cost and mass efficiency with mass production to innovation, quality and speed with customization.

As a result of these changes, HRM configurations have also shifted. Until the 1980s, their underlying core ideology was 'organization first' and they took a collective equality approach. These features have recently changed in favour of an individual equity and market-principle orientation (Bae and Rowley, 2001). The mass recruitment of new graduates and a generalist-orientation has been complemented by practices such as recruitment on demand and a more specialist orientation. Hence, while the seniority-based system has been eroding, the system based on ability and/or performance has been emerging.

Table 8.1   Characteristics of Korean HRM (before and after 1987)

Dimensions	Traditional HRM Features	Some New HRM Features*
Economic Development	· Rapid growth stage · Favourable export markets	· Stable growth stage · Global competition
Wage and Labour Supply	· Relatively low wages · Abundant labour supply	· Relatively high wages · Labour shortage in certain sectors
Competitive Advantages	· Low cost · Mass production	· Innovation/quality/speed · Customization
Basic Directions	· Tradition focused · Undifferentiated equality · Job stability	· Breaking tradition · Differentiated equity · Flexibility
Critical Factors	· Age, educational background and seniority	· (Potential) ability and performance
Core Ideology	· Organization first · Collective equality · Community oriented	· Individual respected · Individual equity · Market principle adopted
Human Resource Flow	· Mass recruitment of new graduates · Job security (lifetime job) · Generalists preferred · Indoctrination and socialization	· Recruitment on demand · Job mobility (lifetime career) · Development of professionals · Promotion by selection
Work Systems	· Tall structure · Line and staff; function based · Position-based job grade system · Broadly-defined jobs	· Flat structure · Team systems · Qualification-based · Skill grade system
Evaluation and Reward	· Seniority(age, tenure)-based monthly salary · Complexity of pay structure · Pay equality pursued · Evaluation to advance in job and grade · No appraisal feedback · Single-rater appraisal	· Ability and performance-based annual pay · Merit pay systems · Evaluation for pay increases · Appraisal feedback · 360° appraisal (multiple-rater appraisal)
Employee Influence	· Relatively low involvement · Relatively low information sharing	· Involvement of knowledge workers and empowerment · More information sharing

* The inclusion of features in this column does not mean that Korean firms are fully utilizing these characteristics; rather that some advanced firms have started to adopt these policies, which gives us information on the direction of development, rather than the levels of use of the ideas, within the current systems.

Sources: Adapted and reprinted from Asia Pacific Business Review, Vol.3(4), Bae, J., Beyond seniority-based systems: A paradigm shift in Korean HRM?, p.97, Copyright (1997), with permission from Frank Cass; also from Journal of World Business, Vol.36(4), Bae, J. and Rowley, C., The impact of globalization on HRM: The case of South Korea, p.411, Copyright (2001), with permission from Elsevier.

The practice of giving lifetime employment has also been eroded. However, this does not mean that all firms have fully utilized these HRM policies, rather that this is the direction being taken. Although HRM practices changed dramatically after 1987, the changes accelerated still further after the 1997 financial crisis.

While most of these elements had already begun to change before 1997, the speed and degree of change has accelerated. For Bae (1997:105),

> the configurations of Korean HRM can be best characterized as a 'seniority-based system with some degree of performance factor' and a 'stability-based system with some flexibility'.

Thus two of the critical dimensions of various HRM functions are resourcing and employment (job security versus flexibility) and evaluation and remuneration (seniority versus performance/ability). In short, the direction of change in Korean HRM is from the combination of lifetime employment and a seniority-based system towards an approach that includes enhanced flexible employment and performance/ability-based elements (Bae and Rowley, 2001).

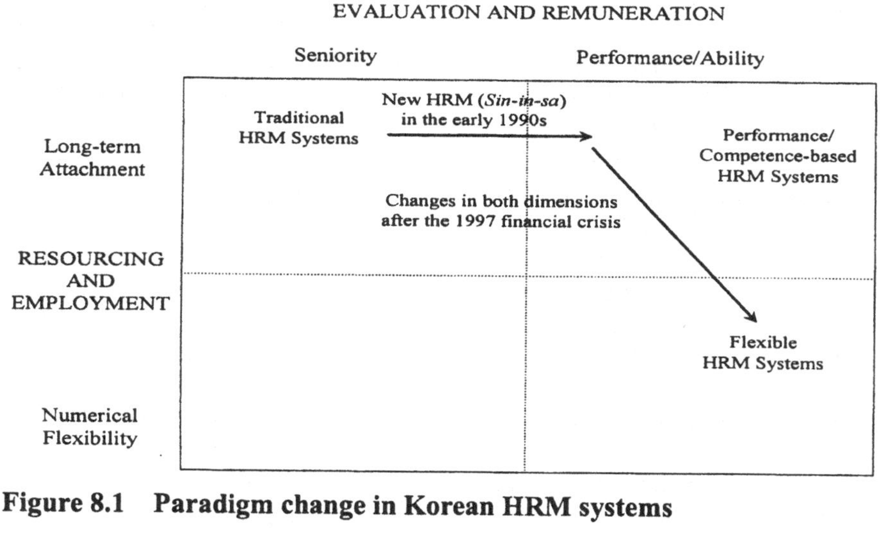

EVALUATION AND REMUNERATION

Seniority   Performance/Ability

Long-term Attachment

Traditional HRM Systems

New HRM (*Sin-in-sa*) in the early 1990s

Performance/ Competence-based HRM Systems

Changes in both dimensions after the 1997 financial crisis

RESOURCING AND EMPLOYMENT

Flexible HRM Systems

Numerical Flexibility

Figure 8.1   Paradigm change in Korean HRM systems

To summarize, traditional HRM structures (i.e., seniority-based, lifetime employment systems) prevailed until the Democracy Declaration of 1987. When wages were dramatically increased, companies began to take a more rational approach, placing greater emphasis on fairness, productivity and performance (Bae, 1997). As a result, performance-based systems have increasingly been adopted by Korean firms since the early 1990s. After the

1997 financial crisis, companies were more interested in HRM systems that emphasized numerical, functional and financial flexibility. This historical trajectory, shifting from traditional HRM through a performance-based system to a flexible system, is summarized in Figure 8.1. As the diagram shows, change in both dimensions (resourcing and employment and evaluation and remuneration) accelerated after the 1997 financial crisis. It seems that the change toward a performance/ability-based system has been regarded as more desirable by both employer and employee, though there has been some disagreement on the methods and programs by which the changes should be adopted. However, the change toward a numerically flexible system showed a lack of consensus.

HRM under Exploratory Pluralism (1987 to 1997): The Period of Experimentation

The key characteristics of this period include industrial restructuring, political democratization and exploratory pluralism. As economic environments worldwide changed drastically, Korean government and management behaviours and practices fell behind. About 15 years ago, the issue of 'industrial restructuring' in Korea was the focus of a special issue of World Development (1988, Vol.16, No.1) as the economy experienced a rapid industrial transition. As political democratization progressed, Korea began to experiment with pluralism after 1987 (Park, 1993).

During this ten-year period (1987-1997), Korean firms adopted and experimented with a large number of new HRM practices. What was their motivation to do so? Broadly speaking, firms wanted to have more efficient and flexible systems that would adapt to the changing environment. The traditional HRM systems had been functioning well until the mid-1980s, but they turned out to be expensive, inefficient and rigid when the environment changed. A more direct and perhaps the main reason for adopting new HRM approaches was as a response to the post-1987 militant unionism and the resulting jump in labour costs. As a result, firms sought to pursue more effective people management strategies. In this section, these new HRM practices are introduced.

New HRM Practices

To overcome the problems of traditional HRM systems, many large Korean companies adopted various new practices in some or all of their HRM functions in the early 1990s. Such new practices covered the following:

- work systems: team basis, skill grade system, separation of rank and position, single job grade system for all employees;
- human resource flow: blind interview, recruitment specialists, more steps in the rank system, promotion by selection, honorary retirement system;
- training and development: internship programs, career development system, 'region expert' program (sending employees to other countries for language and cultural development);
- performance evaluation and remuneration: multiple-rater performance measurement, appraisal feedback, ability- and performance-based payment retaining seniority factor, skill-grade pay, merit pay, monthly salary for production employees.

Although not all Korean companies adopted these practices, this was the first time that such ideas, which were totally unfamiliar to most firms, had been introduced by a number of them at the same time (Bae, 1997).

In 1995, a survey was conducted by the Korea Employers' Federation to explore the extent of the introduction of these new practices (Ahn, 1996). A total of 283 of about 3,000 firms of over 50 employees were covered in the final report. The sample consisted of both manufacturing (71 per cent) and non-manufacturing (29 per cent) firms. The results are summarized in Table 8.2. On average, about 20 per cent of the sample firms had introduced new HRM practices, ranging from 2.5 per cent for 'subordinate/peer performance evaluation' to 43.3 per cent for 'single rate basic pay'. In addition, about nine per cent were considering introducing new HRM practices, implying that more firms would be using the new HRM practices in the future.

Work Systems

The common mode of introducing these new HRM practices will be described by reference to the job grade system. Two of the problems of the job grade system are that it is post-centred and has a dual approach. The standard job grade system in Korean firms was a post grade system, in which employees' job grades followed their ranks in the organization (Bae, 1997). For example, when an employee became a general manager, he or she was automatically promoted to, say, first grade, and the salary level was also automatically increased. Until the late 1980s, job grade systems were regarded as rank systems based on seniority (Bae, 1997). In this system, job grade and rank are related on a one-to-one matching basis. This job grade system is different from either the American-type system (based on the level of difficulty of the task, determined by job analysis and evaluation) or the Japanese system (based on employees' skills and knowledge).

Table 8.2   The extent of the introduction of new HRM practices (N: 271 ~ 281; %)

HRM Areas	New HRM Practices	Introduced	Not Introduced	Under Consideration
	Internships	18.2	73.6	8.2
	Recruitment after fellowship	10.8	85.9	3.2
Recruitment and Career Development	Blind interview	9.8	85.5	4.7
	Recruitment specialists	30.2	57.9	11.9
	Promotion by selection	33.8	56.5	9.7
	Equal promotion opportunities for women	36.2	57.2	6.6
	Career development plan	18.8	65.3	15.9
	Skill grade systems	7.9	92.1	0.0
Work Systems	Separation of post and job grade	40.9	57.0	2.2
	Single job grade system	23.5	71.3	5.1
	Skill-grade pay	25.1	57.0	17.9
	Single rate basic pay	43.3	51.3	5.4
Reward Systems	Individual performance bonus	14.7	72.8	12.9
	Group performance bonus	28.3	58.0	13.8
	Merit pay	7.2	74.2	18.6
	Monthly salary for production employees	27.9	69.3	2.9
	Multiple-rater PE			
	1) Subordinate	1) 2.5	1) 92.1	1) 5.4
	2) Peer	2) 2.5	2) 90.1	2) 7.4
Performance Evaluation (PE)	3) Self	3) 25.8	3) 65.9	3) 8.2
	MBO	21.5	67.2	11.3
	Absolute appraisal	25.3	65.3	9.4
	Appraisal feedback	11.4	78.6	10.0
	Behaviourally anchored ratings	10.9	81.2	8.0
	Honorary retirement	17.3	73.7	10.0
Retirement	Retirement within job-grade systems	10.0	84.9	5.0

Source: Adapted from various tables in Ahn (1996).

The second problem the duality of the job grade system: in other words that fact that there was one scale for production workers (with only about three or four grades) and another for managerial and administrative employees (with about eight grades). As a result, production employees had fewer opportunities for promotion, received lower pay and suffered from worse work conditions (Park and Lee, 1995). To resolve these problems many firms brought in single job grade systems covering both types of employee. As shown in Table 8.2, 23.5 per cent of firms adopted this practice. In addition, the traditional post-centred job grade systems have changed to skill-grade approaches, following the Japanese model. The number of grades has also increased. For example, Samsung increased their job grades to 11 steps within three groups: five junior grades (J1 to J5), three senior grades (S1 to S3) and three manager grades (M1 to M3) (see Table 8.3. Another popular practice was the introduction of the team system, intended to integrate departments and divisions both horizontally and vertically.

Human Resources Flow

In terms of recruitment and selection, some companies operated internship programs and 'blind' interviews (about 10 per cent). Promotion by selection, disregarding incremental promotion up the job ladders, was also adopted by some firms (33.8 per cent). In the past, employees would have had to spend certain periods working at the same job grade in order to be considered for promotion. Under the new HRM systems, most firms began to disregard time served in favour of considering skills, knowledge and abilities for upgrading within skill grade systems.

The previous Korean Labour Standard Act had not allowed the termination of employees without just cause. However, this clause was viewed differently by employers and employees, whose views were totally polarized. While the HRM managers commented to us that it was extremely hard to terminate employees, in contrast employees said they felt their jobs were really insecure. However, the amended law in March 1997 included a clause of 'discharge upon business crisis', which allowed employers to lay people off in the case of financial deterioration, structural adjustment, technical innovation and/or changes to the business so as to enhance productivity. This revision of labour law was expected to help Korean firms to become more flexible. However, some have argued that Korean companies did not widely practice permanent employment even before the amendment (Kang, 1989; Koch, et al., 1995).

Performance Evaluation and Compensation

After 1987, the level of Korean wages rapidly increased. Between 1986-95 nominal and real wages rose at an annual rate of 14.25 per cent and 7.93 per cent, respectively, in all industries and 15.42 per cent and 9.07 per cent, respectively, in manufacturing. These high increases were due to the expansion of the trade unions and the country's strong economic performance (Park and Lee, 1995).

Table 8.3   Changes to the job grade system in the Samsung Electronic Company

Pre-1994		Post-1994		
Job Grade	Minimum Stay	New Job Grade	Position Title	Average Stay
1 A (gap)	-	M (manager) 3	*Susuk bujang* (senior general manager	-
		2	*Bujang* (general manager)	3 years
1 B (eul)	3 years	1	*Chajang* (deputy general manager)	3 years
2 A (gap)	4 years	S (senior) 3	*Sunim* gwajang (senior section chief)	2 years
		2	*Gwajang* (section chief)	2 years
2 B (eul)	2 years	1		2 years
3 A (gap)	3.5 years	J (junior) 5	*Daeri* (deputy section chief)	3.5 years
3 B (eul)	4.5 years	4	*Juim* (senior staff))	2.5 years
		3	*Sawon* (staff member)	2 years
4	2.5 years	2		2.5 years
5	2.5 years	1		2.5 years

Source: Samsung internal material.

To improve fairness and objectivity, many firms have begun to use multi-rater performance evaluation and absolute, rather than the traditional relative, appraisal practices. Furthermore, performance appraisal has moved towards a more developmental role. To achieve this goal, firms began to give feedback to employees (11.4 per cent).

In the area of compensation, skill-grade pay, individual- or group-performance bonuses, monthly rather than hourly pay for production employees and merit pay practices have all been introduced. The most prominent feature of this change was the emphasis on ability and performance rather than seniority.

Training and Development

Many large companies have also launched several programs to promote business-university partnership. In addition, overseas training programs to provide opportunities for training and 're-education' have been introduced. Many companies give employees who have certain qualifications (e.g., language proficiency and high ranks in performance evaluation) the opportunity to study at foreign universities. In Samsung, the 'region expert' program has operated for several years. Samsung sends its brightest junior employees to other countries for a year without any obligation other than to obtain language and make cultural acquaintances: this is seen by some outsiders and commentators as a 'goof off' mission. According to *the Wall Street Journal* (1992), the program costs about $80,000 a year per person.

The Efficacy of New HRM Practices

To evaluate new HRM practices we have employed the concept of 'fit' in three different aspects: internal fit, external fit and social fit.[1] Our first concern is internal fit, which refers to the coordination or congruence between various HRM practices (Wright and McMahan, 1992). Many Korean firms have adopted new HRM practices that seemed attractive to their firms without firstly undertaking a full assessment of their existing approach (Ahn, 1996). Legge (1989) discusses the inherent contradictions in the concept of HRM, though this is not a Korea-specific problem. Take the case of commitment: the basic assumption in pursuing commitment is that it generates desirable outcomes for both individual and organization (Beer, *et al.*, 1985). However, '[t]he possibility of multiple and perhaps competing commitments [to organization, career, job, union, work group, and family] creates a more complex set of issues' (Guest, 1987: 513).

Since Korean firms and HR managers had not paid much attention to the integrated system and the possible tradeoffs between the results of new HRM practices, they seem to have introduced them on an ad hoc, piecemeal basis. This has prevented firms from generating the anticipated outcomes (Bae, 1997).

A second issue is external fit, which refers to the linkages and congruence between HRM practices and organizational goals or business strategy (Lengnick-Hall and Lengnick-Hall, 1988; Wright and McMahan, 1992). This argument is related to two different strategic HRM approaches. Legge (1989: 29) argues that integrating HRM policy with business strategy contradicts the pursuit of the normative 'soft' version of HRM, which puts the stress on the term 'human'. This is because while the former promotes 'a contingent design of HRM policy', the latter supports 'an absolute approach to the design of employment policy'. The external factors that brought about the introduction of new HRM practices to Korea necessitate the 'hard' version of HRM, which emphasizes 'the idea of "resources," that is something to be used dispassionately and in a formally rational manner' (Storey, 1992: 26). Therefore, the underlying assumption of new HRM policy in Korea is that it is desirable to integrate HRM policy with business strategy. However, many firms introduce new HRM practices 'opportunistically rather than strategically' simply because other firms have adopted them, without evaluating their own goals, strategies, or capabilities, as institutional theory would suggest. This is a typical example of poor 'benchmarking'. Some of the internal factors that created the demand for new HRM also require its 'soft' side to be emphasized.

Finally, social fit has been another barrier to the adoption of new HRM practices. While many employers and some employees wanted to do so, the practices were not fully congruent with the Confucian, seniority-based culture and the concept of collectivism, which is deeply rooted in the ethos of the Korean people. This is perhaps the opposite phenomenon to that which occurred when 'lean production' systems, which demand some characteristics of collectivism, were introduced in individualistic societies. According to the description offered by Taira (1996), organization-specific behaviour generated by lean production was in part driven or constrained by broader cultural forces. Hence, such behaviour should be congruent with the culture and society at large.

While Taira's argument is rather macro in the sense of distinguishing culture in the organization from the culture of society as a whole, some UK researchers have focused on the shift of emphasis within organizations (Legge, 1989; Sisson, 1994). Just as the UK's use of HRM has led to potential conflict between emphasizing the virtues of individualism and pursuing collectivist characteristics such as teamwork and functional flexibility (Legge, 1989), Korean new HRM has encountered similar tensions. Many Korean companies are now finding it a challenge to pursue more individualistic and performance-oriented HRM policies at the same time as more collectivist features. Keeping a balance between 'individualism' and 'collectivism' while keeping adverse effects to a minimum is a critical task for many Korean firms. In summary, there has been a wide gap between the 'rhetoric' of new HRM and the 'reality' of new practices.

HRM after the Financial Crisis: Post-1997

Korean HRM has changed tremendously since the 1997 financial crisis. The shifts have occurred in areas such as ideology, recruitment, selection, work systems, evaluation, remuneration and employee influence. However, two major areas that have been particularly influenced by the crisis are pay systems (from seniority to ability or performance) and human resource flow (from lifetime employment to numerical flexibility). These two issues are discussed in this section.

From Seniority-based towards Performance- and Ability-based HRM

Seniority-based elements have been crucial to many Korean HRM functions such as job assignment, performance evaluation, remuneration, promotion, training and so on. Systems can be envisaged as appearing at various stages on the 'seniority versus performance' continuum (Bae, 1997):

- a traditional seniority-based system;
- seniority-based, with some performance factors;
- performance-based, with some seniority factors;
- an ability/performance-based system.

The efficacy of traditional seniority-based pay systems has been increasingly questioned in Korea due to their perceived systemic rigidities and weak motivational effects on individuals (Kim and Park, 1997). As a result, systems have changed to become more performance-based.

There have been changes in Korean remuneration systems, with a lessening of the emphasis on seniority while the importance of 'performance' has grown. Table 8.4 shows that about one third (33 per cent) of firms now have performance-based systems – i.e., (3) or (4). Nonetheless the traditional seniority-based system has remained in use in large numbers of firms (about 42 per cent), with little variation in usage by size or sector. Indeed, some form of seniority basis – i.e., (1) or (2) – accounted for the pay systems of over two thirds (67 per cent) of firms, again with little size or sector variation. The data in Table 8.4 also indicate that almost one fifth of employers (18.9 per cent) believed that the seniority-based system should be discarded, with over half (54.5 per cent) of firms indicating it should be fundamentally changed while retaining its merits. Yet at the same time, over a quarter (26.6 per cent) of firms thought the seniority-based system could be kept on if its perceived defects were remedied.

Table 8.4   Variations in pay systems by size and sector (%)

System Options	Sector		Size (employees)		All Firms (N=278)
	Mfg[b] (N=210)	Non-Mfg (N=68)	Less Than 300 (N=144)	More Than 300 (N=134)	
(1) Traditional Seniority-based	42.4	42.6	43.8	41.3	42.4
(2) Seniority-based with Performance Factor[a]	25.2	22.1	22.8	26.0	24.5
(3) Performance-based with Seniority Factor	29.0	29.4	27.8	30.5	29.1
(4) Ability/ Performance-Based	3.4	5.9	5.6	2.2	4.0

Notes:
a   Original paper labelled this 'Ability-based system, but seniority-based operation'.
b   Mfg: Manufacturing industry.

Source: Park and Ahn (1999).

An example of a performance-based system – merit pay, where the total annual salary is determined in advance based on an individual's ability or performance – presents a striking contrast to traditional seniority-based pay. A January 1999 survey of 4,303 firms with over 100 employees found that 649 (15.1 per cent) had already adopted annual pay; 481 (11.2 per cent) were preparing to do so; and 1,077 (25 per cent) were planning to adopt it at some stage (Korea Ministry of Labour, 1999). Hence, just over one quarter (26.3 per cent) of firms had either made, or were preparing to make, these changes. Indeed, just over half (51.3 per cent) of firms had reached some stage of the process of changing their pay systems. Again, the trends seemed to be common across all size of organization.

The operation of annual pay systems can also be seen among the *chaebols*. Doosan became the first to introduce one in 1994, and SK and SEC followed in 1998. Most firms applied them to managers or more educated staff only. All used a mixed form of the approach by selecting aspects from different pay systems based on basic (annual), performance-, ability- and job-based remuneration. In the case of 'base-up', some firms, such as SEC, Daesang and Hyosung, introduced a uniform annual increase to basic pay regardless of performance or ability levels, while others did not. SEC and Hyosung adopted a zero-sum method, reducing the salary of 'poor' performers while increasing that for 'good' performers by the same amount. Other firms used a 'plus-sum' method where 'good' performers received increases but the pay of 'poor' performers did not go down. Finally, some firms used a cumulative method to determine salary by aggregating the results of performance evaluation.

Employment Adjustment: Towards Numerical Flexibility

Lifetime employment practices are related to several Korean HRM functions. Furthermore, Korean government officials have argued that securing labour market flexibility was one approach to improving competitiveness (echoing similar debates in other countries and regions, such as Australia, the UK and Europe). Thus Korean firms have been encouraged to implement restructuring programs, including massive layoffs and redundancies via the so-called 'honorary retirement plans'. Furthermore, a condition of the post-crisis IMF bailout program was the immediate passing of laws to dismantle lifetime employment.

In the late 1990s, Korea could be classified as 'low' in terms of numerical flexibility and 'moderately high' on functional flexibility (Bae et al, 1997). Such flexibilities have swiftly and extensively increased since then, as indicated in Table 8.5. This locates various HR practices within a typology of labour flexibility and change over time.

During this short, but obviously turbulent, 2-year period, the use of every dimension of flexibility seems to have increased. There have been some spectacular increases in numerical flexibility, via boosting retirements while reducing working hours, overtime and recruitment. Functional flexibility has been increased via redeployment, especially to other departments; and financial flexibility via wage freezes and reducing bonuses and benefits. Thus, to avoid large-scale dismissals, firms explored twin avenues. Firstly, they enhanced functional flexibility by using various methods. Secondly, they boosted numerical flexibility by employing more contingent workers. When we look at employment composition, the ratio of regular to temporary (part-time, outsourced, etc.) employees is 100:23.7. It has been even argued that temporary and part-time workers now outnumber full-time workers (Burton, 2000). Of the four different types of flexibility, the most dramatic change was to financial flexibility (see Table 8.5). Reduction in working hours to achieve internal numerical flexibility and dismissal for external numerical flexibility, were also extensively adopted during this period of turbulence.

Table 8.5   Changes in employment adjustment (# of firms; N=286[a])

Flexibility	Practices	1996	1998	Presence	Change
Numerical (Internal)	Working hours reduction	5	61	v	+++
	Restriction of overtime	11	104	vv	++
	Temporary leave of absence, unpaid	5	24	%	+
	Temporary leave of absence, paid	2	26	%	++
Numerical (External)	Postponement of recruitment	6	29	%	+
	Reduction of recruitment	33	148	vv	+
	Dismissal	2	53	v	+++
	Voluntary retirement	22	72	v	+
	Outsourcing	19	45	%	+
	Dispatch to affiliated company	11	21	%	+
Financial	Base pay reduction	0	41	%	+++
	Freezing of wages	1	78	v	+++
	Bonus reduction	0	116	vv	+++
	Fringe benefits reduction	4	141	vv	+++
Functional [b]	Redeployment after training	5	19	%	+
	Redeployment as salesperson	12	53	v	+
	Redeployment to units with staff shortages	19	95	v	+

Notes:
a   Multiple responses from firms.
b   Functional flexibility typically includes multi-skilling and up-skilling, but practices included here are more broadly related to employment adjustment.

Key (Practice presence):
vv   practice present to a great degree
v   practice present
%   practice present to some degree

Key (Degree of change):
+++   major change between 1996 and 1998
++   change between 1996 and 1998
+   minimal change between 1996 and 1998

Source: Adapted from Bae and Rowley (2001) and various tables from Park and Ahn (1999), conducted in November 1998.

Change also occurred in the period between early 1997 and early 1998, as shown by another survey of 300 firms which was carried out in January – November 1997 and December 1997 – March 1998 (Choi and Lee, 1998). In the first period, virtually one third (32.3 per cent, some 97 firms), had experienced employment adjustments. By the second period, this coverage had spread further, almost doubling to 60.3 per cent (181 firms). For the first period, the specific employment adjustments made were as follows (firms made multiple responses): worker numbers (59 firms, 19.7 per cent), remuneration (32 firms, 10.7 per cent), working hours (60 firms, 20 per cent) and functional flexibility (38 firms, 12.7 per cent). In the second period, the numbers answering in the affirmative to all these types hugely increased: firms changing worker numbers more than doubled (131 firms, 43.7 per cent), those altering remuneration almost quadrupled (116 firms, 38.7 per cent), with almost double the number reporting changes to both working hours (110 firms, 36.7 per cent) and functional flexibility (73 firms, 24.3 per cent). Further probing of 'adjustment in worker number' to the level of specific programs reveals some of the effects of downsizing. For example, there was double the use of both 'freezing or reducing recruitment' – from 45 (15 per cent) to 116 (38.7 per cent) – and 'dismissal', from 21 (7 per cent) to 52 (17.3 per cent). There was also a rise in 'early retirement' from 17 (5.7 per cent) to 24 (8 per cent). These shifts show that many firms had adopted programs for numerical flexibility through reductions in worker numbers.

The cases of individual companies also highlight the adjustments being made. Hyundai Motor Co. had initially planned to dismiss 4,830 of its 45,000 workers, but reduced this to 2,678 and then 1,538. The union went on strike in May 1998 against these redundancies, which was then followed by 6 illegal strikes until a negotiated compromise was reached in August. There were also about 50 instances of physical conflict with management. The final agreement provided for just 277 dismissals, along with lump-sum severance pay.[2] As a result, although Hyundai's workforce still shrank to about 35,000 this was mainly due to 7,226 people taking voluntary retirement plus about 2,000 temporary workers laid off without pay (*Maeil Business Newspaper*, 1999). These conflicts and strikes also cost Hyundai about US $750 million of revenue and its suppliers some US $600 million (Ibid.). The restructuring plans also led to huge costs.

Samsung Electronic Co. (SEC) had 21 worldwide production bases, 53 sales operations in 46 countries and sales of US $16.6 billion (1998) from its 3 main business divisions: Multimedia and Home Appliances, Semiconductors and Information and Communications. SEC was one of the world's largest producers of dynamic random access memory semiconductors. The company acted as something of a trendsetter in HRM, even becoming the object of benchmarking from other Korean firms. About 60,000 employees worked for SEC before 1997. Under the post-crisis restructuring plans, the workforce was to be massively reduced to 40,000, a cut of about one third. SEC managed this process with less overt conflict and attention than Hyundai.

These cases highlight several critical points. Firstly, the government was caught in a dilemma between demanding that *chaebols* restructure and pursuing labour market flexibility through dismissals. It chose a compromise between labour and management instead of rigidly enforcing legal demands. This indicates how difficult it can be to enforce legal clauses (see Bae et al, 1997). Secondly, the examples give conflicting messages about restructuring and downsizing. The fact that actual dismissals were carried out by a *chaebol* – i.e., SEC radically reduced its workforce – could be read as a strong signal that other firms would follow this route. However, the case of Hyundai also shows that unions were able to prevent some redundancies. Thirdly, the strikes, such as those at Hyundai, reflected the severe dislocation faced by Korean managers and workers after the IMF intervention. Layoffs tore families apart and many workers and managers took their own lives.

Table 8.6   HRM activities expected to be outsourced

Rank	HRM Activities for Outsourcing	Feedback (%)
1	Education and training	85%
2	Outplacement	77%
3	Building up and utilization of HR information systems	77%
4	Job analysis	68%
5	Employee recruitment and selection	56%
6	Salary pay and operation	53%

Source: Park and Yu (2001).

Another phenomenon relevant to flexibility is the increased use of outsourcing for HRM activities. A survey of 107 HR professionals (HR managers and professors or researchers in HRM areas) conducted by the Korea Labour Institute in the spring of 1999 identified several areas which were about to be outsourced (see Table 8.6).

Flexibility: A Final Choice?

The recent paradigm changes in management do not necessarily require flexibility alone to be enhanced. In fact, competing forces are operating simultaneously. While the pressures of neo-liberalism-based globalization encourage more flexibility, learning-based knowledge management emphasizes knowledge creation and sharing. In addition, the Korean economy has been put under pressure to take the technological and production upgrading, rather than the cost minimization, route to competitiveness. One issue is that the pressures of globalization erode the key ingredients of knowledge management and the pro-competition technological upgrading strategy (Bae and Rowley, 2001). Enhancing market functions and competition has weakened the harmony and cooperation of organizational members and the high-care climate, both of which are needed for successful knowledge management. Korean firms have turned away from their earlier 'over-investment' (characterized by high employment security and training commitment, but with contributions through immediate jobs) towards 'under-investment' employment relationships (characterized by full commitment from employees, but with high numerical flexibility). One example of this trend is the 12.2 per cent cut in Korean training investment by firms between 1997-98 (Cho et al., 1999).

In addition, enhanced flexibility in employment adjustment may bring with it some problems, especially in Asian cultures. The flexibility route is not necessary the best choice: rather, it may generate a series of trade-offs. Interestingly, less regulated or high-flexibility economies (e.g., the UK) do not necessarily out-perform (e.g., in terms of GDP, productivity and worker conditions and benefits) more regulated or 'rigid' ones (e.g., Germany, France) (Bae and Rowley, 2001). For instance, in times of crisis MNEs in the UK will first of all try to close down plants because of the less restrictive regulations that make redundancies quicker, easier and cheaper in comparison to low-flexibility economies (Bae and Rowley, 2001). Yet, in the long run, this route produces a downward spiral, in which firms reduce their investment in training and dynamic productivity as the incentives for these are reduced. The lack of training then reduces other possibilities, such as 'mass customization' which requires substantial training for employees to operate and use to make the firm competitive. Eventually, this reduced competitiveness may lead to another downsizing program being required.

A recent report (Samsung Economic Research Institute, 1999) has raised serious questions about labour flexibilities and pointed out countervailing trends elsewhere. The report concludes that Korean firms would benefit from 'mutual' rather than 'unbalanced' (i.e., over- or under-) investment, employee-organization relationship approaches (cf Tsui et al., 1997), with some return to longer-term employment relationships.

The phenomenon of widespread downsizing and the resulting concerns about its use can be partly explained by institutional theory (McKinley et al, 1995). According to this, firms adopt downsizing not because of its 'effectiveness', but due to three specific social forces and factors. Firstly, 'constraining' forces shift as downsizing, once viewed negatively, becomes positively interpreted and gains legitimacy. This shift in social constraints subsequently encourages firms to conform to newly legitimate structures. Secondly, 'cloning' forces pressurize firms to mimic the actions of leading companies in the sector. Thirdly, 'learning' forces are shaped through learning processes in educational institutions and professional associations. Together these forces push firms to adopt the currently prevailing institutional rules.

This framework can be applied to Korea. From the mid-1980s on firms experimented with various 'new' management approaches, including total quality management, business process re-engineering, team-based work systems and so on. Many of these approaches were adopted not because of their economic effectiveness, but rather to align the firm with institutional forces. For example, for Lee and Kim (1999) the take-up of team-based systems is explained better by institutional legitimacy rather than economic rationality. Likewise, downsizing was implemented by many firms after the 1997 crisis when restructuring plans contained workforce reductions, due to institutional legitimacy. More recently, firms have begun recruiting for the same reason – because other prestigious firms were doing so.

Chapter Summary

We have explained the changes to traditional HRM systems during the late 1980s and early 1990s. As environments changed, various challenges to the efficacy of the existing systems emerged. Accordingly, *sininsa* (new HRM) systems evolved. The guiding principles of the new systems were ability/performance orientation, rationalization and fairness (Bae, 1997). Before the *sininsa* systems could be fully established, however, the Asian crisis hit Korea in 1997. This unexpected and turbulent environmental crisis increased the pressure on Korean HRM transformation. Two main changes at the time were to remuneration (from a seniority-based to performance- or ability-based system) and to the employment system (from lifetime employment to numerical flexibility).

The previous and present chapters have dealt with the origins and evolution of HRM in Korea. We will now wrap up this chapter by comparing the key characteristics of HRM in each period. Before providing the comparative picture, we propose the general trajectory of the evolution of HRM as follows (Bae, 1999):

- primitive personnel management (PM): each personnel-related function has not yet been fully developed, and there is no independent personnel unit;
- PM: most personnel-related functions have been established but no

coordination exists, with the personnel-related sub-unit usually under the general affairs unit;

- HRM: most personnel-related functions have been coordinated into a system but this is not aligned to business strategies and goals, although an independent HRM unit exists;
- strategic HRM (SHRM): a coherent HRM system is well aligned to organizational strategic directions both reactively and proactively.

Table 8.7 The characteristics of HRM by period

Period	HRM Level	Characteristics
Colonial Period (1910-1945)	Primitive personnel management (PM)	• Some personnel functions emerged (e.g., recruitment and compensation) • Personnel units (usually general affairs) started to be established
Rebuilding Period (1945-1961)	Mostly primitive PM, but PM in major companies	• Various labour laws (1953) provided both guidance and restrictions • Personnel administration of US military diffused to public then private companies
Industrialization Period (1962-1987)	PM during early days, but HRM later on	• Most firms established independent HRM units • Formalization of HRM progressed • HRM functions individually developed in 1960s and 1970s • HRM system (integrated and coordinated) appeared in 1980s • Seniority system, the salary step and lifetime employment institutionalized
Restructuring Period (1987-1997)	HRM and some strategic HRM	• Seniority-based system eroding • Performance-based system adopted • Various experimentation with new HRM practices in the name of new HRM system (sininsa jedo)
Post-crisis Period (Post-1997)	Toward strategic HRM	• Lifetime employment eroding • Labour market flexibility pursued • Linkage of HRM to business goals and strategy emphasized • New roles and competences of HRM professionals defined and education programs for HR managers provided

We outline the level of evolution and the main features of HRM for each period in Figure 8.9. Before the start of the industrialization process, most firms remained at the primitive level except for some major companies. During the early stages of industrialization (in the 1960s and 1970s), the level of personnel management prevailed in most firms. From the 1980s onward, the HRM level began to take deep root in Korean firms and from the 1990s, they started to implement strategic HRM. The extent of its use has increased since the crisis period.

Notes

1   The contents in this section were abridged from Bae (1997).
2   Severance pay was equivalent to 7 months' gross salary for those who had worked for less than 5 years, 8 months' for 5-10 years and 9 months' for over 10 years.

References

Ahn, H.-T. (1996), *The Current Situations And Future Directions Of New Personnel Management Systems In Korean Firms*, The Korea Employers' Federation, Seoul. (In Korean.)

Bae, J. (1997), 'Beyond seniority-based systems: A paradigm shift in Korean HRM?', *Asia Pacific Business Review*, vol.3, no.4, pp.82-110.

Bae, J. (1999), 'Competitive Advantage and Human Resource Management: Beyond Strategic Human Resource Management', *Korean Journal of Management*, vol.7, no.2, pp.1-45. (In Korean.)

Bae, J. and Rowley, C. (2001), 'The impact of globalization on HRM: The case of Korea', *Journal of World Business*, vol.36, no.4, pp.402-428.

Bae, J., Rowley, C., Kim, D. and Lawler, J. (1997), 'Korean industrial relations at the crossroads: The recent labour troubles', *Asia Pacific Business Review*, vol.3, no.3, pp.148-160.

Beer, M., Spector, B., Lawrence, P.R., Mills, D.Q. and Walton, R.E. (1985), *Human Resource Management: A General Manager's Perspective*, Free Press, New York.

Cho, Y.J., Pak, H.Y. and Wagnert, S. (1999), 'Training in a changing Korea', *Training and Development*, May, pp.98-99.

Choi, K. and Lee, K. (1998), *Woorinara Giupeui Goyongjojung Siltae* (Employment Adjustment in Korean firms: Survey of 1998), vol II, Korea Labour Institute, Seoul.

Guest, D.E. (1987), 'Human Resource Management And Industrial Relations', *Journal of Management Studies*, vol.24, no.5, pp.503-521.

Kang, T.W. (1989), *Is Korea the Next Japan?: Understanding the Structure, Strategy, and Tactics of America's Next Competitor*, Free Press, New York.

Kim, D., and Park, S. (1997), 'Changing patterns of pay systems in Japan and Korea: From seniority to performance', *International Journal of Employment Studies*, vol.5, no.2, pp.117-134.

Koch, M., Nam, S.H. and Steers, R.M. (1995), 'Human resource management in South Korea', in L.F. Moore and P.D. Jennings (eds), *Human Resource Management On The Pacific Rim: Institutions, Practices, And Attitudes*, Walter de Gruyter, Berlin and New York, pp.217-242.

Korea Ministry of Labour (1999), *A Survey Report on Annual Pay Systems and Gain-Sharing Plans*. Korea Ministry of Labour, Seoul. (In Korean.)

Lee, K. and Kim, D. (1999), 'Rationality and legitimacy as factors influencing adoption of teams', in *Proceedings of the Annual Conference of the Korean Association of Personnel Administration*, Seoul, pp.25-47. (In Korean.)

Legge, K. (1989), 'Human resource management: a critical analysis', in J. Storey (ed), *New Perspectives On Human Resource Management*, Routledge, London and New York, pp.19-40.

Lengnick-Hall, C.A. and Lengnick-Hall, M.L. (1988), 'Strategic Human Resources Management: A Review of the Literature and a Proposed Typology', *Academy of Management Review*, vol.13, no.3, pp.454-470.

Leonard, D. and Sensiper, S. (1998), 'The role of tacit knowledge in group innovation', *California Management Review*, vol.40, no.3, pp.112-132.

Maeil Business Newspaper (1999), August 25.

Marchington, M. and Wilkinson, A. (1996), *Core Personnel and Development*, Institute of Personnel Development, London.

McKinley, W., Sanchez, C.M. and Schick A.G (1995), 'Organizational downsizing: Constraining, cloning, learning', *Academy of Management Executive*, vol.9, no.3, pp.32-44.

Nonaka, I. (1991), 'The Knowledge-Creation Company', *Harvard Business Review*, Nov/Dec, pp.96-104.

Park, J. and Ahn, H. (1999), *The Changes and Future Direction of Korean Employment Practices*, The Korea Employers' Federation, Seoul. (In Korean.)

Park, S.-I. (1993), 'The Role of the State in Industrial Relations: The Case of Korea', *Comparative Labor Law Journal*, vol.14, no.3, pp.321-338.

Park, W. and Yu, G. (2001), 'Paradigm shift and changing role of HRM in Korea: Analysis of the HRM experts' opinions and its implication', *The Korean Personnel Administration Journal*, vol.25, no.1, pp.347-369.

Park, Y.-B. and Lee, M.B. (1995), 'Economic development, globalization, and practices in industrial relations and human resource management in Korea', in A. Verma, T.A. Kochan and R.D. Lansbury (eds), *Employment Relations in the Growing Asian Economies*, Routledge, London and New York.

Samsung Economic Research Institute (1999), *Multiple Approaches to the Employment Relationship and Strategic Choices of Korean Firms*.

Sisson, K. (1994), 'Personnel management: paradigms, practice and prospects' in K. Sisson (ed), *Personnel Management: A Comprehensive Guide To Theory And Practice In Britain*, (2nd ed), Blackwell, Oxford, pp.3-50.

Storey, J. (1992), *Developments in the Management of Human Resources*, Routledge, London.

Taira, K. (1996), 'Rejoinder To Open Peer Commentaries On Koji Taira's "Compatibility of Human Resource Management, Industrial Relations, and Engineering Under Mass Production and Lean Production"', *Applied Psychology: An International Review*, vol.45, no.2, pp.146-152.

Tsui, A.S., Pearce, J.L., Porter, L.W. and Tripoli A.M. (1997), 'Alternative approaches to the employee-organization relationship: Does investment in employees pay off?', *Academy of Management Journal*, vol.40, no.5, pp.1089-1121.

Ulrich, D. (1997), *Human resource champions: The next agenda for adding value and delivering results*, Harvard Business School Press, Boston, MA.

Wall Street Journal (1992), 30th December, p.1.

Wright, P.M. and McMahan, G.C. (1992), 'Theoretical Perspectives For Strategic Human Resource Management', *Journal of Management*, vol.18, no.2, pp.295-320.

PART IV
ILLUSTRATIONS OF KOREAN EMPLOYMENT RELATIONS AND HRM SYSTEMS

9 Employment Relations and HRM in Practice: Case Studies

Introduction

This chapter uses actual cases to give a realistic picture of Korean employment relations (ER) in the workplace. Two case studies are described: one unionized and one non-union organization. Both belong to the electronic industry, and are ranked among the 'big three' in the sector in Korea. As shown in Table 9.1, LG Electronics (Case 1) produces an array of electronic household appliances, whereas Samsung SDI (Case 2) specializes in electronic display products. LG Electronics is also bigger than Samsung SDI in terms of size of workforce.

Both companies are considered highly innovative role models in terms of their sophisticated human resource management (HRM) and cooperative ER. They have both received government awards from the Ministry of Labour (the New Labour-Management Standard Award) for their excellent ER in the late 1990s (Kim et al., 2000). Thus, they are well-developed demonstrations of the Korean style of ER. In the following sections each case study company is discussed in terms of organizational characteristics and business strategy, ER, workplace innovations, HRM and organizational performance.[1]

Case 1: LG Electronics (A Unionized Company)[2]

Organizational Characteristics and Business Strategy

LG Electronics was established in January 1958, and has been a front runner in the Korean electronics industry ever since. It produced the first radios in Korea in the 1950s, and subsequently manufactured various household electronic appliances such as TV sets, electric fans, refrigerators and electric washers until the 1970s. From the 1980s on, the main product lines moved from such appliances to digital devices such as PDAs, CD-ROM drives, laptop computers and digital TV sets. Since the late 1990s, LG Electronics has concentrated on three product lines: 1) digital media (VCR, personal computers, CD-ROM drives, audio, cordless phones, VCR tapes, PCB); 2) digital appliances (refrigerators, electric washers, air conditioners, vacuum cleaners, compressors, general motors); and 3) digital display products (TV, PC monitors, CPT, CDT). In other words, the company covers all types of electronic products.

Table 9.1   Descriptions of the two organizations

Companies	Case 1 LG Electronics	Case 2 Samsung SDI
Industry	Electronics	Electronics
Main products	All types of household electronic appliances (VCR, PC, CD-ROM drives, audio, cordless phones, refrigerators, electric washers, vacuum cleaners, air conditioners, TV, PC monitors, CPT and CDT)	Display products (CPT, CDT, LCD and VFD)
Employment size	50,000	21,500
Union status	Unionized	Non-union

LG Electronics employs over 50,000 workers worldwide in 8 domestic plants, 60 overseas production and sales facilities and 39 overseas branches. The overseas businesses have expanded greatly since the 1980s, as illustrated by its acquisition of Zenith (an American-based TV producer) in 1995. Indeed, LG Electronics is one of the global players in the world electronics industry. Its overseas sales (US$78,422 million) were approximately three times domestic sales (US$26,696 million) in 1999.

LG Electronics has three business goals in the 21st century: (1) to concentrate on the most competent and high value-added products to improve profitability (instead of market share) in the global market; (2) to identify and strengthen the firm's four core competencies of marketing, technology, design and networking; and (3) to enhance a performance-oriented corporate culture based on the three core values of innovation, openness and partnership. To accomplish these business goals, LG Electronics has formulated two catchphrases specifying its business strategies. The first of these is 'value creation for customers', which stresses that the satisfaction of internal and external customers is LG Electronics' ultimate goal. The second is 'respect for human assets'. The underlying philosophy of this catchphrase is that satisfied employees are able to satisfy customers. Thus, the maximization of customer and employee satisfaction is the fundamental principle underpinning LG Electronics' business strategy.

ER

The labour union of LG Electronics was first established on May 30, 1963. The union currently has around 12,000 members, and is affiliated to the FKTU. The 40-year history of labour relations in LG Electronics can be divided into the following four stages.

The first stage (1963-1987) was characterized by a unilateral, paternalistic management and a dormant union. The company dominated the employee organization through control-oriented labour policies and various paternalistic personnel practices. Wages and working conditions in LG Electronics were considered superior to its domestic counterparts. Although the union was established in 1963, it was not truly independent of the employer. There was not a single strike during this period.

The second stage (1987-1989), which was influenced by the nationwide strike waves of the Great Labour Struggle in 1987, was dominated by adversarial labour relations. A series of wildcat strikes were initiated by disguised workers (i.e., former radical college students who tried to organize and agitate workers to build up an aggressive union movement) in 1987. Strikers argued that the existing union was a company union, and demanded more autonomy. The wildcat strike in 1987 lasted 9 days and demanded wage increases and humane treatment of employees. A series of further strikes with similar demands continued until 1989 (Kim and Park, 1992). After the strike waves, a more independent and aggressive union leadership was elected, and a period of adversarial labour relations began.

The strikes significantly weakened the company's economic competitiveness as a result of a decrease in sales over this period of approximately 600 billion won and its frequent failures to meet delivery dates. After the strikes LG Electronics' market share was surpassed by that of its nonunionized domestic competitor (i.e., Samsung Electronics). The general impression was that this development was at least partly due to the adversarial nature of labour relations at the time.

Labour-management cooperation characterized the labour relations of the third stage (1990-1994). Both parties were extremely aware of the heavy costs of their previously adversarial approach, and of the urgent need to build up trust. The company announced the principle of people-oriented management, 'respect for human assets'. Labour and management agreed on the new catchphrase 'management who respects employees, employees who understand the business'. Much to the general surprise of observers, 12 union leaders announced in LG's January 1994 TV advertisements that 'we will be responsible for product quality', symbolizing the new cooperative spirit of labour relations.

Although such labour-management cooperation was retained at the affective and attitudinal level, the next period (1995-present day) saw both parties make an effort to establish a more structural and institutionalized level of union participation. This fourth stage was characterized by the term 'labour-management partnership'. The union voluntarily initiated and participated in various workplace innovations, initiating actions such as quality improvement, productivity enhancement and problem-solving programs. It also began to participate in managing the workplace. For example, union officers were included as members of the company's promotion committees, and the self-managing work teams introduced in 1995 were run by representatives of both management and labour.

The labour-management partnership of LG Electronics seemed to help the company successfully overcome the 1997-1998 financial crisis.[3] The sudden and sharp decline in demand for products resulting from the crisis forced the company to close down its less profitable business units and to reduce the size of the workforce. The company and union agreed on the introduction of early retirement programs with monetary incentives, and employees submitted their retirement applications to the union, not the firm. Eventually, 500 union members (i.e., mostly production workers), and approximately 1,000 office and technical employees accepted early retirement packages. Whereas many Korean companies (e.g., Daewoo Motor, Hyundai Motor and Korea Telecom) had suffered from extreme labour disputes in the process of employment reduction, there were no strikes over such issues in LG Electronics. When wage bargaining began during the financial crisis, the union accepted the company's initial offer without further negotiations in order to help it survive the temporary financial distress. Needless to say, trust and partnership between labour and management led to such non-competitive behaviour.

Workplace Innovations

From 1995, LG Electronics implemented the TPC (Total Productivity Control) and TPM (Total Production Maintenance) programs to enhance productivity. The Six Sigma program, a more comprehensive process innovation, was introduced in 1996. Six Sigma refers to the measuring, analysing, improving and controlling of business processes until they are near to perfection. The fundamental objective of the methodology is the implementation of a measurement-based strategy that focuses on process improvement. Six Sigma perfection means a quality level with no more than 3.4 errors per million opportunities. It started as a statistical tool to improve product quality, but has now become a total management tool and philosophical method for changing corporate culture.

In LG Electronics, the Six Sigma program was implemented with the full cooperation of union leadership, and made rapid progress. In 1996, there were 22 company specialists in Six Sigma, and 9 Six Sigma projects were successfully accomplished. In 1997, the concept was extended to the R&D area, and the number of defects in new models decreased by 70 per cent. By 1998, Six Sigma was being applied to all the company's work processes and in 1999, a quality level of 4.1 sigma, a very high standard, was reached. The Six Sigma program enabled the completion of a total of 1,662 projects and saved 133.3 billion won of production costs in 1999.

LG Electronics also adopted the Six Sigma program's quality certification system ('belt system') in order to build up its roster of quality specialists with problem-solving abilities. There are 4 stages in the belt system: master black belt (MBB, the highest quality specialist), black belt (BB), green belt (GB) and white belt (WB). The Six Sigma program in LG Electronics produced 56 specialists with MBBs and 159 with BBs. In 2000, LG Electronics acquired the Underwriters Laboratories (UL) quality marks as a result of the success of its Six Sigma program.

Another innovation from LG Electronics was its adoption of self-managing teams in 1995 by benchmarking high performance work organizations in the U.S. such as Saturn, NUMMI, Motorola and Xerox. LG was one of the first Korean companies to reorganize based on the concept of self-management. As the life cycle of electronic goods becomes shorter and customers want more diverse products, a mass production system is regarded as too rigid and burdensome because of its high initial set-up costs. Self-managing teams based upon cell manufacturing, and a multi-skilled labour force which can modify lines very easily and quickly with cheaper set-up costs, are one response to this challenge.

In the self-managing teams deployed in the Kumi plant (called the Tuk-Tak system) four multi-skilled production workers in modular-cell systems conducted the whole process of production including assembly, inspection, maintenance and packaging. These self-managing teams produced custom-tailored large TV sets, which constitute highly value-added, non-standardized products. The approach was shown to improve productivity and decrease production time. After self-managing teams had been introduced, the number of TV sets produced per employee increased from 3.13 to 5.13 (64 per cent) and unit production time decreased from 102 minutes to 32.6 minutes (66 per cent). In the Pyung-Tack plant, self-managing teams (called Barobaro teams) produced laptop computers in a cell production process. The teams conducted problem solving, process improvement, production planning and assembly. The evidence showed that after their introduction there were clear improvements in the areas of occupational safety and health, productivity, quality and employee morale and satisfaction.

HRM

LG Electronics launched the Knowledge-building Committee in November 1989 to build a learning organization by cultivating a learning culture and enhancing employees' knowledge and skills. A unique feature of the Knowledge-building Committee is the use of the concept of management by objectives (MBO) in promoting knowledge building. That is, individual goals for education and training are set up between supervisors and employees every year, progress is periodically checked and if necessary, the goals modified, and then progress is evaluated at the end of the year. The progress made by each individual is used in promotion decision-making.

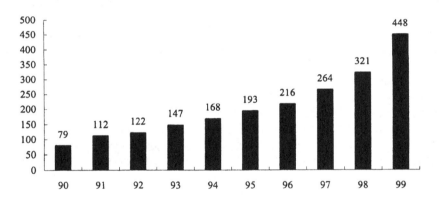

Figure 9.1   Production value per employee, 1990-1999 (in million won)

LG Electronics employs an extensive system of information sharing. Since 1993, three-day joint labour-management workshops have been held twice a year in order to promote open communication between managers and union leaders. Monthly seminars and quarterly committee meetings between labour and management are also held to discuss outstanding issues. All employees participate in discussing current issues in an Open Forum twice a year. The company also operates informal communication channels between junior employees and middle managers (called, respectively, Junior Board and Fresh Board). In addition, there is a 'speak-up' system in which if front-line workers express their voices and concerns to top management, they must receive a response within 15 days. Also, the response must be posted on the intranet bulletin board so that all employees can read it. To eliminate the status barriers between executives and employees and promote its egalitarian philosophy, the company has abolished all preferential practices such as executive-only restaurants and parking lots.

From 1994 on, a merit-based HRM system replaced the traditional seniority-based approach. Whereas traditional promotion had relied heavily on seniority, after the mid-1990s junior employees with excellent potential were promoted to high managerial positions regardless of their length of service. To strengthen union participation in managerial decision-making, union officers were included in promotion committees. Also, blue-collar workers were given the opportunity to be promoted to managerial and executive posts if they passed examinations and showed aptitude. These practices have significantly mitigated the psychological barrier between blue- and white-collar employees in LG Electronics.

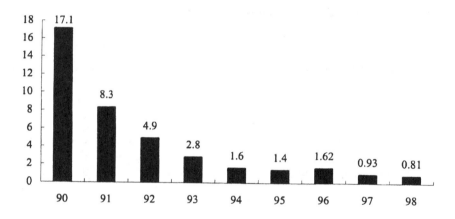

Figure 9.2   Defect rates (TV, VCR, MWO, REF, W/M), 1990-1998 (%)

Various incentive programs are in place to reward superior performance and attract talented employees. A profit-sharing program based upon economic value-added (EVA, which is after-tax profits minus the opportunity costs of capital) was launched in 1999. Profit sharing provides employees with a company-wide bonus based on a portion of company EVA when it exceeds a predetermined level. Merit bonuses up to 1-year salary are paid for excellent performance. Promising employees are given company stock to improve loyalty and identity. In order to recruit promising talent from the external labour market, a signing bonus system was adopted. Finally, to enhance motivation for self-directed learning, monthly incentives are provided for quality specialists with MBBs, BBs, GBs and WBs under the Six Sigma system.

Organizational Performance

The labour-management partnership is believed to have led to the significant enhancement of various organizational outcomes. As shown in Figure 9.1, between 1990-1999 productivity increased on average by 20 per cent every year. That is, the value of production per employee rose from 79 million won in 1990 to 448 in 1999, an almost 6-fold increase in 9 years. The defect rate for 5 main products (TV, VCR, MWO, REF and W/M) decreased from 17.1 in 1990 to 0.81 in 1998 (see Figure 9.2). At the same time, occupational accident rates in LG Electronics fell from 0.24 in 1991 to 0.076 in 1999. These ratios were much lower than the industry average. For example, in 1998 the average accident rate in the electronics industry was 0.88, whereas that in LG Electronics was only 0.099 (see Table 9.2).

Table 9.2   Occupational accident rates, 1991-1999 (%)

Years	1991	1992	1993	1994	1995	1996	1997	1998	1999
LG Electronics	0.24	0.09	0.10	0.10	0.13	0.15	0.15	0.099	0.076
Industry Average	1.61	1.52	1.30	1.18	0.98	0.88	0.81	0.88	-

The increase in productivity and decrease in defects and accidents resulted in a steady sales increase. As shown in Figure 9.3, sales rose from 2,605 billion won in 1989 to 10,327.2 billion won in 1999, a four-fold increase. At the same time, profits continued to increase from 316 billion won in 1998, to 338.1 billion won in 1999, and to 927.3 billion won in 2000.

In telephone interviews with the first author of this book in August 2002, both the senior labour relations manager, Manjin Han, and the union president, Seok-Chun Chang, mentioned that they had no doubt that the cooperative nature of labour relations at LG and the extent of union participation had made significant contributions to the persistent improvement in organizational performance which LG had enjoyed despite the 1997-1998 nationwide economic crisis. Whereas non-union management seemed to be the norm in the high-tech electronics industry (as shown in the cases of IBM, HP, Motorola, Samsung Electronics and Samsung SDI) the interaction of labour and management at LG Electronics illustrated that a unionized company in the electronics industry was able to compete with or even outperform their nonunionized competitors.

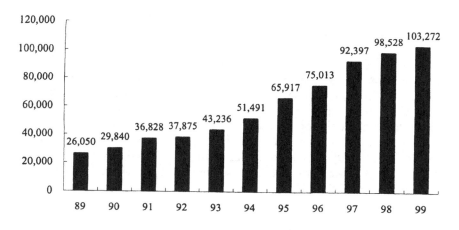

Figure 9.3 Sales trend, 1989-1999 (in 100 million won)

Case 2: Samsung SDI (A Non-union Establishment)

Organizational Characteristics and Business Strategy

Samsung SDI is a non-union company with a thirty-year history. As at summer 2002, it had the biggest share of the world market for CPT (Color Picture Tubes) and CDT (Color Display Tubes), and the second biggest market shares for LCD (Liquid Crystal Displays) and VFD (Vacuum Fluorescent Displays). Samsung SDI has three plants in Korea and 9 overseas plants, and employs approximately 21,500 people including 7,700 in domestic plants and 13,800 in overseas plants.

The case study outlined here focuses on the Pusan plant, one of the company's three domestic plants. Pusan employed approximately 7,400 workers as at September 2002 (4,100 regular and 3,300 contingent employees), and manufactured CPT, CDT, LCD and VFD. The vision of Samsung SDI is to be a 'True Leader in the Digital World'. Specifically, it aims to be the best and largest company in the display products market within 10 years by acquiring the biggest market share in four products: CRT (Cathode Ray Tube), PDP (Plasma Display Panel), mobile display products and batteries.

Competition in the display products market has been intense, and is heavily influenced by rapid technological development. Samsung SDI's main competitors in the CRT market are Phillips, Sony, Hitachi, Toshiba and LG Electronics, whereas in the LCD market they are up against Epson and

Motorola. In the VFD market, two Japanese manufacturers, Futaba and Noritake, are the main players. Whereas Samsung SDI has previously focused on the mass production of low value-added products, its current business strategy is to produce highly value-added, diverse display products. The core competencies involved in obtaining competitive advantage in the high-end market are agility, responsiveness, leading-edge technology and the ability to provide a whole array of products (i.e., total solutions). To ensure it can deploy these strategic tools, Samsung SDI has made substantial investments in research and development for leading-edge products and built up a staff of multi-skilled knowledge workers. For example, in Samsung SDI 10 per cent of all employees work for the R&D sector, and approximately 6 per cent of revenue is spent in this business area.

ER

Few unions exist among the dozens of companies in the Samsung business group, and Samsung SDI is no exception. The non-union policy was heavily influenced by the founding father of the group, Lee Byung Chul. In some sense, Samsung SDI can be considered as a doctrinaire non-union company, because it attempts to maintain its non-union status at any cost (Foulkes, 1980).[4] Samsung SDI operates one of the most active forms of non-union employee representation in Korea, along with POSCO.

Whereas the Pusan plant has traditionally had the worst record of ER of the company's three domestic plants, the situation has improved considerably since the late 1990s. The history of ER in Samsung SDI can be divided into four stages.

The first stage (1970-1986) was characterized by employer-dominated labour relations. From the early 1970s, an employees' council was established to improve working conditions and deal with grievances and complaints. One of its underlying purposes was to prevent the emergence of radical and aggressive unionism. It was an employer-dominated organization, because the company actually appointed council officers and members without genuine input from its employees. Thus, the works council did not truly represent the concerns and interests of rank and file members, and the majority of lower-level employees neither trusted it nor participated in its activities.

The second stage (1987-1996) was characterized by the eruption of a large-scale wildcat strike and a subsequent period of adversarial labour relations. The stage kicked off in 1987 with a 13-day wildcat strike (August 28 through September 10), influenced by the nationwide waves of labour disputes during the Great Labour Struggle of the same year. Strikers demanded higher wages, better working conditions and an autonomous labour unions to replace the company-dominated employees' council.

As a result of this, the worst strike in the history of Samsung SDI, a labour-management committee (LMC) was established in 1988. Although the LMC is not a union, it functions in a similar way. That is, employees directly elect labour representatives to the LMC, including four full-time officers. The LMC handles employee grievances and complaints and acts as a forum for labour and management to conduct annual wage bargaining. The labour representatives of the LMC are considered much more autonomous than the members of the previous employees' council.

The establishment of the autonomous LMC in 1988 signalled the beginning of bilateral and adversarial labour relations in the Pusan plant, and more professional management of the process. In particular, responding to the aggression of labour, the company formulated and implemented a 'new human resource system' (NHRS) in 1995 in order to improve employee satisfaction by enhancing working conditions and improving employment security. The key features of the NHRS included: (1) personnel management based upon fairness; (2) the highest level of compensation and fringe benefits in the industry; (3) a guarantee of almost lifetime employment for employees; (4) extensive training and education; and (5) performance-based HRM in terms of staffing, promotion and compensation. Since the mid-1990s, the NHRS has been regarded as a symbol of Samsung-style non-union management. It seems to have been successful in improving employee satisfaction and calming the more aggressive demands of the labour force.

The third stage (1997-1998) represented a crisis for the NHRS when it was challenged by the Asian economic emergency. During this period, Samsung SDI had to rationalize its business lines and labour force. In spring 1998, approximately 50 middle-level managers in the Pusan plant took early retirement, which was regarded as a *de facto* layoff program. Furthermore, through the extensive usage of outsourcing and subcontracting, the number of regular production workers in the Pusan plant decreased from approximately 7,000 to 5,000. Wages were cut by approximately 10 per cent and some fringe benefits such as summer vacation allowances were abolished or temporarily restricted.

Such employment restructuring and worsening of working conditions were determined unilaterally by management without the full consensus of the labour representatives on the LMC who, together with employees, opposed the measures. Several demonstrations were held in front of the Seoul headquarters of Samsung SDI. The weakening of the principle of guaranteed employment was viewed by employees as a failure of the NHRS. After these incidents, labour relations in the plant rapidly deteriorated and the number of grievances rose substantially while employees' commitment and loyalty to the company declined.

The deterioration in labour relations was followed by a sudden increase in the defect rate in 1997 (see Figure 9.4). This, taken with the depression that followed the financial crisis, seemed to result in a decrease in sales and consequent financial loss in 1997, as shown in Figures 10.6 and 10.7. This was the first time in the history of Samsung SDI that a loss had been made. Furthermore, rumour spread that head office were considering closing down the Pusan plant and moving the production facility to China where there were no serious labour problems.

However, the fourth stage (1999 – present day) was characterized by labour-management cooperation. The previous round of labour disputes led both sides to realize the costs of adversarial labour relations and recognize the urgent need for more cooperative and participative labour relations to overcome the competitiveness crisis. In particular, the company actively initiated the promotion of information sharing, trust building and partnership between labour and management. Since 1999, labour and management have jointly drawn up a new set of 'rules of the game' including (1) an employment guarantee agreement, (2) an expanded role for the LMC and (3) profit sharing. In March 1999, an agreement was reached that there would be no further employment reduction without the consent of the labour representatives on the LMC. A series of labour-management joint seminars was also held in order to set up a task force to bring about a greater degree of information sharing and employee participation. Finally, labour and management agreed to implement profit sharing. This provided employees with company-wide bonuses based on a portion of company EVA when it exceeded a predetermined level. Both the general manager of the plant, Lee Jung-Hwa, and the chair of the LMC labour representatives, Dae-Chul Park, agreed that the labour-management cooperation agreement of 2000 had made a great contribution to the subsequent improvement in labour relations within the plant.

Labour-management cooperation in the non-union Pusan plant mainly takes place through the LMC. The overall, plant-level LMC has 3 department-level sub-LMCs. The plant LMC has 66 members (33 employee and 33 company representatives, including a labour chairperson and a management chairperson). It has five sub-committees to deal with grievances, health and safety, research and statistics, employee welfare and recreation. The LMC holds a meeting once every two months to discuss various topics such as employee benefits, discipline, education and training plans and handling and resolving grievances. More importantly, the LMC conducts wage bargaining, and produces a non-union labour agreement. The labour agreement does not have the legal protections prescribed by labour law and is regarded as a gentlemen's agreement. However, no party has yet violated its provisions.

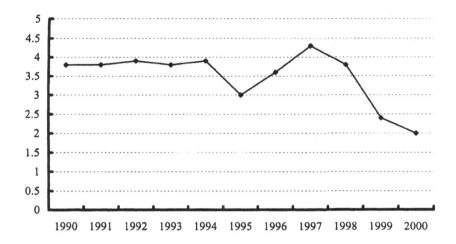

Figure 9.4   Defect rates, 1990-2000 (%)

Alongside these practices, the HRM department in Samsung SDI relies on various approaches to maintain its non-union status such as communicating the non-union philosophy, practicing sophisticated and fair HRM, and improving employees' job satisfaction and organizational commitment. The company continues to invest heavily in HRM: the size of the department is believed to be much larger than that of its unionized counterparts and, indeed, to be among the largest in the electronics industry as a whole.

Workplace Innovations

Workplace innovations at Samsung SDI began in the 1970s with quality circles, and continued through the 1980s with total quality circles, total productive maintenance (TPM) and total productivity innovations (TPI). The ISO 9000 project and process innovations (PI) were introduced in the early 1990s. By the mid-1990s Six Sigma had been adopted in combination with supply chain management (SCM) in logistics, and enterprise resource planning (ERP) in MIS. Since then Six Sigma has symbolized workplace innovation in Samsung SDI.

In the process of implementing Six Sigma, Samsung SDI extensively benchmarked other programs in Motorola, Citibank, Saturn and Federal Express by visiting the companies and researching their experiences. The Six Sigma program in Samsung SDI has three objectives: (1) to reduce production costs by improving business processes; (2) to accomplish the near total prevention of defects; and (3) to build up the numbers of quality specialists. A quality committee composed of labour representatives of the LMC, managers of the quality department and manufacturing managers, meets monthly. The program is accompanied by an extensive employee suggestion system. Monetary rewards are provided for useful suggestions at the individual- and group-levels (up to US$1000 for individuals and US$10,000 for groups). An average of 5.5 suggestions per employee was implemented between 1998 and 2000.

The positive outcomes of the Six Sigma program are apparent in the various performance indicators. As shown in Figure 9.4, the defect rate decreased sharply from 4.3 in 1997 to 2.0 in 2000, which is at least partially due to Six Sigma. Numerous quality improvement projects have also been conducted under its auspices since 1996: 622 such projects were completed during the 1996-1999 period, and in the first half of 2001 alone a further 69 had been achieved. As shown in Figure 9.5, the level of cost savings has jumped since the first introduction of Six Sigma in the mid-1990s, reaching 4,436 million won in 1999 from 500 million won in 1995.

Samsung SDI established a Six Sigma Academy to educate its employees and build up a roster of quality specialists with problem-solving abilities. Under the quality certification system ('belt system') of Six Sigma, there are four degrees of quality specialists: master black belt (MBB), black belt (BB), green belt (GB) and white belt (WB). The quality certificate is used as an important determinant of promotion. For example, an employee must acquire at least GB to be promoted to assistant manager. If he or she obtains a BB or MBB, more promotion points are accumulated. As a result, all the employees of Samsung SDI have achieved white belts. The number of employees with GBs rose from 710 in 1998 to 1,228 in 1999 and 1,565 in 2000. Thus, approximately 20 per cent of total employees obtained GBs. The number of employees with BBs and MBBs also jumped from 39 in 1999 to 275 in 2000, almost a 7-fold increase in a year.

HRM

In order to be the best producer of highly value-added display products, multi-skilled knowledge workers are indispensable. Samsung SDI spent 3.6 per cent of payroll costs on education and training, a very high percentage even among high-performance firms such as Xerox, NUMMI, Saturn, IBM and Motorola. Samsung SDI not only makes substantial investments in education and training, but also creates incentives to encourage both individual and organizational learning. Under the learning evaluation system, every year each employee sets up learning objectives and learning themes with the consent of his/her supervisor. They then carry out periodic interviews to check progress and discuss what to do to accelerate learning, before a final evaluation by the supervisor at year-end. Based upon the evaluation, employees earn learning points, which are among the factors determining promotion.

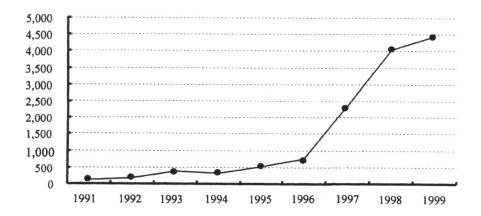

Figure 9.5 Cost savings, 1991-1999 (in million won)

In March 1999, labour and management agreed to implement a profit-sharing program. The profit-sharing program is based upon the concept of EVA: on average 15 per cent of EVA generated above a pre-determined level is paid to employees. Employees receive a different percentage of the EVA depending on the performance of their department. During the 1999-2001 period, individual employees received profit sharing bonuses every year, with the average amount roughly equal to 20 per cent of yearly salary. Project incentives are also provided: if a project generates profits of more than 200 million won (US$167,000) at the department-level or 2 billion won (US$1,670,000) at the company level, all the participants receive cash rewards depending on their contributions to its success.

Samsung SDI is now using a very convenient human resource information system called Personal Decision Support System (PDSS). The PDSS is an intranet database covering all areas of HRM such as recruiting, staffing, education and training, evaluation, compensation and benefits. For example, each employee can enter their opinions and grievances through the intranet, and conduct self-appraisal through the same source. Each employee can also use the intranet to verify the results of their performance appraisal and find details of their salary increase. Of course, all of these processes are confidential and each employee has a unique password. The PDSS greatly reduces the time and red tape involved in processing personnel documents.

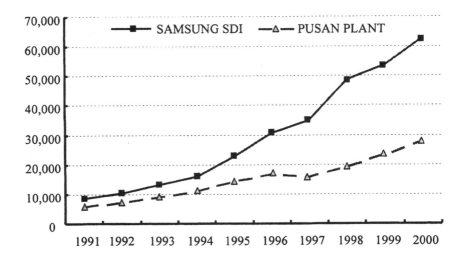

Figure 9.6   Sales trend, 1991-2000 (in 100 million won)

The company uses various methods for information sharing and vertical and horizontal communication. Top managers communicate corporate information and details of the financial situation to all employees in the monthly meeting. Also, the company encourages various less formal meetings, such as brown-bag meetings and cookie meetings and subsidizes their associated expenses. It is noteworthy that Samsung SDI makes extensive use of its intranet for communication between the company and employees. Cyber-bulletin boards on the company home page are heavily used for rapid transmission of corporate information, reports of grievances and complaints and exchanges of opinion about business and employment issues. The use of the intranet for labour-management communication saves a lot of time and effort, and seems to accomplish virtual electronic democracy within the plant.

'Green management' is the catchphrase used in the areas of occupational safety and health and environmental issues. Its goal is to completely prevent occupational accidents, occupational diseases and pollution at the workplace. The company invests 2 per cent of its revenue every year (approximately US$25 billion) in programs for better employee relations and community relations. Consequently, occupational accident rates have remained at very low levels: 0.04 per cent in 1998 and 1999, against the industry average of 0.2 per cent. The company has also received international recognition in the environmental area through the award of BS 7750, BS8800 and ISO 14001.

Organizational Performance

Organizational performance appears to be heavily influenced by the quality of labour relations and the success of workplace innovations. As labour relations deteriorated around the 1997-1998 financial crisis, most indicators of organizational performance declined. As shown in Figure 9.4, the defect rate increased from 3.0 in 1995 to 4.3 in 1997, and sales and profit (which may also have been influenced by the general business downturn) declined for the first time in company history. Specifically, the amount of sales decreased from 1,662.3 billion won in 1996 to 1,554.3 billion won in 1997, and profits were -17.8 billion won in 1996 and -24.9 billion won in 1997 (see figures 10.6 and 10.7).

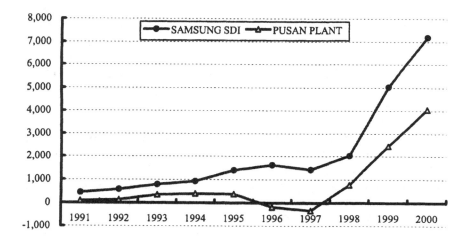

Figure 9.7   Pre-tax profits, 1991-2000 (in 100 million won)

In the subsequent period, the improvement in labour relations was accompanied by a recovery in organizational performance. The defect rate fell steadily from 3.8 per cent in 1998, to 2.4 per cent in 1999 and 2 per cent in 2000. Sales also showed a rapid recovery, increasing from 1,227.3 billion won in 1997 to 2,487.6 billion won in 2000. The company became profitable again in 1998 (e.g., 77.6 billion won in 1998, 245.6 billion won in 1999, and 357.6 billion won in 2000). The improvement in labour relations was followed by a decline in voluntary turnover. The turnover rate of the Pusan plant fell from 1.1 per cent in 1996 and 1997 to 0.7 per cent in 1998 and 1999. Plant managers and labour representatives of the LMC unanimously attributed the recovery in performance to three factors: (1) improved labour relations and labour-management cooperation since 1999; (2) the success of workplace innovations such as the Six Sigma program; and (3) the recovery of the overall economy after the crisis.

Chapter Summary

It is interesting to note that both organizations experienced serious labour disputes (i.e., extreme conflict in the late 1980s in LG Electronics; wildcat strikes in 1988 and 1998 in Samsung SDI), which caused them to modify significantly the basic philosophy and framework of their labour relations. These labour disputes eventually persuaded both parties to choose the path of labour-management cooperation and participation. Both organizations have many similarities: extensive knowledge building, sophisticated HRM, workplace innovations and the use of an employee representation body (i.e., union and non-union employee representation). The two organizations also differ in terms of their union status, the extent to which they utilize employees' knowledge and potential and the fundamental nature of their labour-management relations. Table 9.3 summarizes the main characteristics of the two cases.

The LG Electronics case illustrates one of the most extensive systems of employee and union involvement in any Korean organization. It is one of the rare Korean examples of explicitly benchmarking team systems in U.S. high performance work organizations such as Saturn and Xerox. In the high-tech electronics industry, most of LG's competitors are non-union firms including Samsung Electronics, Samsung SDI, IBM, Motorola and HP. Labour and management in LG Electronics have showed that a unionized company can outperforms its non-union competitors in some areas by making use of the collective voice function of trade unionism. Indeed, compared to its non-union competitors in Korea, LG Electronics has constructed a more comprehensive and effective system of employee and union involvement, and has successfully overcome the financial crisis with the union's full cooperation. However, although LG Electronics shows very active union participation in the workplace level (i.e., the lowest) and the collective bargaining level (i.e., the middle), this is not practiced at the strategic level (i.e., the highest) in processes such as product development, new investment and corporate restructuring. This may be part of the future agenda for labour and management in this company.

Table 9.3   Comparison of the two organizations

Companies	Case 1 LG Electronics	Case 2 Samsung SDI
Business strategy	Providing an array of household electronic appliances	Focusing on high-end electronic display products
Production type	Close to team production emphasizing employee involvement	Close to lean production emphasizing top-down quality programs
ER	Experienced extreme labour disputes in the late 1980s; Union-management partnership based upon union participation	Experienced labour disputes in 1988 and 1998; Non-union employee representation based upon L-M cooperation
Workplace innovations	Six Sigma Self-managing teams	Six Sigma Suggestion systems
HRM	Knowledge-building and learning Various incentive systems Information sharing Merit-based promotion and staffing	Extensive learning and training system Various incentive systems Information sharing Merit-based promotion and staffing

The work organization of Samsung SDI is close to the lean production model, emphasizing TQM, Six Sigma and other management–initiated innovations. The enormous effort and resources invested in workplace innovations and human resources is very impressive. Samsung SDI successfully operates an extensive system of open communication, information sharing and non-union employee representation. Although it has done well to cultivate the attitudinal aspect of labour relations (i.e., labour-management cooperation), the structural and institutional aspects of labour relations (i.e., employee participation through formal mechanisms) are not yet fully developed. Whereas the former is less stable depending on the orientation, commitment and personality of incumbents, the latter is a more secure and stable (and so more desirable) system of employee participation. Specifically, the employee involvement systems at Samsung SDI rely mainly on suggestions and committees, and do not give employees full decision-making responsibility as do self-managing teams. In this sense, employee involvement systems have room to be more active and extensive in the future.

Notes

1　See Kim et al. (2000) for more detailed descriptions of these cases.
2　The authors would like to acknowledge the invaluable contribution of Byung Hoon Lee to this case study.
3　According to a telephone interview with LG Electronics Union President, Seok Chun Chang, on July 22, 2002.
4　According to doctrinaire non-union management, maintaining non-union status is one of a series of explicit management goals, and the management has attempted to achieve this by utilizing a positive approach (e.g., excellent and fair HRM), a negative approach (e.g., discrimination against union activists) or both. Another type of non-union management is philosophy-laden non-union management. Under this regime, sound and superior HRM naturally leads to high satisfaction and low interest in unionism. Thus, in this context non-union status is not a managerial goal, but a natural by-product of excellent HRM (Foulkes, 1980).

References

Foulkes, F.K. (1980), *Personnel Policies in Large Nonunion Companies,* Prentice-Hall, Englewood Cliffs, New Jersey.

Kim, D.-O., Lee, B.H., Kim, H.K. and Cho, N.H. (2000), *Analysis of Exemplary Cases of New Labor-Management Standard,* The Ministry of Labour, Seoul. (In Korean.)

Kim, T.G. and Park, J.S. (1992), *Case Studies of Labor Relations: Focusing on Large Manufacturing Firms,* Korea Labour Institute, Seoul. (In Korean.)

PART V
CONCLUSION

10 Summary and Conclusion: Korean Employment Relations and HRM at the Crossroads

In this chapter, we summarize the main findings and themes of this book, assess the current status of Korean employment relations (ER) and human resource management (HRM) and discuss the prospects for the future. We will then conclude by outlining the policy implications of our findings for the state, employers and the labour force.

Overview of Korean ER and HRM since 1890

Two significant incidents have greatly influenced Korean ER and HRM: the Great Labour Struggle in 1987 and the 1997-1998 Financial Crisis. Both events not only had a profound impact on the socio-economic lives of Koreans, but also functioned as historical junctures that shifted the status quo and opened up new eras for ER and HRM.

ER Through History

Let us first address the characteristics of ER by period. As shown in Figure 10.1, ER systems can be assumed to vary along two key dimensions: (1) the nature and degree of employers' and labour's participation in policy-making and (2) the nature of state labour policy, representing whether the government relies on authoritarian or democratic methods to determine and enforce its labour policy. Based upon these two dimensions, national ER systems may be expected to cluster into one of three systems: state corporatism, pluralism and societal corporatism. We believe that the Korean employment system since the late 19th century has gradually moved from state corporatism, through exploratory pluralism and finally to an experiment with societal corporatism.

Firstly, ER during the pre-1987 period can be characterized by state corporatism. In this framework, the authoritarian state enforces social peace not by co-opting and incorporating but repressing and excluding the autonomous articulation of labour's demands in a situation where the nation lacks the resources to respond effectively and legitimately to these demands

197

within the framework of a liberal democratic society (Schmitter, 1974). As discussed in Chapter 4, for almost a hundred years, from 1890 to 1986, the Japanese military government and successive Korean governments continued to suppress and exclude the autonomous labour movement, although the goals and means of this oppression varied from government to government.

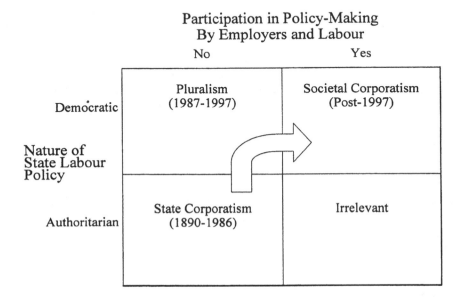

Figure 10.1 Characteristics of ER by period

Secondly, after the Great Labour Struggle in 1987 that awakened Korean workers and led them to form an unprecedentedly aggressive labour movement, the state increasingly realized the limitations of its traditional, authoritarian policies and made the effort to seek out an alternative paradigm. These attempts resulted in experiments with pluralism during the 1987-1996 period along with the income policy and central wage bargaining of 1993 and 1994. Although not all of these experiments resulted in the intended outcomes, we believe that the 1987-1996 period can be best characterized by the term exploratory pluralism.

Finally, the Korean industrial relations system had not yet stabilized when the sudden financial crisis of 1997 took place and all parties experienced serious conflicts and hardships. It is noteworthy that ER actors attempted to effect a transformation from authoritarian corporatism to democratic corporatism in the wake of the crisis. Needless to say, the crisis consciousness of the time greatly facilitated the formation of the Tripartite

Commission. Although the early success of democratic corporatism (i.e., the Social Compact agreed by the three parties in February 1998) played a big part in helping the country overcome the financial crunch, the effectiveness of the Commission since then has been questionable. Its early success and subsequent malfunctioning seem to reflect the current problems and difficulties that are affecting ER in Korea. That is, the vestiges of authoritarian corporatism, an overly aggressive labour movement and the deeply entrenched hostility of employers all inhibited the Tripartite Commission's effective functioning.

HRM Through History

As with ER, the characteristics of HRM were also affected by two major incidents. HRM systems can be classified along two dimensions: (1) evaluation and remuneration and (2) resourcing and flexibility (see Figure 10.2). The first dimension represents whether firms use seniority or performance/ability as the basis of evaluation and remuneration. The second dimension denotes whether firms pursue internal labour markets and long-term attachments, or numerical flexibility. Based on these dimensions, Korean HRM systems, we propose, have shifted from 'seniority-based HRM' (pre-1987) through 'performance-based HRM' (1987-1996) to the current 'flexibility-based HRM' (post-1997).

Firstly, HRM systems pre-1987 can be characterized as seniority-based. Under this system, seniority played a critical role in HRM-related decisions such as recruitment, promotion, evaluation and pay and termination. In addition, given the undeveloped nature of external labour markets, firms relied more on internal movement, so mass recruitment from new graduates was the preferred strategy. Flexibility was pursued through functional mobility within firms and also attrition. Such seniority-based HRM systems functioned well until the mid-1980s. However, the rapid increase in wages, the inefficiency of systems and low productivity made it impossible for firms to gain their competitive advantage through their people.

Secondly, after the 1987 Great Labour Struggle, firms started to adopt new HRM (*sininsa*) systems to enhance fairness, rationalization and efficiency. During this period (1987-1996), while there was little adjustment on the resourcing and flexibility dimension, the evaluation and remuneration dimension shifted from the seniority to the mixed approach by bringing in some performance/ability factors. As explained in Chapter 8, Korean firms experimented with various new HRM practices. Hence, the HRM of this period is best characterized as involving exploratory performance-based systems.

Finally, HRM systems of post-1997 are best described as flexibility-based. While many large corporations weathered the 1997 financial crisis, some *chaebols* (e.g., Hanbo, Halla, Sammi and Kia) went bankrupt before and after it. Under the crisis, such large firms launched massive restructuring efforts to rearrange their operations around core businesses and to withdraw from non-core businesses (e.g., M&A, management buyout, spin- or split-off, outsourcing, debt for equity swap, downsizing and early retirement programs). Under these circumstances, Korean government and firms pursued enhanced labour market flexibility. At the same time, the evaluation and remuneration dimension also shifted further toward performance/ability factors after the crisis, as shown in Figure 10.2.

Evaluation and Remuneration

		Seniority	Mixed	Performance and Ability
Resourcing and Flexibility	Internal Labor Market and Long-term Attachment	Traditional Seniority-based HRM (Pre-1987) →	Exploratory Performance-based HRM (1987-1996) ↘	
	Dual Approach (Core vs. Peripheral)		Exploratory Flexibility-based HRM (Post-1997)	
	High Numerical Flexibility			

Figure 10.2   Characteristics of HRM systems by period

Figure 10.3 summarizes the characteristics of both ER and HRM systems by period. However, our intention is not to propose clear-cut and distinctive features for each period, nor to suggest that most firms/unions adopted similar systems as those outlined here. Rather we seek to delineate the main aspects of change in ER/HRM systems according to period. The direction, scope and speed of change were actually not identical.

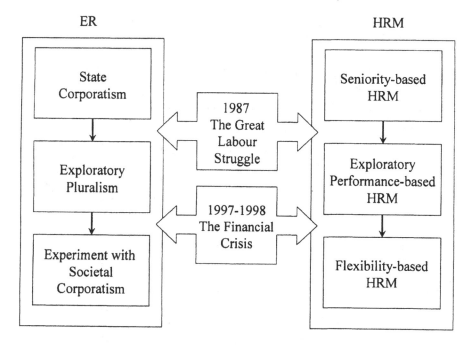

Figure 10.3   Characteristics of ER and HRM by period

Outstanding Issues in ER

In the following sections, we will discuss the outstanding issues in ER. These issues include: (1) the excessive level of labour disputes in recent years; (2) the under-institutionalization of collective bargaining; and (3) disputes over basic labour rights.

Excessive Level of Labour Disputes in Recent Years

Korean ER are well known as having an adversarial and conflict-oriented nature. In some countries, ER are considered to be one of the factors contributing to economic success, such as co-determination and participative approaches in Germany and Sweden and labour-management cooperation in Japan. However, the hostile labour relations and excessive number of labour disputes in Korea in recent years are regarded as a main obstacle to the economic development and upgrading of the country. The serious and potentially explosive 'labour problems' in Korea has been recognized by foreign observers (Wilkinson, 1994) as well as domestic experts (Kim, 1993), and seem to have been further exacerbated by disputes over employment restructuring drives following the crisis.

Table 10.1   Workdays lost due to strikes and lockouts per 1,000 employees

Year	Korea	Japan	Taiwan	Australia	France	Germany	U.S.A.
1985	7.9	6.1	0	225.0	50.3	1.5	74.9
1986	8.5	5.8	0	241.6	59.0	1.2	122.4
1987	755.8	5.8	0.3	220.9	54.6	1.4	45.0
1988	562.0	3.8	1.6	266.4	69.2	1.8	43.0
1989	611.3	4.7	4.3	184.1	43.8	4.1	164.2
1990	409.8	3.0	0.1	209.1	27.6	14.6	57.0
1991	286.8	1.9	0	249.0	25.8	4.6	44.6
1992	131.5	4.5	2.4	147.4	18.7	47.1	38.5
1993	110.9	2.2	0	99.5	26.8	18.3	37.9
1994	120.4	1.6	0	75.6	26.2	7.1	46.5
1995	30.7	1.4	7.5	78.8	40.4	7.7	52.4
1996	68.4	0.8	0.4	131.4	22.8	3.1	43.7
1997	33.6	2.0	-	75.1	19.8	1.6	36.7
1998	119.1	1.9	-	72.1	17.1	0.5	40.6
1999	109.1	1.6	-	86.9	-	2.4	15.5
2000	144.1	0.7	-	60.5	-	0.3	155.0

Source: Korea Labour Institute (2000) *Overseas Labour Statistics.*

As shown in Table 10.1, the number of workdays lost due to strikes and lockouts per 1000 employees in Korea has exceeded that of other major economies in most of the years since 1987. Whereas the number of workdays lost declined in the late 1990s in other countries, in Korea they increased and indeed reached another peak (i.e., 119.1 days in 1998, 109.1 days in 1999, and 144.1 days in 2000). That is, the number of workdays lost per 1,000 employees in Korea in 1999 was more than 200 times greater than Germany and Taiwan and more than 60 times greater than in Japan. Consequently, the direct cost of strikes in Korea, assuming other factors to be equal, currently seems to be the highest of the major economies.

Foreign observers also give Korean ER a very low rating. For example, the International Institute for Management Development (IMD) based in Switzerland consistently rates the competitiveness of Korean ER systems very poorly. That is, Korea was ranked 41st among 46 countries in 1997, 46th among 47 countries in 1999 and 47th among 49 countries in 2002 (IMD, Various years).

As economic competition among nations intensifies, the advantage conferred by participative management and labour-management cooperation becomes more and more important. However, the 'strike-proneness' and excessive level of labour disputes has certainly hurt the competitiveness of the Korean economy in overseas markets in recent years. Thus, one of the most urgent tasks for the three actors in ER is to devise an employment system that at least does not hinder, if it cannot enhance, national economic competitiveness.

Under-institutionalization of Collective Bargaining

A related issue is the under-institutionalized nature of ER, which is closely related to the illegality of labour disputes and the imprisonment of union activists in Korea. As shown in Table 10.2, illegal strikes constitute a substantial portion of all strikes in Korea. Since 1987 when 94.1 per cent of the 3,749 strikes held were illegal, the proportion of illegal actions had steadily decreased to 14.9 per cent in 1995. However, this increased again after the 1997 financial crisis, reaching 48.0 per cent in 1999.

Illegal strikes are not unique to Korea. Indeed, they take place in other countries such as Sweden (Korpi, 1981), the U.S. (Ichniowski, 1988; Olson, 1986), Canada (Hebdon, 1998) and Taiwan (Wilkinson, 1994). In the U.S. and Canada, illegal strikes have taken place mainly in the public sector, and account for only a small portion of the total number of strikes (Hendon, 1998; Ichniowski, 1988; Olson, 1986). However, illegal work stoppages in Korea occur in the private sector, mainly involve the violation of procedural rules, and account for a substantial portion of the total number of strikes.

Furthermore, successive Korean governments have imprisoned labour activists mainly for conducting illegal strikes. Among the 104 workers who were in prison as of July 2001, 54.8 per cent (57 of 104 workers) had been sentenced for the violation of procedural rules such as violating the order of the Regional Labour Relations Commission to stop labour disputes and illegally occupying the public roads. Twenty-six per cent (27 of 104) had been involved in violence during labour disputes such as throwing fire bottles. Ten per cent (10 of 104) had been imprisoned because of their involvement in the communist movement (The Korea Labour Daily News, 7/12/2001).

We believe that two main reasons for the proliferation of illegal strikes and the resultant imprisonment of labour leaders are: (1) very restrictive labour laws and government policies repressing strike activities and (2) a lack of respect for the labour laws among labour leaders. That is, the Korean labour laws use a very restricted definition of legal strikes. In order to satisfy them, each strike has to go through a majority vote in a secret ballot, and a mandatory mediation procedure is required before it can go ahead. Workers can strike only to address immediate economic matters, so strikes over other issues such as grievances, downsizing and unpopular government policies are all considered illegal. Also, in organizations performing 'essential public service' strikes are virtually banned. That is, the definition of illegal strikes in Korea is much broader than that used in other OECD countries.

Table 10.2   Statistics on illegal strikes in Korea

Year	Number of strikes[a]	Number of illegal strikes[b]	Ratio of illegal strikes to total strikes (%)
1987	3,749	3,529	94.1
1988	1,873	1,491	79.6
1989	1,616	1,107	68.5
1990	322	183	56.8
1991	234	93	39.7
1992	235	84	35.7
1993	144	35	24.3
1994	121	43	35.5
1995	88	13	14.9
1996	85	13	15.2
1997	78	17	21.7
1998	129	55	42.6
1999	198	95	48.0
2000	250	67	26.8
2001	235	55	23.4

Sources:
[a]   Korea Labour Institute (2001) *KLI Labour Statistics*.
[b]   Ministry of Labour (2002) Internal Documents.

Labour activists believe that the laws are unreasonably restrictive. They believe that conduct which is illegal in Korea would be legal in most OECD countries, and argue that the laws on striking are neither legitimate nor fair. Because labour leaders believe that strikers have been unfairly victimized by a state that still retains traces of its previous adherence to authoritarian corporatism, there is a widespread tendency among them to disrespect the law.

The government attempts to prevent illegal strikes by making the penalties for doing so harsh enough to discourage people from taking part. This has so far failed to reduce the number of illegal strikes. On the contrary, it seems that enforcing harsh penalties such as imprisonment of leaders and enormous fines for unions and strikers actually makes people feel the unfairness of the system more acutely, increases the bitterness of labour-state conflicts, results in the further radicalization of the labour movement, and actually increases the likelihood of there being an illegal strike in the next round of bargaining. Thus, the harsh labour laws and penalties for strikers seem to act as the starting point of a vicious circle. To summarize, the proliferation of illegal strikes indicates the inability of the legal system to resolve employees' discontent and the under-institutionalization of labour movement. Arresting this vicious circle is another urgent task for the three actors of ER.

Disputes over Basic Labour Rights

Since the early 1990s, when Korea joined the ILO and OECD, disputes over the guaranteeing of basic labour rights have intensified. The relevant issues include: (1) the right of government employees and college professors to organize and bargain collectively; (2) the reduction of legal working hours from 44 to 40 hours per week; (3) the universal prohibition of work stoppages at organizations performing public services; (4) disputes over employers' payment of the salaries of full-time union officers; and (5) the prohibition of multiple unions at a workplace. We will describe these issues in turn.

First, the right of government employees to organize and bargain collectively has not yet been recognized in Korea. Although works councils for government employees were allowed by the Social Compact in February 1998, these councils do not have the right to bargain or strike. Some groups of government employees have sought to form genuine unions, and indeed two illegal (that is, not recognized by the government) such unions are currently operating and from time to time initiate illegal strikes.

Similarly, professors' unions are not legally permitted in Korea, although teachers' unionism (covering elementary, middle and high school teachers) was legalized in 1999. A substantial minority of college professors have showed a keen interest in unionism, forming the Korean Professors Union in the fall of 2001. However, this is not recognized under current labour laws, and thus remains technically illegal.

Second, despite the steady reduction in working hours in Korea since the mid-1980s, the average number of hours worked (i.e., 47.5 hours per week in 2000) is still the longest of OECD member countries. Although the government and labour leaders have attempted to revise the Labour Standards Act to shorten the legal working hours from 44 to 40 hours per week, the attempt has not been successful mainly due to the strong opposition of employer groups. The Tripartite Commission was equally unable to reach an agreement on the nationwide implementation of such a reduction. Currently, the 40-hour workweek is practiced only in the banking industry as a result of a voluntary collective bargaining agreement between labour and management in that sector. It is uncertain whether the shorter workweek will be implemented more widely in the near future.

Third, current labour laws severely limit the right to strike at organizations performing 'essential public services', such as public transportation, public utilities, electricity and gas, banking, public broadcasting, medical services, petroleum refining and telecommunications. In these organizations, strikes are virtually prohibited and compulsory arbitration is required in most cases. Both the FKTU and the KCTU have argued that the definition of 'essential public services' is too broad and infringes the constitutional right to collective action. The government and employers argue that narrowing the definition is likely to worsen the problem of excessive labour disputes. Although labour interests have insisted on the modification of this provision, it is unlikely that they will succeed in the near future due to the opposition of the government and employers.

Fourth and fifth, current labour laws do not allow multiple unionism at the enterprise level. Although the multiple unionism was agreed upon as part of the Social Compact in February 1998 and subsequent enactment was complete, the effective dates were postponed to January 2007. Also, the payment of full-time union officers' salaries (who remain at the same time employees of the company) by employers will be prohibited from January 2007. Both employers and labour are paying keen attention to these issues, because both provisions may have a substantial impact on the power relationships between labour and employers in the workplace.

In general, labour centers (both the FKTU and the KCTU), supported by international organizations such as the ILO, the OECD and the ICFTU (International Confederation of Free Trade Unions), have argued that Korean labour practices fall short of international standards and the labour laws should be revised immediately to guarantee the rights discussed above. On the other hand, the government and employers' organizations such as the KEF have asserted that given the stage of economic development that Korea has reached and the extremely aggressive nature of the labour movement, improvement of these basic rights will give labour too much power and result in excessive labour disputes, which will diminish Korea's economic competitiveness still further. The position taken by the government and employers has been that although basic labour rights should eventually be provided, employers need some time to adjust to the changes, and these rights should be granted on a step-by-step basis.

Policy Implications for ER

Among all the OECD member countries, the 'labour problems' in Korea seem to be among the most acute and serious. First of all, the relationships between the three actors are so tense and adversarial that one can hardly even find comparable examples among other OECD member countries. These antagonistic relationships seem to make it impossible to improve the competitiveness of the current ER system, so any attempts to reform it may have to start by improving and cultivating these relationships. We believe that the ER system in Korea is currently confronting two key tasks: (1) in the short term, reducing the adversarialism of ER; and (2) in the longer term, enhancing the competitiveness of the ER system by adopting high performance work systems. In the following sections, we will discuss the policy implications for the government, labour and employers in turn.

Implications for the Government

In terms of the labour laws, we recommend that the government should revise the legal framework so it becomes comparable to the labour standards recommended by the ILO, OECD and ICFTU. As mentioned in Chapter 5, after Korea joined the ILO in 1991 and the OECD in 1996, successive Korean governments were subject to international pressure to improve labour standards. In the process of joining the OECD, the Korean government even made a formal commitment to reform the existing laws and regulations on ER in line with internationally accepted standards such as freedom of association and collective bargaining. The issues under consideration include the establishment of multiple unions in a single workplace, the right of government employees to organize, the right to strike in organizations performing public services, trade union membership of dismissed or unemployed workers, payment by companies of their full-time union officials, a very strict definition of legal strikes, and the imprisonment of unionists for union activities.

Everyone seems to appreciate that the current labour standards fall short of international standards, and that this is why unions doubt the legitimacy and fairness of current legal provisions and publicly defy the authority of the law. It is recommended that the government relax the legal restrictions on the above issues to bring the legal framework into line with other OECD countries. After this legal reform, it may become easier for the government to enforce the law on illegal union activities with legitimacy and authority.

Although the Korean government has a long tradition of suppressing the labour movement, it has increasingly lost its control over labour and employers since the 1987 Great Labour Struggle. Perhaps due to its history of state corporatism, however, the government still shows a tendency to intervene heavily in private sector labour disputes. Since many of the union activities during such disputes are technically illegal, the government (i.e., the police and regional offices of the Ministry of Labour) has to be involved in order to regulate illegal behaviour. However, one undesirable consequence of such excessive state intervention is the weakening of autonomous collective bargaining between labour and management. In many cases, labour disputes result in labour-state conflicts (i.e., between strikers and the police) and employers play only a minor role in concluding the dispute. The KCTU has argued that in some extreme cases employers do not bargain in good faith, knowing this will lead to a bargaining impasse and an illegal work stoppage, and then wait for state intervention. For voluntary collective bargaining to function properly, it would be desirable for the government to provide more room for discussion between labour and management by limiting its intervention. In this sense, the above-mentioned labour law reform (e.g., relaxing the strict definition of legal strikes) would also help.

It is important to find ways to actively utilize the Tripartite Commission. Since the Social Compacts in January 1998, the Tripartite Commission has failed to produce any agreements. Although a few important items were discussed in the Tripartite Commission such as permission for government employees to join unions and the reduction of working hours, these issues were not agreed upon. In order to ameliorate the antagonistic relationships between the three actors, the importance of the Tripartite Commission as a communication channel among parties cannot be overemphasized.

One reason for the malfunctioning of the Tripartite Commission is the non-participation of the KCTU after its withdrawal from the commission in February 1999. Because the KCTU represents a substantial segment of the labour movement (i.e., approximately 40 per cent of all union members in Korea), its absence from the Commission greatly weakens its representativeness and legitimacy. Thus, in order for the Commission to function effectively, the first step should be to persuade the KCTU to rejoin. However, it is not desirable for the Tripartite Commission to become yet another mechanism for state intervention in private sector labour relations. Most importantly, reconstructing voluntary and autonomous collective bargaining is an important aspect of reforming ER in Korea. Thus, as far as operating the Commission is concerned, it may be more constructive for the government to play only a mediator role, arbitrating the relationship between labour and employer groups.

Implications for Unions

The labour movement in Korea is divided into two streams. The FKTU, with a membership of approximately 850,000, represents a more conservative, economic unionism with a keen interest in 'bread and butter' issues, whereas the KCTU, with approximately 650,000 members, stands for a more progressive and aggressive unionism with a heavy emphasis on broader political and social agendas. Although the KCTU accounts for only 43 per cent of all union members in Korea, its affiliated unions have been responsible for 70-80 per cent of the total strikes in recent years. Strike statistics show that KCTU affiliated unions are much more likely to be involved in illegal strikes than FKTU affiliated unions. More important, the membership of the KCTU has been increasing since the mid-1990s, mainly by absorbing former FKTU-affiliated union members, who prefer the KCTU's more aggressive strategy to the conservative policy of the FKTU. While some predict that the KCTU will eventually outgrow the FKTU, at the moment it can be safely said that it represents the main driving force of the labour movement.

We would emphasize, for both the FKTU and the KCTU, the importance of a responsible unionism that can be accepted by employers and the state. Also, the history of labour movement shows that in the long run the fate of labour organizations greatly depends on public opinion, which favours or disfavours a particular approach. When a particular type of labour organization is shunned by both employers and the government, its long-term viability is likely to be questionable. The proliferation of illegal strikes and the repeated occurrences of general strikes seem to make most employers frightened of the aggressiveness of the labour movement, and lead them to adopt a strategy of union-avoidance at all costs.

Indeed, a substantial numbers of Korean employers have already moved their facilities and plants to China and South Asia, mainly to take advantage of relatively cheap labour costs and the absence of an aggressive labour movement in these regions. Also, we know that the biggest concern of foreign investors operating facilities in Korea is the aggressive and unrestrained labour movement. Such a reputation can hurt workers as well as unions by depriving them of job opportunities in the long run. Labour centres, especially the KCTU, may have to tone down their radical rhetoric, avoid illegal protests and adopt a softer – and legal – approach to negotiations and collective actions, so that employers and the government (and indeed neutral citizens) can accept them as reliable and responsible participants in ER.

When employers push corporate restructuring or try to implement workplace innovations, unions can take three options: 'just say no' (opposition), 'sit tight and wait' (passive involvement), or active participation (Eaton and Voos, 1989). Korean unions, especially those affiliated with the KCTU, almost always prefer the opposition strategy. This leaves no room for negotiations with employers over the details of inevitable restructuring or the necessary innovations that can have a significant effect on their members' well-being. For example, when downsizing was an inevitable choice for organizations that wanted to survive, the unions were not involved in the important decisions made about the layoffs procedure, the choice of victims and their financial relief packages (Jung, 1999).

For union leaders, this experience indicates a need for a change to their traditional strategy. If employment restructuring or innovations are inevitable, it would be constructive for them to be actively involved in the decision-making process so as to protect their members. Under these circumstances, active participation is more effective than opposition in representing their members' immediate concerns. It also provides an important opportunity to obtain real and equal partnership in the workplace. We believe that participation in important corporate decisions is a promising approach toward responsible unionism.

Implications for Employers

Employers need to play a more active role in labour negotiation. Given that the government is heavily involved in labour disputes (in particular, over legal issues), it seems inevitable that employers have a limited role. However, their frequent reliance on government intervention hinders autonomous collective bargaining, which implies the weakening of internal problem-solving abilities in the workplace. Whenever possible, employers need to pursue autonomous dispute resolution between labour and management rather than resorting to third-party intervention.

In dealing with labour organizations, employers have two options: control or utilization. The control strategy focuses on weakening unions to minimize their negative effects, such as monopolization, whereas the utilization strategy emphasizes the positive potential of unions such as their function as a collective voice. One common feature of high performance work organizations (such as Saturn, Xerox, Corning, NUMMI and AT&T) is that they attempt to use labour organization to its fullest potential through union participation and employee involvement. Even exemplary non-union companies (such as Motorola, IBM and HP) choose to solicit and utilize employees' views through non-union employee representative bodies (Kaufman and Taras, 2000).

In Korea, although there are some exceptional organizations that practice HPWO (e.g., Samsung SDI and LG Electronics, as shown in Chapter 9), most surveys have revealed that typical Korean employers seem to pay too much attention to weakening or avoiding labour organizations rather than using their potential. In order to become world-class high-performing organizations, simply minimizing the costs of unionism is not enough: maximizing the benefits of unionism seems to be an important element of successful employment strategies. We recommend that employers should extensively utilize the collective voice function of unionism through the incorporation of unions and employees in managerial decision-making.

Outstanding Issues in HRM

Some outstanding issues in HRM include: (1) human resource professionals and their competencies; (2) changing roles of HRM departments; and (3) the war for talents.

Human Resource Professionals and Their Competencies

There is a long-standing misconception that anybody can do HRM tasks and roles without having any special competence. Many HRM managers in Korea have been excluded from involvement in competence development and strategic decision-making. Koch, Nam and Steers (1995) assessed the degree of professionalism of HR in Korea using data collected from 88 managers. The items used for the assessment were as follows (per cent agreeing with the item in brackets):

- a body of specialized knowledge including standardized terminology (14 per cent);
- widely recognized certification based on standardized qualifications (18 per cent);
- code of ethics (31 per cent);
- members oriented towards a service objective (2 per cent);
- recognized by the general public as a profession (18 per cent);
- limited access to the field, based upon acquisition of standard skills/knowledge (26 per cent);
- a professional society or association that, among other things, represents and gives voice to the entire field (22 per cent);
- practitioners are licensed (15 per cent);
- close collegiality among practitioners (31 per cent).

The results suggest that Korean HRM managers do not regard themselves as representing a distinct profession. Koch et al. (1995) also compared the results obtained from Korean managers with those from their Canadian counterparts and found that Canadian HR managers responded more positively to almost all items the assessing professionalism. However, after the 1997 financial crisis, Korean companies began to recognize the importance of recruitment, retention and outplacement. Accordingly, their perception of HRM managers changed. In addition, the self-perception of professionalism among HR managers is also explicitly emerging.

Some companies have launched education programs for HRM professionals (e.g., Samsung Electronic, the LG group and the Doosan group). Some companies and institutions (such as LG group and Korea Management Association) now provide intensive classes for HR managers to prepare for HRM certification exams, which are administered by the Human Resource Certification Institute, affiliated to the Society for HRM. To help employees achieve both Professional in Human Resources (PHR) and Senior Professional in Human Resources (SPHR), the LG group and Korea Management Association ran courses on management practice, general employment practice, staffing, human resource development, compensation and benefits, employee and labour relations and health, safety and security.

Samsung Electronic Company (SEC) has provided the most intensive of the education programs for HRM managers, putting them through a five-week program since 1999. The program covers five different areas such as strategic management, organizational theory, strategic HRM, human resource practices and ER. The course is delivered through lectures with some workshops and case analyses. Up to the end of 2002, the programs had been run six times with 20-25 HRM managers attending each time. In addition, SEC also provided one-week advance courses for senior HRM managers, focusing on strategic issues, to encourage them to become strategic partners.

The LG Academy, an LG-affiliated training and development institute, launched the HR University in 2002 to provide more systematic educational programs for HRM managers and enhance HRM competences through formal curricula. One of the programs of the HR University is HRM Strategy and Audit, which is designed for senior HRM professionals who have functional HRM skills and knowledge. The program lasts for 4 days, focusing on strategic general and HRM rather than functional areas. It started in 2001 and the programs have been operated twice so far. Similarly, the Doosan group also ran HRD programs for HRM managers from their affiliated firms. The program deals with strategic HRM, HRM functional areas, special topics such as e-HRM and some computer applications and simulations. All these training and development programs for HR managers reflect the shifting perception toward the strategic importance of HR professionals in the firms. This issue is also closely related to the changing roles of HRM departments, to which we now turn.

Changing Roles of HRM Departments

The roles of HRM organizations have changed in recently times from being just administrative support to becoming strategic partners and change agents. Ulrich (1997) suggests four different roles of HRM: management of strategic human resources (focusing on future/strategic issues and processes), management of transformation and change (focusing on future/strategic issues and people), management of firm infrastructure (focusing on day-to-day/operational issues and processes) and management of employee contributions (focusing on day-to-day/operational issues and people). Using this framework, we surveyed 107 large and small companies in Korea. HRM managers responded that their companies recognized the four roles at the rate of, on average, about 29 per cent (strategic HRM), 34 per cent (infrastructure management), 23 per cent (employee contribution management) and 25 per cent (change management). When they were asked about the changes over the preceding 2-3 years, the proportions changed to 35 per cent, 26 per cent, 24 per cent and 29 per cent respectively. The roles of strategic HRM and change management are now expected to increase. If this is so, HRM managers need to develop new competences and discard some of the old ones.

Table 10.3   Change in perspectives on HRM (%)

Employee champion or advocate	29 12	Current Future	40 68	Strategic partner
Reactive change agent for management	63 32	Current Future	17 57	Proactive change agent
Internal-oriented for organizational issues	57 22	Current Future	17 48	External-oriented for social issues
Focused on operational issues in organization	68 16	Current Future	14 75	Focused on business goals and strategies
Efficient management of human resources	53 38	Current Future	23 49	Internal consultants for line managers
Seniority-based HRM	70 2	Current Future	12 96	Ability/performance-based HRM
Results-oriented HRM	51 26	Current Future	24 54	Process-oriented HRM
Task-centred HRM	26 47	Current Future	50 38	People-centred HRM
Generalist orientation	62 6	Current Future	11 84	Specialist orientation
Paternalism-based HRM	71 3	Current Future	9 91	Contract-based HRM
Authoritarian approach	70 4	Current Future	10 91	Democratic approach

Source: Park and Yu (2001).

A survey by Park and Yu (2001) also revealed recent changes to the role of HRM in Korean firms (see Table 10.3). The results show that, among others, HR professionals of the future will become strategic partners rather than employee champions, and proactive rather than reactive change agents. In addition, the most conspicuous role change is the shift from seniority-based HRM toward ability/performance-based HRM.

On the other hand, the nature of HRM-related units has also changed. A survey of 74 companies conducted by the Korea Personnel Improvement Association in 2000 showed that about 80 per cent of them had an independent HRM department. The number of employees per HR officer was on average about 199. However, the HRM organization can have several different names including Department (Part, Team, Group, Unit, or Section) of Administrative Support, Human Resource Management, Human Resource Planning, Personnel Administration, Human Resource and Industrial Relations, Planning and Coordination, Human Resource Development, General Affairs and so on (see Table 10.4). The frequencies of each name for the HRM unit were HR(M) Team (or Unit, Division, or Department) (about 40 per cent, 30 firms); Personnel Unit and its variants (32.4 per cent, 24 firms); HR Development Unit or its variants (12.2 per cent, 9 firms); and traditional names such as General Affairs (14.9 per cent, 11 companies). Some companies used mixed names such as 'Personnel and Finance Department' and 'Personnel and General Affairs Team'. This nomenclature reflects the changing roles of the HRM unit and suggests that Korean firms are continually searching for the new roles of HRM in the future.

War for Talents[1]

After the 1997 financial crisis, Korean venture firms started to scout for experienced engineers from big corporations. As a result, mobility increased. Big corporations responded to the change in labour markets by employing multiple strategies. Firms divided employees into three different groups and took a different approach to each. For core employees, firms used an attraction strategy (i.e., dashing into the war for talent) and retention strategy (i.e., taking measures to keep core employees). For full-time employees who were poor performers, firms took a replacement strategy (i.e., dismissing under-performing employees) and outplacement strategy[2] (i.e., providing information and training for job switching). Finally, for contingent workers, firms employed a transactional and outsourcing strategy (i.e., contract-based, short-term approach). All of these strategies had been unfamiliar to most Korean firms before the crisis.

Table 10.4   Names of HRM unit in Korean companies (in 2000)

Name of HRM Unit	Number	Per cent
Human Resource (Management) Team/Unit/Division/Department/Section[a]	30	40.5
Personnel Team/Unit/Division/ Department/Section[b]	24	32.4
Human Resource (or Personnel) Development Team/Unit/Division/ Department/Section[c]	9	12.2
General Affairs (or General Administration) Team/Unit/Division/Department/Section[d]	11	14.9
Total	74	100

Notes: The names in the table are typical ones and these categories also include some mixed names such as:
a   Human Resources and Labour Relations Division;
b   Personnel & Finance Department, Personnel & General Affairs Team, Personnel & Planning Group and Personnel Affairs Section;
c   HRD & General Affairs Team; and
d   Management Team and Planning & Management Team.

Dual (core vs. peripheral) or multiple approaches were also observed. Bae and Chen (2002) found that the scores of the same sample of firms studied in terms of HRM practices (measured by selective staffing, job security, performance-based pay, extensive training and employee involvement) all increased in 2000 compared to 1996. This implies that firms used HPWS for core employees but pursued numerical flexibility through contingent workers.

The recent adoption of flexibility-oriented practices (e.g., downsizing, early retirement and outsourcing) and the erosion of the seniority-based and lifetime employment systems have lowered the average age of companies' workforce. However, as in many advanced economies, Korea has the problem of the aging workforce. The percentage of people over 65 in 2000 is 7.2 per cent. It is estimated that the ratio will be 15.1 per cent in 2020 and 23.1 per cent in 2030. The average life expectancy in Korea is 75.9 in 2000, but this will improve to 80.7 and 81.5 in 2020 and 2030 respectively. Early retirement and poor external labour markets may generate high social costs. This is a critical policy issue to be resolved and there will be a need to develop public policy to ensure productive aging (or welfare arrangements). At the firm level, several factors prevent older employees from being taken on. Tall and bureaucratic organizational structures clearly differentiate boss from subordinate and reveal one's position on the ladders. In this system, promotion is an important index of success, especially for aged employees, making it difficult to bring them in. More specifically, the current pay system requires firms to bear high labour costs. It may need to be changed in a way that will lessen this burden. Finally, perception and culture also play negative role. Older people will have rarely worked for a younger boss in Korea. Without a change in culture and attitude, other changes in structure and system would not function.

Among the aforementioned response strategies, the war for talent (i.e., an attraction strategy to recruit top talent) seems to be the most prominent contemporary issue. The term 'war for talent' became well known to many people after the McKinsey & Company report on people management strategy was published by Harvard Business School Press in 2001. Korean firms have been actively involved in recruiting and retaining top-quality talent. Korean *chaebol* groups such as Samsung, LG, SK, Hyundai Motor, Hanwha, Doosan and Kumho dashed into the war. They all announced that exceptional people would be recruited regardless of nationality and ethnic group. Firms would provide a fast-track system, signing bonus, stock options and so on. The Samsung group declared that attracting and retaining top talents would account for about 40 per cent in the evaluation of the CEOs of Samsung-affiliated firms. It is important to note that CEOs personally take care of this issue. To ensure the retention of core employees, Samsung also provides a mentoring system, makes the top talent people get to compose their teams of the best quality people, and enables dual-ladder career paths, succession planning and fellowship for R&D people. One critical barrier to 'the war for talent' in Korean firms is the perception of internal equity. Breaking down the established pay structure, promotion ladder and rigid work structure is a critical issue that remains to be resolved.

Discussion and Implications in HRM

The efficacy of the various experiments and tremendous changes in Korean HRM in the 1990s still require a balanced assessment. Here we raise two questions for discussion and consider their implications: (1) what action should be taken to gain competitive advantage through experiments in HRM? and (2) what is the role of Asian values in the age of a global standard?

Competitive Advantage through HRM: 'Fit' Revisited

The relationships between globalization, 'best practice' and competitive advantage are much more complicated than is often thought. In terms of 'best practice' effects, according to resource-based theory, competitive advantage comes about through building up of imitation barriers (Barney, 1991). Without valuable resources (such as 'best practices'), firms suffer competitive disadvantage resulting in poorer performance. However, benchmarking 'best practices' would only bring competitive parity, producing normal performance, because other firms would adopt them as well. Only after firms build imitation barriers can 'best practices' bring competitive advantage (Barney and Wright, 1998). This implies 'best practices' do not generate competitive advantage by themselves (Bae, Rowley and Sohn, 2001).

How can management create those imitation barriers? One way is to develop 'high fit'. Up until the 1980s, there was a good alignment between Korean culture, corporate philosophy and management practices. The Confucian culture supported in-group harmony and paternalistic leadership. With this cultural milieu, 'owner managers' had an 'employee-first philosophy' and took care of employees and their families. To achieve this kind of orientation firms offered lifetime employment, seniority-based pay systems and allowances for family members (e.g., for children's education). Employees therefore displayed loyalty and commitment, even sometimes sacrificing their personal leisure time. All these factors were the driving force for Korea's rapid economic development. This configuration was a source of competitive advantage for Korean firms.

However, efforts were made to produce new configurations in the 1990s to enable firms to respond effectively to environmental changes. Two major such changes were towards flexibility and performance-based approaches. While flexibility and performance may have come to be more valued elements in Korean HRM, the transfer of best practices is one thing: making them effective is quite another. To be effective, the shift in HRM system architecture demands consistent policy mixes and practices (Becker and Gerhart, 1996). For example, the movement towards performance-based systems may require firms to attempt to reduce the well-known tendency towards subjective behaviour and increase the objective measurement of employee performance, using state-of-the-art 360-degree appraisal systems.

However, we still need to pay attention to the contextual limitations on such policies and practices in the Asian context. As discussed in Chapter 3, this issue can be discussed in terms of congruence at both national level (i.e., fit between government and policies, labour/product/capital markets, culture and social climates and organizational architecture) and firm level (i.e., between hardware and software). At the national level, although public and private policies promote employment flexibility, external labour markets are not yet fully developed. While firms have begun to put increasing weight on performance and competence, the seniority factor in the social culture still seems to be robust. More critically, most of the restructuring and downsizing efforts brought in after the 1997 financial crisis were implemented without much consideration of employee input. As a result, it is hard to achieve internalization of newly adopted practices (i.e., satisfaction with, commitment to and psychological ownership of, the practices) (Kostova, 1999). In addition, in turbulent environments, since pursuing 'static fit' is not enough, attaining 'dynamic fit' is essential (cf., Ghemawat and Ricart I Costa, 1993; Wright and Snell, 1998). In summary, stressing the need to 'gain competitive advantage through people' is one thing, actual attainment of it another.

Asian Value[3] and the Global Standard

Globalization and the digital economy have pushed firms to incorporate the so-called 'global standard' through benchmarking 'best practices'. This sort of global pressure does not allow deviance from the standards. After the 1997 Asian crisis, many commentators and researchers discussed the efficacy of the Asian model in general and the Korean developmental model in particular (Korean Political Science Research Group, 1998; Jwa and Lee, 2000; Rowley and Bae, 1998; Rowley, Sohn and Bae, 2001). It seemed that neo-liberalism-based transformation was the only way out of the crisis. Many in academia and business world had something of a changes-are-good mentality. Afterwards, many lost their sense of direction. However, there was no agreement on this issue. Furthermore, as discussed in Chapter 3, various evaluations were placed on Confucian values in connection with economic development. Although global standard forces imply convergence in HRM, divergence is also strongly supported (cf., Bae and Rowley, 2001).

This trend also had an impacted on HRM. It can be argued that Korean HRM has changed direction from a community-based, towards a more competition-based, system. Traditional HRM was characterized by a community orientation and paternalistic relationships. Its basic values were harmony, care and equality. It was not uncommon for managers to take responsibility not only for subordinates' work, but also for their personal and family lives. After firms began to adopt more flexible and performance-based practices, the characteristics of HRM shifted towards a greater 'transaction' orientation, market principles and contract. The basic norm for this is, in contrast to before, competition.

A problem firms face is not simply absorbing this second set of norms, but rather totally discarding the first set so as to enable the wholesale and uncritical adoption of the second (Bae and Rowley, 2001). Evidence of this difficulty is the recent outflow to venture firms of the core employees of large companies who have grown disappointed with the changes in HRM. Without the 'high care' climate and family-like organizational community, employees are becoming more sceptical about giving their loyalty. This reduced commitment and work ethic has been noted generally and specifically, as with the lack of loyalty and associated problems following the dismissals at Samsung Life Insurance (Lee, 1998). Ironically, some Western firms have recently emphasized greater 'relationship' over 'transaction' orientations (Keltner and Finegold, 1996), prioritizing trust and commitment for knowledge creation and sharing and valuing high care climates (Leonard and Sensiper, 1998; Nonaka, 1991; Von Krogh, 1998). This can be seen in the 'partnership' agreements signed between management and unions in some UK companies since the 1990s.

Practitioners need to be careful not to change things that may well be hard to recover in case high recovery costs should come to exceed the benefits generated from the changes. For instance, during the recent downsizing many Korean firms lost their 'human touch' and broke the 'psychological contract' of long-term attachment and trust. Now many human resource managers in Korean firms will comment that it has become hard for them to expect loyalty from employees, and more difficult to motivate and retain them. Therefore, one task for firms is to ensure that they do not simply discard 'community' for 'transaction' orientations, but can achieve the simultaneous realization of multiple values (cf Goudzwaard, 1979): in other words, that they pursue both Korean values and values from foreign countries (Bae and Rowley, 2001).

Concluding Remarks: Threats or Opportunities?

As a latecomer to economically advanced nations, Korea has relied on borrowing or learning from advanced economies to achieve national industrialization (Rowley and Bae, 1998). Korean ER and HRM systems also started out by learning from either Japanese systems or American systems. If we compare Korean, US and Japanese systems, the Korean model (e.g., lifetime employment, collective activities within firms and seniority basis) is typically positioned between the other two. Hence, the evolution of Korean ER and HRM systems can be characterized by an eclectic approach. Since the mid 1980s, Korean firms have conducted various experiments to identify new management and ER/HRM systems. One critical problem with this is that few of the systems arrived at by such experimentation were institutionalized effectively. Their adoption was typically focused more on short-term 'quick fixes' rather than a long-term orientation towards fundamental changes; on a hardware approach (e.g., structure and systems) rather than software (e.g., culture and cognition); on formal implementation rather than internalization in terms of people's attitudes and perceptions; and on diffusion based on institutional theory than rational efforts based on strategic choice. All these characteristics saw many Korean ER/HRM systems become a vicious circle. Therefore, we would argue that one critical task facing both ER and HRM systems is their institutionalization. The recent turbulence of the environmental has threatened ER/HRM systems by making it more difficult than ever before to institutionalize them. Stakeholders in ER/HRM systems have very different perspectives (e.g., neo-liberalism, societal corporatism and pluralism). However, although it may require a painful process of negotiation and accommodation, now is perhaps the right time for the Korean government, firms and employers and employees and unions to take the opportunity to formulate better systems.

Notes

1   The term 'war for talent' has been popularly used since McKinsey & Company initiated a project and published a book titled 'The war for talent'.
2   This strategy is, of course, also used for core talents who want to quit voluntarily. However, these core employees usually do not need help from the firm to switch jobs.
3   Although we refer to 'Asian values' here, this does not necessarily mean that all Asian countries share the same values. We recognize that there are variations between countries in this region. As mentioned in Chapter 3, though Japan and China are characterized by collectivism, Japanese emphasize loyalty to the firm, but Chinese stress loyalty to and solidarity with the inner circle of family.

References

Bae, J. and Chen, S. (2002), 'Gaining global competitive advantage through human resources: The cases of MNCs operating in Korea and Taiwan', paper presented at the University of Illinois Center for Human Resource Management Conference on *Human Resource Management: Global Perspectives*, Oak Brook, IL. Sept. 19-20.

Bae, J., and Rowley, C. (2001), 'The impact of globalization on HRM: The case of Korea', *Journal of World Business*, vol.36, no.4, pp.402-428.

Bae, J., Rowley, C. and Sohn, T. (2001), 'Conclusion – Knowledge, Learning, and Change in Korean Management', *Asia Pacific Business Review*, vol.7, no.4, pp.182-200.

Barney, J.B. (1991), 'Firm resources and sustained competitive advantage', *Journal of Management*, vol.17, pp.99-120.

Barney, J.B. and Wright, P.M. (1998), 'On becoming a strategic partner: The role of human resources in gaining competitive advantage', *Human Resource Management*, vol.37, no.1, pp.31-46.

Becker, B. and Gerhart, B. (1996), 'The impact of human resource management on organizational performance: Progress and prospects', *Academy of Management Journal*, vol.39, no.4, pp.779-801.

Eaton, A.E. and Voos, P.B. (1989), 'The Ability of Unions to Adapt to Innovative Workplace Arrangements', *American Economic Review*, vol.79, no.2, pp.172-176.

Ghemawat, P., and Ricart I Costa, J.E. (1993), 'The organizational tension between static and dynamic efficiency', *Strategic Management Journal*, vol.14, pp.59-73.

Goudzwaard, B. (1979), *Capitalism and Progress: A Diagnosis of Western Society*, Wedge, Toronto.

Hebdon, R. (1998), 'Behavioral Determinants of Public Sector Illegal Strikes: Cases from Canada and the U.S', *Relations Industrielles / Industrial Relations*, vol.53, no.4, pp.667-690.

Ichniowski, C. (1988), 'Police Recognition Strikes: Illegal and Ill-fated', *Journal of Labor Research*, vol.9, no.2, pp.183-197.

International Institute for Management Development (Various years), *IMD's World Competitiveness Yearbook*, IMD, Lausanne.

Jung, E.H. (1999), *Economic Crisis and Industrial Relations in Korea*, Korea Labor and Society Institute and Friedrich Ebert Stiftung, Seoul. (In Korean.)

Jwa, S. and Lee, I.K. (2000), (eds), *Korean Chaebol in Transition: Road ahead and agenda*, Korea Economic Research Institute, Seoul.

Kaufman, B.E. and Taras, D.G. (2000), (eds), *Nonunion Employee Representation: History, Contemporary Practice, and Policy*, M. E. Sharpe, New York.

Keltner, B. and Finegold, D. (1996), 'Adding value in banking: Human resource innovations for service firms', *Sloan Management Review*, Fall, pp.57-68.

Kim, D.-O. (1993), 'Analysis of Labour Disputes in Korea and Japan: The Search for an Alternative Model', *European Sociological Review*, vol.9, no.2, pp.139-154.

Koch, M., Nam, S.H. and Steers, R.M. (1995), 'Human resource management in South Korea', in L.F. Moore and P.D. Jennings (eds), *Human resource management on the Pacific Rim*, Walter de Gruyter, Berlin and New York, pp.217-242.

The Korea Labour Daily News (2001), *Rapid Increase of Worker Arrests*, July 12.

Korea Labour Institute (2000), *Overseas Labour Statistics*, Korea Labour Institute, Seoul. (In Korean.)

Korea Labour Institute (2001), *KLI Labour Statistics*, Korea Labour Institute, Seoul. (In Korean.)

Korea Ministry of Labour (2002), Internal Document, Korea Ministry of Labour, Seoul. (In Korean.)

Korean Political Science Research Group (1998), (eds), *Did the developmental model in East Asian fail?* Samin, Seoul.

Korpi, W. (1981), 'Unofficial Strikes in Sweden', *British Journal of Industrial Relations*, vol.19, no.1, pp.66-86.

Kostova, T. (1999), 'Transnational transfer of strategic organizational practices: A contextual perspective', *Academy of Management Review*, vol.24, no.2, pp.308-324.

Lee, H.C. (1998), 'Transformation of employment practices in Korean businesses', *International Studies of Management and Organisation*, vol.28, no.4, pp.26-39.

Leonard, D. and Sensiper, S. (1998), 'The role of tacit knowledge in group innovation', *California Management Review*, vol.40, no.3, pp.112-132.

Nonaka, I. (1991), 'The Knowledge-Creation Company', *Harvard Business Review*, Nov/Dec, pp.96-104.

Olson, C. (1986), 'Strikes, Strike Penalties, and Arbitration in Six States', *Industrial and Labour Relations Review*, vol.39, no.4, pp.539-551.

Park, W. and Yu, G. (2001), 'Paradigm shift and changing role of HRM in Korea: Analysis of the HRM experts' opinions and its implication', *The Korean Personnel Administration Journal*, vol.25, no.1, pp.347-369.

Rowley, C. and Bae, J. (1998), (eds), *Korean Businesses: Internal and External Industrialization*, Frank Cass, London and Portland, OR.

Rowley, C., Sohn, T. and Bae, J. (2001), (eds), Managing Korean Business: Organization, Culture, Human Resources and Change, Frank Cass, London and Portland, OR.

Schmitter, P.C. (1974), 'Still the Century of Corporatism?', The Review of Politics, vol.36, no.1, pp.85-131.

Von Krogh, G. (1998), 'Care in knowledge creation', *California Management Review*, vol.40, no.3, pp.133-153.

Wilkinson, B. (1994), *Labour And Industry In The Asia-Pacific: Lessons From The Newly-Industrialized Countries*, Walter de Gruyter, New York.

Wright, P.L. and Snell, S.A. (1998), 'Toward a unifying framework for exploring fit and flexibility in strategic human resource management', *Academy of Management Review*, vol.23, no.4, pp.756-772.

Index

C

T

Printed in the United States
by Baker & Taylor Publisher Services